The Logic of Information

The Logic of Information

A Theory of Philosophy as Conceptual Design

Luciano Floridi

OXFORD
UNIVERSITY PRESS

OXFORD

UNIVERSITY PRESS

Great Clarendon Street, Oxford, OX2 6DP,
United Kingdom

Oxford University Press is a department of the University of Oxford.
It furthers the University's objective of excellence in research, scholarship,
and education by publishing worldwide. Oxford is a registered trade mark of
Oxford University Press in the UK and in certain other countries

First Edition published in 2019

Impression: 5

Published in the United States of America by Oxford University Press
198 Madison Avenue, New York, NY 10016, United States of America

British Library Cataloguing in Publication Data

Data available

Library of Congress Control Number: 2018953774

ISBN 978-0-19-883363-5

Printed and bound by
CPI Group (UK) Ltd, Croydon, CR0 4YY

Contents

Part I. Philosophy's Open Questions

Part II. Philosophy as Conceptual Design

Preface

The title of this book contains two words that are semantically very loaded, "logic" and "information". Before I say anything about its contents, I better explain how I use each of them.

Consider "logic" first. Philosophy is often concerned with the study of structural properties of systems—whether empirical, like political organizations, or conceptual, like scientific theories—and their dynamics.[1] Before the advent of modern mathematical logic, such structural studies might have been considered to be part of logic broadly understood.[2] Today, this would be very misleading. But so would be the use of labels such as "informal logic"[3] and "philosophical logic",[4] already appropriated by other branches of philosophy. Thus, for lack of a better expression, I have chosen to refer to such structural studies as "conceptual logic". A conceptual logic is what we have in mind when we ask questions about the abstract properties, principles, mechanisms, or dynamics characterizing or underpinning systems like international relations, a bureaucracy, a scientific theory, or the internal arrangement of elements in a device to perform a specific task. A conceptual logic focuses on formal features that are independent of specific implementations or idiosyncratic contingencies, on types rather than tokens, on invariants and their mutual relations, and on state transitions that are generalizable. This is the sense in which "logic" should be understood in the title of this book.

Next, take "information". What remains unclear in the previous explanation is exactly what further qualifies as a conceptual logic of a system. Later in this book, I shall use a more precise vocabulary and talk about the "model" (semantic information about) of a "system" (the referent "abouted" by some semantic information). This means that the overall question I address across this book, and hence its subtitle, can be phrased more precisely by asking: what is the conceptual logic of information-modelling (i.e. generating a description of some structural properties of) a system? Note that, once unpacked, this question is not *ontological* but *epistemological*. It is not about the intrinsic, conceptual logic of a system in itself, but rather about the conceptual logic of the model (i.e. information) of a system, and how we design[5] it. If this is

---

[1] See Alexander (1964, p. 8).

[2] For an enlightening reconstruction of the late modern developments of logic between Kant and Frege see Heis (2012).

[3] See two excellent examples: Sinnott-Armstrong and Fogelin (2015), Walton and Brinton (2016).

[4] See two excellent examples: Burgess (2009), Sainsbury (2001).

[5] Parsons (2016) is a great source for a philosophical analysis of the debate on the concept of design. The book is also an essential starting point to frame the proposal made in this book. It dedicates quite some space to the debate on modernism. It is a must-read for anyone interested in understanding the conceptual nature of design together with the excellent Dunne and Raby (2013). These works, together with Barthes (1981) and Flusser (1999), have deeply influenced my views on the topic.

unclear, compare the conceptual logic of a watch's mechanism with the conceptual logic of the design of a watch. The focus is really about a conceptual logic of the design of a system, understood as a specific kind of conceptual logic of information about (the design of the model of) a system; and not any kind of information, but that particular kind we call *semantic* or *factual* information, that is, information about something. Thus, "information" in the title of this book is not the sort of quantitative, probabilistic, signal-based concept that one may find in an engineering textbook (what is sometimes called Shannon information)—although I shall use that too in the following chapters— but the well-formed, meaningful, and truthful kind that one may find in a tourist guide about Rome.

Focusing on the logic of a model rather than on the logic of a system captured by a model means that this book is closely linked with some of the epistemological ideas I supported in a previous book, entitled *The Philosophy of Information* (Floridi 2011c). However, this is not a book in the epistemological tradition. It is rather a book on the logic of design and hence of making, transforming, refining, and improving the objects of our knowledge. So, it is not a book about ontology either, at least not in the classic sense. For some philosophers, it may be obvious that the conceptual logic of semantic information is the deep, conceptual logic of the world. Or, to put it in the vocabulary just introduced, that the logic of a model of a system is the logic of the system. In this, Hegel, Marx, the first Wittgenstein, and the atomistic Russell appear to share the same view. I am not so sure. Actually, I really doubt it, but, most importantly, this is not an issue that needs to be resolved here. We can all refrain from stepping into any ontological discussion, and phrase anything that we need to discuss epistemologically, and therefore more safely in terms of commitment. If, as a bonus, some readers may believe that we pay one and get two, as it were—that is, if anyone is convinced that by developing a conceptual logic of the model we shall also have obtained a conceptual logic of the corresponding system—I shall not complain, but neither shall I join them.

Putting the two clarifications together, this book is a study in the *conceptual logic* of *semantic information*. The next thing I should be candid about is that it is a *constructionist* study.

The scientific-realist reader should not be alarmed. If anything, this is a pragmatist book about a world that needs to be modelled correctly in order to be made meaningful satisfactorily. I never seriously question for a moment the recalcitrant and often grating presence of outside realities. Actually, I have little patience for self-indulgent and irresponsible speculations about logically possible situations involving brains in a vat, dreaming butterflies, or Matrix-like pills. In the best scenarios, they were once devised to help discuss valuable philosophical questions. They have now become scholastic puzzles that engage only professional academics.

At the same time, the naïve realist may rightly be a bit suspicious. Because the constructionism I develop in this book is still of a Kantian kind (more on Kant below). The starting point defended in this book, as in my previous works, is that we do not have access to the world in itself, something I am not even sure one can explain in full.

We always access any reality through specific interfaces, what I shall define in Chapter 2 as *levels of abstraction*, borrowing a conceptual framework from computer science. The world provides the data, to be understood as constraining affordances, and we transform them into information, like semantic engines. But such transformation or repurposing (see Chapter 4) is not equivalent to portraying, or picturing, or photographing, or photocopying anything. It is more like cooking: the dish does not represent the ingredients, it uses them to make something else out of them, yet the reality of the dish and its properties hugely depend on the reality and the properties of the ingredients. Models are not representations understood as pictures, but interpretations understood as data elaborations, of systems. Thus, the whole book may also be read as an articulation and defence of the thesis that *knowledge is design*, and that philosophy is the ultimate form of *conceptual design*.

There is one more clarification I should make. Shifting from representing to interpreting the world may be controversial. We shall see that it raises problems in terms of quality of the outcome (Chapter 5) and scepticism about its truthfulness (Chapters 6 and 7). But it is not new and it can easily be mistaken for something that I criticize throughout the book: a passive understanding of knowledge as being always about something already present in the world. This Platonic view, to be found also in Descartes, is too reductive. Modelling is not just dealing with what there is; it is often designing what there could, or should be. Having a different word helps here: a *blueprint* is a model of something that does not yet exist but that we want to design, not of something that is already there and that we want to explain, for example. So, this book is a *constructionist* study in the *conceptual logic* of *semantic information* both as a *model* (*mimesis*) and as a *blueprint* (*poiesis*). We have reached the full description. And this can now be used to contextualize this book within the wider project for the foundation of the philosophy of information.

This is the third volume in a tetralogy that includes *The Philosophy of Information* (volume one (Floridi 2011c)) and *The Ethics of Information* (volume two (Floridi 2013b)). I began labelling the tetralogy *Principia Philosophiae Informationis* not as a sign of bottomless hubris—although it may well be—but as an internal pun among some colleagues. In a sort of rowing-like competition, I joked that it was time for Oxford to catch up with Cambridge on the 3–0 scoring about "principia". Not a pun that many find funny, or even intelligible.

Within the *Principia* project, this book occupies a middle ground between the first and the second volume. However, as the reader should expect, the three volumes are all written as stand-alone, so this book too can be read without any knowledge of anything else I have ever published. Yet the three volumes are complementary. The essential message from volume one is quite straightforward. Semantic information is well-formed, meaningful, and truthful data; knowledge is relevant semantic information properly accounted for; humans are the only known semantic engines and conscious informational organisms who can design and understand semantic artefacts, and thus develop a growing knowledge of reality; and reality is the totality of information (notice the crucial absence of 'semantic'). Against that background, volume two investigates the foundations of the ethics of informational organisms (inforgs) like us, which flourish in informational environments (infosphere), and are responsible for their construction and well-being. In short, volume two is about the ethics of inforgs in the infosphere. Thus, in a classic Kantian move, we are shifting from theoretical to pragmatic philosophy. I already mentioned that this third volume, insofar as it focuses on the conceptual logic of semantic information as a *model*, is linked with the epistemological analysis provided in *The Philosophy of Information*. And insofar as it focuses on the conceptual logic of semantic information as a *blueprint*, it offers a bridge towards the normative analysis provided in *The Ethics of Information*. This discusses, among other things, what duties, rights, and responsibilities are associated with the poietic practices that characterize our existence, from making sense of the world to changing it according to what we consider normatively right or morally good. By working like a hinge between the two previous books, this third one prepares the basis for volume four, on *The Politics of Information*. There, the epistemological, conceptual, and normative constructionism supports the study of the design opportunities we have in understanding and shaping what I like to call "the human project" in our information societies.

The three volumes may be understood as seeking to invert four misconceptions, easily explainable by using the classic communication model introduced by Shannon: sender, message, receiver, channel. Epistemology focuses too much on the passive receiver/consumer of knowledge, when it should be concerned with the active sender/producer, because knowing is constructing. Ethics focuses too much on the sender/agent, when it should be concerned with the receiver/patient, because the keys to being good are care, respect, and tolerance. Metaphysics focuses too much on the relata, the sender/producer/agent/receiver/consumer/patient, which it conceives as entities, when it should be concerned with the message/relations, because dynamic structures constitute the structured. And logic focuses too much on channels of communication as justifying or grounding our conclusions, when it should be concerned with channels that enable us to extract (and transfer) information from a variety of sources reliably, because the logic of information design is a logic of relata and clusters of relations, rather than a logic of things as bearers of predicates. I will be utterly amazed if even one of these u-turns in our philosophical paradigms will be successful.

Let me now turn to a quick overview of the contents. The task of this third volume is still that of contributing to the development of a philosophy of our time for our time, as I have written more than once. As in the previous two volumes, it does so systematically (conceptual architecture is pursued as a valuable feature of philosophical thinking) rather than exhaustively, by pursuing two goals.

The first goal is meta-theoretical and is fulfilled by Part I. This comprises the first three chapters. There, I offer an interpretation of philosophical questions as open questions (Chapter 1), of philosophy as the conceptual design of such questions and of their answers (Chapter 2), and of constructionism as the best way of approaching such a way of doing philosophy (Chapter 3).

On the basis of this first part, the second part pursues not a meta-theoretical but a theoretical investigation. In Chapter 4, I investigate how a constructionist philosophy as conceptual design can interpret perception and testimony as data providers. This leads to the discussion of two further issues: the quality of the information that we are able to elaborate on the basis of such data (Chapter 5); and the truthfulness of the information constructed, namely the sceptical challenge faced by a constructionist interpretation of semantic information, and its related modelling processes (Chapter 6). In Chapters 7 and 8 I return to the features of a constructionist logic to analyse the value of information closure for the consistency of our models of the world, and the possibility of expanding such models even through fallacious reasoning. In Chapter 9, I finally define what the maker's knowledge could be, once we interpret ourselves as the designers responsible for our own understanding of the world. The book ends with a detailed analysis of what conceptual logic may underpin our designing activities, seen as depending on constraints and a relation of "*a* makes *b* a sufficient solution" (Chapter 10). The ten chapters are strictly related, so I have added internal references whenever it might be useful. They could be read in a slightly different order, as one of the anonymous referees pointed out. I agree. I offer here the structure that I find more helpful, but, for example, some readers may wish to go to the end of the story first, and learn about the logic of design as a conceptual logic of information before approaching any other chapter.

In terms of its philosophical roots, like volumes one and two, this too is a German book, written from a post-analytic continental-divide perspective, which I have the impression is increasingly fading away. The careful reader will easily place this work in the tradition linking pragmatism, especially Charles Sanders Peirce, with the philosophy of technology, especially Herbert Simon.[6] Unlike volume one, and even more than volume two, this third volume is much less neo-Kantian than I expected it to be. And contrary to volume two, it is also less Platonic and Cartesian. In short, writing it has made me aware that I may be moving out of the shadows of my three philosophical heroes. Not a plan, but this is what happens when you follow your reasoning wherever it leads you. *Amici Plato, Cartesius et Kant, sed magis amica veritas*. In *The Ethics of Information*, I wrote that "some books write their authors". I now have the impression that only bad books are fully controlled by their authors. They are called airport novels and telenovelas. Let me illustrate this with an anecdote.

One day, when I was a boy, my mother found me distressed because I had just read about the death of Porthos, one of the four musketeers, in Dumas' *The Man in the Iron Mask* (1847–50, now (Dumas 2008)). There was not much she could do, but she tried to console me by pointing out that I was not alone. Dumas himself had been deeply upset by the death of his character. She recounted the story according to which a maiden had found Dumas crying because Porthos was dead. This seemed to me perfectly

---

[6] The reader interested in exploring these connections may wish to consult Allo (2010) and Durante (2017).

reasonable. It was a very sad moment indeed. But what struck me at the time, and made me forget my sadness, was the alleged explanation that Dumas offered when asked why he, the omnipotent author, could not change the story of his own literary character. He said that Porthos *had* to die. That seemed to me to express, better than anything else I had experienced at the time, the force of a theorem, the strength of logical coherence, the inescapable, constraining grip of dynamic structures, which have features and interact in ways that are utterly independent of our wills and desires. You can choose the *if*, but not the *then*. Dumas was a great writer because he felt powerless. Porthos' death was the inexorable conclusion, given the development of the plot. That evening I thanked my mother for the lesson in logical thinking, and felt a bit less upset: necessity is somewhat soothing. Many years later, I went to check the episode again. It still saddens me. But I found a line that seems very appropriate to conclude this anecdote. " 'Parbleu!' said Porthos again, with laughter that he did not even attempt to restrain, 'when a thing is explained to me I understand it; begone, and give me the light.' "

Regarding the style and structure of this book, as I wrote in the preface of volumes one and two, I remain painfully aware that this third volume too is not a page-turner, to put it mildly, despite my attempts to make it as interesting and reader-friendly as possible. I remain convinced that *esoteric* (in the technical sense) research in philosophy is the only way of developing new ideas. But *exoteric* philosophy has its crucial place. It is like the more accessible and relevant tip of the more obscure and yet necessary part of the iceberg under the surface of everyday life. The reader interested in a much lighter reading may wish to check *The Fourth Revolution: How the Infosphere is Reshaping Human Reality* (Floridi 2014a) or perhaps the even easier (Floridi 2010b).

This book will require not only graduate-level knowledge of philosophy, patience, and time but also an open mind. The last three are scarce resources. For in the last two decades or so of debates, I have been made fully aware—sometimes in ways less friendly than I wish—that some of the ideas I defend in the following pages are controversial. I have also seen how often mistakes are made by relying on "systemic attractors": if a new idea looks a bit like an old idea we already have, then the old one is a magnet to which the new one is powerfully attracted, almost irresistibly. We end up thinking that "that new" is really just like "this old", and if we do not like "this old" then we dislike "that new" as well. Bad philosophy indeed, but it takes mental strength and exercise to resist such a powerful shift. In the case of this book, I am sure some readers will be tempted to conclude that it is an anti-realist, anti-naturalist attempt to let the sceptic and the relativist have the final word about logic, knowledge, and science. So, let me say this as clearly as I can, quoting Margaret Thatcher: no, no, no. There are many ways of being anti-sceptic and anti-relativist, and being a realist constructionist is one of them. I actually believe that it is the best option we have today. The reader does not have to follow me that far. But no mistake should be made about the direction I am taking.

As in the previous two volumes, two features that I thought might help the reader to access the contents of this book more easily are the summaries and conclusions at the beginning and at the end of each chapter, and some redundancy. Regarding the first feature, I know it is slightly unorthodox, but the solution, already adopted in volumes one and two, of starting each chapter with a 'Previously in Chapter x...', should enable the reader to browse the text, or fast-forward entire chapters of it, without losing the essential plot. Science-fiction fans, who recognize the reference to *Battlestar Galactica*, may consider this third volume as the equivalent of season three.

Regarding the second feature, while editing the final version of the book, I decided to leave in the chapters some repetitions and some rephrasing of recurrent themes, whenever I thought that the place where the original content had been introduced was too distant, either in terms of pages or in terms of theoretical context. If sometimes the reader experiences some *déjà vu* I hope it will be to the advantage of clarity, as a feature and not a bug.

A final word now on what the reader will not find in the following pages. This is not an introduction to formal logic from an informational perspective (a book that should be written) or to some modal logic of "S is informed that p". Nor do I seek to provide an exhaustive investigation of all the issues that may go under the label of "logic of information". In particular, I hope to work more extensively on testimony, epistemic luck, and causality in the future. They are a topic just touched upon in the following chapters. The book is not a textbook on information theory or on the sort of topics discussed in undergraduate courses entitled "Introduction to (library and) information science" either.[7] The reader interested in such topics might wish to look at *The Routledge Handbook of Philosophy of Information* (Floridi 2016) or at *Information—A Very Short Introduction* (Floridi 2010b). This book is about the roots of some of the logical problems of our time, not their leaves. It is about design.

---

[7] I discussed the relationship between the philosophy of information and library and information science in Floridi (2002a, 2004b).

Acknowledgements

After the experience of the first two volumes, I am bound to acknowledge here some of the things I already acknowledged there. The repetition does not diminish but reinforces my deep gratitude.

As before, I could not have worked on such a long-term project without dividing it into some feasible and much smaller tasks. Some of the earliest bits of this book date to 1999, although most of the work was done between 2011 and 2017. I am glad to see that so many different components still fitted together in the end. Of course, I hope this is the symptom of a well-planned project, but I am afraid that, the older I get, the more likely it is that it may actually be due to some mental resistance to change, also known as sclerosis. Old people do not change their minds easily.

As for the previous two volumes, many of the ideas and contents presented in the chapters were initially tested as conference presentations or (sometimes inclusive or) journal articles. The bibliographic details are in the list of references. This systematic and gradual way of working is laborious, but it seems to be fruitful and it may also be inevitable, given the innovative nature of the field. It does require a perseverance and commitment that I hope are not ill-exercised. I wished to assess the ideas presented in this volume as thoroughly as possible, and publishing the articles gave me the opportunity and privilege to enjoy a vast amount of feedback, from a very large number of excellent colleagues and anonymous referees. If I do not thank all of them here, this is not for lack of manners or mere reason of space, but because the appropriate acknowledgements can be found in the corresponding, published articles.

There are, however, some people I would like to mention explicitly because they played a significant role throughout the project and during the revisions of the final text. Kia first of all. She and I have been married for as long as I have been working on the whole *Principia* project. Without her, I would have never had the confidence to undertake such a task, and the spiritual energy to complete it. It requires a huge amount of serenity to invest so much time in philosophical thinking, and Kia is my muse. I am repeating something I already wrote in the previous volume: she keeps making our life blissful, and I am very grateful to her for the endless hours we spend talking about the topics of the *Principia*, for all her sharp suggestions, and for her lovely patience with an utterly obsessed, single-minded, overly focused husband, who must be unbearable to anyone else. I wish I could claim to have contributed to her research in neuroscience even half as much as she has to my philosophical development. Between the second and this third volume we moved into the house of our dreams. Mill Barn is the perfect place to think.

Patrick Allo, Selmer Bringsjord, Min Chen, Marcello D'Agostino, Massimo Durante, Giuseppe Primiero, Sebastian Sequoiah-Grayson, Ugo Pagallo, Mariarosaria Taddeo,

David Watson, and James Williams, as well as several members and visitors of the Digital Ethics Lab at Oxford during the past years, were very generous with their time and provided numerous opportunities for discussion and further reflection on the topics analysed in this book.

A very long list of meetings, conferences, and workshops (the details are in the published articles listed in the References section) provided stimulating and fruitful venues to elaborate and further test some of the ideas presented in this book. I have learnt a lot from the colleagues I met there, though I wish I had been able to learn more.

Peter Momtchiloff was pivotal for the realization of all three volumes, both because of his foresighted invitation to publish them with OUP, and because of his support and firm patience, when it seemed that I would never complete them.

The anonymous reviewers appointed by OUP were incredibly helpful with their comments and suggestions. I was impressed especially by one of them for her or his careful reading and very insightful recommendations. I wish I could thank her or him in person.

Jessica Antonio and Louise Parker, my personal assistants at different times, provided the exceptional support and impeccable managerial skills without which I could not have completed this project.

I would also like to thank all the people who made the task of working on this book more difficult than it should have been. Sometimes friction is essential to make progress.

Finally, this book was made possible by the very generous and friendly support of the Universidad Carlos III de Madrid, where I spent a fruitful and quiet period of research as the 2015 Chair of Excellence, thanks also to the support of the Santander programme. The colleagues at Carlos III, and especially Ilia Galan Diez, provided the best intellectual and social environment to develop some of the ideas presented in the following pages. I am immensely grateful for the privilege. The book is dedicated to them.

List of Most Common Acronyms

A   agent, Alice
B   agent, Bob
C   agent, Carol
ICTs   Information and Communication Technologies
LoA   Level of Abstraction
PI   Philosophy of Information

The use of Alice as synonymous with Agent is not merely an Oxford-related reference. The reader acquainted with the literature on quantum information will recognize in Alice, Bob, Carol, and Dave the more memorable and concrete placeholder names for otherwise abstract agents or particles; see http://en.wikipedia.org/wiki/Alice_and_ Bob, retrieved January 2018.

List of Figures

PART I

Philosophy's Open Questions

Advanced research develops at an ever-faster pace, so it is becoming increasingly hard to anticipate its future. This holds true in any field of investigation, including philosophy, where the scope and varied nature of the discipline make forecasting its development perhaps an even more challenging task. At the same time, there seems to be a growing demand for philosophical understanding, in a world in which conceptual problems, ethical issues, social and political tensions, economic imbalances, religious and cultural clashes, international conflicts, and environmental challenges have acquired global dimensions and visibly affect the lives of billions of people simultaneously. The world needs more philosophical insights and more ideas on how to cope with a complex future. It needs conceptual theorizing and philosophical answers. Therefore, it is simply irresponsible to dismiss philosophy as a useless waste of time, with cheap jokes, populistic rhetoric, and unscientific remarks, as Stephen Hawking (more on him in Chapter 1), Neil deGrasse Tyson, or Bill Nye have done. True, philosophy has its ups and downs, as I shall argue in Chapter 1, but so have other disciplines, and it is essential that we should try to identify the most promising lines of philosophical research, and anticipate trends in which it might be worth investing our intellectual efforts and dwindling resources. What kind of philosophy are we developing? And what kind of philosophy should we be fostering? These are difficult questions. They also represent a classic *leit-motif* in the history of philosophy, because no serious philosophy worth pursuing shies away from the reflection on its own status. It comes with the job, as they say. They are also questions that should be asked preferably to (I did not write by) experts.[1] The main

---

[1] They have been; see for example Schlette (1968), Leaman (1998), Bencivenga (2006), Dietrich and Weber (2011), and Floridi (2013a). In the latter case, I sought to collect views from philosophers who are also editors in chief of influential philosophical journals and philosophy editors of important publishing houses. They may contribute particularly helpful perspectives on the future of philosophical research because they enjoy a privileged role with respect to its current state. Not only are they likely to have a better sense of what is the most promising work in progress, and what kind of fruitful patterns might be emerging, as the journals' long backlogs of forthcoming articles and publishers' long-term editorial plans clearly suggest. They are also the ones who may have an overall perspective about what is not published, and for what reasons. As in the case of negative results, this too is valuable information. According to a widely cited piece of research, (Fanelli 2012), every year there is a 6 per cent decrease in the publication number of scientific papers with negative results. It would be interesting to compare this situation to philosophical journals.

questions to address are inevitably indexical: what now, what next, what for. The strategy is always, to quote Schlick:[2]

to ask the question, 'What will be the future of philosophy?' entirely from the point of view of the philosopher. However, to answer the question we shall have to use the method of the historian because we shall not be able to say what the future of philosophy will be except in so far as our conclusions are derived from our knowledge of its past and its present.

Inevitably, readers of this book will have their own answers. In this first part of the book, I present my own. I hope they are convincing, but even if they are not, they should be helpful in understanding how I approach the philosophical questions discussed in the second part.

For in the best scenarios, when new research topics begin to emerge, it is conceivable that attempts at studying them might initially be unsuccessful, and yet, the presence of such failures may still betray the importance of the topic itself. Finally, editorial strategies and choices also contribute to shaping the future of the discipline, so editors seem to be well positioned to discuss the future of philosophical research.

[2] Schlick (1932), republished in Schlick (1979).

1

What is a Philosophical Question?

Summary

There are many ways of understanding the nature of philosophical questions. One may consider their morphology, semantics, relevance, or scope. This chapter introduces a different approach, based on the kind of informational resources required to answer them. The result is a definition of philosophical questions as questions whose answers are in principle *open* to informed, rational, and honest disagreement, *ultimate* but *not absolute, closed* under further questioning, possibly *constrained* by empirical and logico-mathematical resources, but requiring *noetic* resources to be answered. The chapter concludes with a discussion of some of the consequences of this definition for a conception of philosophy as the study (or 'science') of open questions, which uses conceptual design to analyse and answer them. That is the topic of Chapter 2.

1. Introduction: Russell's 'such ultimate questions'

In 1912, Russell published *The Problems of Philosophy* (Russell 1912). A hundred years later, it is still a classic introduction to philosophy, accessible to beginners and insightful for experts. As the reader probably knows, it is a tiny book. In such a short space, Russell explicitly chooses to privilege epistemological problems over metaphysical ones. As he writes in the preface:

In the following pages, I have confined myself in the main to those problems of philosophy in regard to which I thought it possible to say something positive and constructive, since merely negative criticism seemed out of place. For this reason, theory of knowledge occupies a larger space than metaphysics in the present volume, and some topics much discussed by philosophers are treated very briefly, if at all.   (Russell 1912, p. 1)

Such an epistemological orientation makes the book especially suitable for an informational interpretation, as the analysis of the problem of sense data shows, for example. Yet, in this chapter, I do not wish to engage with Russell's selection of philosophical questions, with his own formulation of them, or even with the answers he advocates. Instead, I intend to concentrate on only one paragraph. It is the first of the book, and the following pages may be read, in a Whiteheadian sense (Whitehead 1978, p. 39), as a long footnote to it:

Is there any knowledge in the world which is so certain that no reasonable man could doubt it? This question, which at first sight might not seem difficult, is really one of the most difficult that can be asked. When we have realized the obstacles in the way of a straightforward and confident answer, we shall be well launched on the study of philosophy—for *philosophy is merely the attempt to answer such ultimate questions* [my italics], not carelessly and dogmatically, as we do in ordinary life and even in the sciences, but critically, after exploring all that makes such questions puzzling, and after realizing all the vagueness and confusion that underlie our ordinary ideas.   (Russell 1912, p. 1)

What I intend to present is an interpretation of 'such', 'ultimate', and 'questions' and some of its consequences for the conception of philosophy that I shall defend in the rest of the book. Before I do so, let me remove three sources of potential confusion.

First, I shall follow Russell in not distinguishing between *philosophical problems*, which he mentions in the preface, and *philosophical questions*, which he mentions in the first paragraph. I shall assume that the latter are mere linguistic expressions of the former, that this holds true also for the distinction between philosophical *solutions* and philosophical *answers*, and hence that the two couples of concepts can safely be used interchangeably. This is less trivial than it may seem because there is a significant difference between heuristics, understood as the method of *problem* solving (Pearl 1984), and erotetics, that is, the logic of *questions* and answers (Belnap and Steel 1976).

Second, when talking about *philosophical questions and answers*, I shall not presuppose them to be equivalent to *philosophers' questions and answers*. I take the latter to be degenerate cases of the former, to borrow a technical term[3] from mathematics that I will fully discuss at the end of Chapter 2.[4] They can be criticized as expressions of mere scholasticism.[5]

Third, I agree with Russell that the task of philosophy is twofold: the analysis of questions must precede, but then should also be followed by, the synthesis of answers. A philosophy without clear questions is sterile, but without convincing answers it is an abortion.

2. The Variety of Questions

There are many interesting ways of analysing questions. Some of them easily lend themselves to a metaphilosophical application. In particular, one may begin by concentrating on their *morphology*, and describe philosophical questions as *definitional* ('wh-...' kind of questions) or *existential* (as in 'existential quantifier', not as in Sartre). Textbook examples include: what is truth? What should I do? Why do we behave

---

[3] From a similar perspective, one may argue that *War and Peace* is a transcendental novel: http://www.salon.com/2015/01/11/leo_tolstoys_theory_of_everything.
[4] See also Floridi (2012a).   [5] As done in Dennett (2006), Floridi (2011c).

altruistically? Who am I? Is there a God? Can there be justice? And because of the classic 'ti esti...' ('what is...') format, one may hold that philosophical questions are therefore Socratic questions. In a well-known article, Uygur suggested as much:

> My main object is to *scrutinize the typical structure of a genuine philosophical question* without regard to the stage of research it might animate. My chief concern is to *describe* only the salient characteristics of a philosophical question. I see my task in showing what is contained in such a question; I want to throw light on what is asked in it, trying to point out, as correctly as I can, the basic form of a question proper to philosophy.   (Uygur 1964, p. 65)

This is a good start, but it does raise a difficulty: the philosophical specificity of Socratic questions soon appears to lie in their *topics* rather than in their *morphology*. Because one may object that it is because Socratic questions are about truth, duty, altruism, personal identity, God, or justice that they are philosophical. If so, their philosophical specificity would be primarily a matter of *reference*: their morphology would be a mere means to a more important end, that of unveiling the problematicity of their concep-tual targets. I suppose one could imagine a language in which all wh- and existential questions can only be expressed as propositional wants or needs (e.g. 'I need to know that *p*' or 'I must know whether *p*') and still fully maintain the philosophical nature of such wants and needs. So perhaps this is correct. Maybe there are intrinsically philo-sophical contents (*sense*) or topics (*reference*) from which relevant questions inherit a corresponding philosophical value, like moons illuminated by their suns. But even this cannot be the whole story. There is still at least one important aspect missing. Even with the right morphology and semantic features, Socratic questions may start from, but are not about, this particular empirical truth, or that idiosyncratic act of altruism. Moreover, in philosophy we do not seek to know whether there is a God or there can be justice in the fantasy world of Tolkien's *Lord of the Rings*. Therefore, *scope* and *relevance* are also important. For this reason, we also tend to qualify Socratic questions as abstract, universal, sometimes timeless,[6] and as important for us, our lives, choices, practical and intellectual pursuits, preferences, and moral behaviours. I am not sure this will not do. Russell seems to have thought that it did. As we shall see in section 7, this is why, I take it, he spoke of philosophical questions as '*ultimate* questions'. Indeed, a careful mixture of morphology, semantics, scope, and relevance has served the philo-sophical profession well for a long time. So, far be it from me to criticize it. What I would like to suggest is that there is another approach, compatible with the Socratic interpretation outlined above, which can help to clarify further what philosophical questions are and cannot be *today*. The chronological clause is important. Russell could not have been acquainted with the approach that I wish to advocate, because the latter

---

[6] Schlick (1932) already had some very convincing arguments against interpreting philosophy as the science of the general or a super-science. Yet his arguments seem to have gone unheard: see, for example, Dewey (1956) or Schlette (1968), two cases in which such an interpretation is still quite popular (it is also discussed in Glaeser (1969), rather approvingly), and what Dummett (2010) suggests about Quine and the naturalization project.

is based on a simple but ground-breaking lesson we have learned from studies in computational complexity since the 1960s: a lesson that had its roots in the work of Alan Turing (Fortnow and Homer 2003), who was born the same year Russell published his book. It seems that 1912 was some kind of accidental threshold.

3. A Resource-oriented Approach to the Nature of Questions

To understand the approach to the nature of philosophical questions that I intend to advocate, we need to take a step back.

Turing gave us a clear analysis of what an algorithm is. This is crucial in order to shift our perspective on the nature of computational problems, because having a standard way of formulating algorithms means having a universal parameter to calculate the complexity of the problems that such algorithms are supposed to solve. Thus, a Turing Machine works a bit like the standard metre in Paris. The result, a few decades after Turing's ground-breaking research, is that, in computational theory, one investigates the nature of problems by looking at their complexity, understood as the degree of difficulty of solving them, by studying the resources required to solve them.[7] This means that one does not focus on the specific *morphology* of the problems—because this is where having a universal model, such as a Turing machine, helps us not to be side-tracked—on their *semantic features*—because we are interested in whole classes of problems independently of their specific content and topic—or on their *scope* and *relevance*—because we are interested in their complexity, independently of their timeless applicability. Rather, one investigates the complexity of computational problems by studying the quantity and quality of *resources* it would take to solve them. This usually means considering the amount of *time* (number of steps) or *space* (quantity of memory) required. In this way, it becomes possible to study classes of problems that share the same degree of complexity, and to structure such classes in hierarchies of different degrees of complexity.

The importance of such a shift in perspective may be easily conveyed by means of a simple analogy. When studying animals, one may concentrate on their morphology (e.g. quadruped), or reproductive method (e.g. oviparous), or indeed many other features, such as their habitat (e.g. palustre, or swamp animal). Or one may consider what it takes it to keep an animal alive. According to this diet-oriented approach, a class of animals could be catalogued as frugivore, or fruit eater, for example. This is more or less what happens in computational theory: classes of computational problems are organized in terms of their complexity understood as the kind of resources they (would) consume in order to be solved.

---

[7] An excellent introduction is provided by Sipser (2012). I have provided a simple and philosophically oriented outline of computational complexity in Floridi (1999).

The previous analogy should help to clarify the resource-oriented approach adopted below: we can study questions by considering the resources required by their answers. It should also dispel any concern about the strategy I shall follow. It is not my intention to try the impossible, that is, to classify and study philosophical problems on the basis of their computational complexity. On the contrary, later in the chapter it will become obvious that this should be considered an outdated, Leibnizian dream. In philosophy, there are no experiments and no calculations, for reasons that will soon be obvious. What I wish to borrow, from computational complexity theory, is only the simple, yet very powerful, insight that the nature of problems may be fruitfully studied by focusing on what it may take in principle to solve them, rather than on their form, meaning, reference, scope, and relevance.

Equipped with this new conceptual tool and a different approach, let us now return to our initial attempt to clarify what a philosophical question is.

4. Three Kinds of Question

Questions may be of many kinds;[8] think of Socrates' rhetorical questions, for example, or his testing questions. And therefore they may serve a variety of purposes; for example, implicitly asserting that p, or explicitly checking whether Alice knows that p. However, it seems clear that, in this context (recall Russell's book), we are discussing questions as genuine requests for information[9] or *queries*: we are looking for an answer we do not have but would like to obtain.[10] It follows that, from a resource-oriented approach, and simplifying a bit,[11] we may distinguish between different kinds of questions as *queries* (henceforth I shall drop this qualification), depending on what kind of information it would take to answer them.

Obviously, some questions require empirical information to be answered, as when Alice asks Bob who is coming to their party on Saturday, and whether any guest is vegetarian. Equally obviously, some other questions require logico-mathematical information to be answered,[12] as when Alice asks Bob how many people might be coming

---

[8] Analyses abound. In connection with the nature of philosophical questions, Cohen (1929) already provided a clear analysis of the other senses that I disregard in this chapter, and further bibliographical references.

[9] "The question has usually been described as a request for information" (Cohen 1929); see also Llewelyn (1964) for an analysis of questions as ways to elicit information—what I have called queries.

[10] The proposal in Cohen (1929)—critically discussed by Llewelyn (1964), but see also Carnap, C. I. Lewis, Reichenbach, Ryle, Hamblin, and Presley—to construe questions as propositional functions is perfectly compatible with the theses defended in this chapter, but its adoption would merely burden the text with an unnecessary complication.

[11] I am simplifying here because, of course, hybrid cases are very common, combining features of more than one class (hence my use of the inclusive "or" in the text), but this refinement only makes things more obscure without helping to make the point any more convincing, so I shall rely on the reader's intelligence.

[12] Whether logico-mathematical resources may be defined as logico-mathematical *information* is a difficult issue because the informational nature of logic and hence mathematics is problematic; see Hintikka's "scandal of deduction" (Hintikka 1973). I shall not discuss this issue here. For a full discussion and a constructive proposal see D'Agostino and Floridi (2009).

if each guest brings a spouse, and whether there is one chair per person. However, still other questions may be answered by neither empirical nor logico-mathematical information (or a combination of the two), as when Alice asks Bob whether they should have a party on Saturday at all, or why it may be preferable to anticipate it to Friday. In this case, no matter how much empirical and logico-mathematical information Bob may use to formulate his answer, he may still fail to address Alice's question convincingly. This is repeatedly stressed in many contexts by philosophers of almost any school. To quote Uygur again:

the question 'Is consciousness a mechanism or organism?' requires primarily a thorough investigation of the respective concepts 'mechanism' and 'organism.' The ground for treating philosophical questions is thus not various world-facts—e.g. machines or living beings—but different discourses embodying these concepts.   (Uygur 1964, p. 67)

It gets worse. For Alice might marshal an equal amount of empirical or (inclusive or, I shall not repeat this clarification unless it is necessary) logico-mathematical information to formulate an answer different from Bob's, even if she and Bob may still be well informed, reasonable, sensible to each other's perspectives, and honestly willing to compromise. For this reason, I shall call this third kind of questions *open* to informed, rational, and honest disagreement. The reader will have guessed that philosophical questions are open questions, in the following sense.

5. Philosophical Questions as Open Questions

Empirical and logico-mathematical questions are in principle closed, whereas philosophical questions are in principle open. By this I do not mean to suggest that people necessarily agree on how to answer empirical and logico-mathematical questions (I wish). Nor am I suggesting that the relevant empirical or logico-mathematical information is always available as a resource to formulate a correct answer to any empirical and logico-mathematical questions (more wishful thinking). What I am suggesting is that empirical and logico-mathematical questions are such that, once we have the necessary and sufficient resources to formulate a correct answer, any further disagreement on that formulated answer may speak volumes about the parties involved but says nothing about the answer itself. This is how I interpret Kant (and I may be forcing this interpretation on him) when he writes:

there are sciences the very nature of which requires that every question arising within their domain should be completely answerable in terms of what is known, inasmuch as the answer must issue from the same sources from which the question proceeds. In these sciences it is not permissible to plead unavoidable ignorance; the solution can be demanded.

(Kant 2007, A 476/B 504)

If Alice and Bob disagree on who or how many people did come to their party, one of them is un- or misinformed, or irrational, or confused, or perhaps just stubborn, or a bit of all these. But if they disagree on whether the party should take (or should have taken) place at all (or on Friday rather than on Saturday), they may both be perfectly informed, rational, and open-minded. Philosophical questions are questions not answerable empirically or mathematically, with observations or calculations. They are open questions, that is, questions that remain in principle open to informed, rational, and honest disagreement, even after all the relevant observations and calculations have become available and the answers have been formulated.

Let us suppose for the moment that such definition is entirely correct (it is not, and it will need to be refined). Assuming that some questions are indeed open, how can we recognize them? A good test for the genuinely open nature of a question may look like the following.

Recall that questions are here understood as genuine requests for information. In ordinary circumstances—for example, barring circumstances in which one may wish to double-check whether one has received the correct piece of information, and so on—if the communication goes well and one receives the requested information, it would be unreasonable to reiterate the question. If Alice asks Bob: 'How many people are coming to the party?' and Bob answers, 'eight', then, in ordinary circumstances, assuming that Alice has fully and clearly understood Bob's answer, it would be unreasonable of Alice to reiterate the question, because she could not hope to be better informed by doing so. To use Wittgenstein's famous analogy, she would be buying another issue of the same newspaper to double-check the news (Wittgenstein 2001, § 265). Not a smart move. However, if it is reasonable to reiterate the question, as a request for further information, after having received any amount of relevant empirical or logico-mathematical information, then clearly one is asking a question that cannot be satisfied by the answer just received. Now this is what happens with open questions. Bob may ask Alice why they are organizing a party on Saturday, and all the empirical facts or observations and logico-mathematical proofs or calculations available will not make it unreasonable to keep asking the typical 'yes, but...' question: 'yes, I understand who is coming and what food we are serving and..., but why are we organizing a party on Saturday?' The careful reader will recognize in this test of 'reasonably reiterable query' a family resemblance with the open question argument developed by E. G. Moore (1993a) in his *Principia Ethica* to deal with the naturalistic fallacy.[13] The affinity is strong, and not accidental, since in both cases it is a form of antinaturalism that is driving the reasoning. A full discussion of this topic, and its relevance for a non-naturalist philosophy, will have to wait until Chapter 3, but I shall briefly return to it in section 7 below, when discussing the nature of philosophical questions as *ultimate* open questions, *closed* under questioning.

The definition of philosophical questions as open questions is a first approximation that needs to be refined, because it needs to be defended against four main objections. This will be the task of sections 6, 7, 8, and 9, respectively. At the end of such a defence,

---

[13] For a recent presentation see Strandberg (2004).

the definition will be more precise and cogent. But it will still need to be unpacked in order to see its implications. This task is left to the final section, which concludes the chapter. Before we look at the objections and replies, the definition can already be used to stop some vandalism: Hume's.

The reader may recall the following, famous quotation from Hume:

> When we run over libraries, persuaded of these principles, what havoc must we make? If we take in our hand any volume; of divinity or school metaphysics, for instance; let us ask, does it contain any *abstract reasoning concerning quantity or number*? [my italics] Does it contain any *experimental reasoning concerning matter of fact and existence*? [my italics]
>
> (Hume 2000, sec. XII, part III, 165)

Hume's 'experimental reasoning concerning matter of fact and existence' and his 'abstract reasoning concerning quantity or number' are just the empirical and logico-mathematical information mentioned above. As a consequence, if the answers to Hume's two questions (both empirical, by the way) are affirmative, then what I am suggesting is that we should search elsewhere, because that is science, not yet philosophy. But if the answers are negative, then it would be foolish to follow Hume's pyromaniac advice:

> Commit it then to the flames: for it can contain nothing but sophistry and illusion.
>
> (Hume 2000, sec. XII, part III, 165)

This is silly, for we would be throwing into the flames both the baby and the bath water (including Hume's philosophical books, by the way), if only the idiom allowed one to say so. Many questions that are not answerable by means of empirical or logico-mathematical information are also not a matter of 'sophistry and illusion'. Indeed, there is much space in between, represented by open (philosophical) questions of the highest importance. Most of what matters is often to be found in such an open space. Part of the careful task of a philosopher is to disentangle open questions from 'sophistry and illusion', rather than impatiently and intolerantly throwing the whole lot into the fire. Unfortunately, some people disagree and prefer Hume's vandalism. This is the first objection.

6. First Objection: There are No Open Questions

If philosophical questions are open questions, in principle unanswerable empirically or logico-mathematically, one may argue that such a definition is correct but includes too little, indeed nothing at all, and ends up being self-defeating. For one may accept that questions are in principle answerable *only* by resort to empirical or logico-mathematical information, so that anything else is just *reducible confusion* (open questions are actually closed) or *eliminable nonsense* (open questions are actually meaningless). Ultimately, the objection continues, there is no space between questions answerable by facts or observations and questions answerable by proofs or calculations, apart from a combination of the two kinds of resources. If the definition is correct, it makes the set of philosophical questions empty, either because they are reducible to empirical or logico-mathematical questions or because they can be fully eliminated, once they are shown to be meaningless questions. This is not merely an academic position. Famously, Schlick argued:

Thus, the fate of all 'philosophical problems' is this: some of them will disappear by being shown to be mistakes and misunderstandings of our language and the others will be found to be ordinary scientific questions in disguise. These remarks, I think, determine the whole future of philosophy.   (Originally Schlick 1932, see now 1979, vol. 2 p. 221)

Philosophers have often been the source of such Humean friendly fire. There is a simplistic way of reading the Vienna Circle as supporting a similar kind of intolerant vandalism. I write 'simplistic' because philosophers like Schlick were much more refined and interpreted philosophy as a necessary semantic *activity* rather than a science, following Wittgenstein (the ensuing quotation, provided by Schlick, is from the *Tractatus*, 4.112):

The view which I am advocating has at the present time been most clearly expressed by Ludwig Wittgenstein; he states his point in these sentences: 'The objection of philosophy is the logical clarification of thoughts. Philosophy is not a theory but an activity. The result of philosophy is not a number of "philosophical propositions", but to make propositions clear'. This is exactly the view which I have been trying to explain here.   (Schlick 1932)

The very idea of philosophy as a dissolution of its own problems as pseudo-problems (Sorensen 1993) is sympathetic to this first objection. It is a recurring temptation for impatient people. Recently, one of the most radical and vociferous advocates of such anti-philosophical position has been Stephen Hawking. In *The Grand Design—New Answers to the Ultimate Questions of Life*, we read:

We each exist for but a short time, and in that time explore but a small part of the whole universe. But humans are a curious species. We wonder, we seek *answers*. Living in this vast world that is by turns kind and cruel, and gazing at the immense heavens above, people have always asked a multitude of *questions*: How can we understand the world in which we find ourselves? How does the universe behave? What is the nature of reality? Where did all this come from? Did the universe need a creator? Most of us do not spend most of our time worrying about these questions, but almost all of us worry about them some of the time. Traditionally these are questions for philosophy, but *philosophy is dead*. Philosophy has not kept up with modern developments in science, particularly physics. Scientists have become the bearers of the torch of discovery in our quest for knowledge.   (Hawking and Mlodinow 2010, my italics)

Although this is not the place in which to discuss such a *boutade*—the reader interested in following the debate about it may find (Norris 2011) enlightening—it is worth considering Hawking's position in so far as it helps to clarify the self-reflective nature of philosophical questions and hence answer the first objection.

Hume and Hawking are right in holding that, if one assumes that philosophical questions are *closed* questions—if philosophy is in the business of dealing with 'experimental reasoning concerning matter of fact and existence', 'abstract reasoning concerning quantity or number', and 'discovery in our quest for knowledge'—then philosophy is dead, because it has (or at least it should have) outsourced the task of answering such questions to investigations that can help themselves to the right empirical or logico-mathematical resources; to science, to put it simply. In light of the previous section, however, it is equally sensible to read the previous inference as a *modus tollens*: since open questions are not reducible or eliminable, philosophy does not (have to) outsource them, so it is in a healthy state and in business. Indeed, one may argue that the more the world becomes a place where choices, strategies, policies, and interpretations matter, the more we need philosophy as an essential art of designing the right answers. But I am anticipating. Going back to the previous argument, the result is that we are caught in a classic stalemate whereby 'one philosopher's *modus ponens* is another's *modus tollens*', as the phrase goes. End of the story? Not quite, because this, that is, the stalemate itself, starts looking like an open question in and of itself, but even if one is still reluctant to step up the metatheoretical level, where questions begin to require a different kind of resources to be answerable in principle— impatient arsonists often show such reluctance—it is at least clear that the stalemate can be resolved by agreeing on whether there actually are genuinely open questions. One can use the same appeal to observations and calculations that supporters of the *modus tollens* advocate, to turn such an argument against them: factually, the burden seems entirely on the shoulders of people like Hawking. For it seems very hard to deny that many, if not most, of the significant and consequential questions we deal with in our life are open. Should Bob propose to Alice? Should they get married? Is it a good idea for them to have children? How can they cope with the loss of their parents? What sense can they make of their life together? Is Alice's career worth Bob's sacrifices? And if Bob later on cheats on Alice, should she forgive him, if he repents? Or should they divorce, even if they have children? Daily, unexciting problems, one may object, that do not deserve to be qualified as philosophical. I disagree, but suppose the objection sticks. There is, of course, a classic move that hinges on the peculiar self-reflective nature of philosophy itself. For, whatever philosophy is, every schoolboy knows that asking this question means philosophizing, Aristotle *docet*; and every schoolgirl is aware that disagreeing on whether philosophy is dead or alive has the same self-reflective effect of making one do philosophy, therefore providing a practical answer. Likewise, discussing whether there are genuinely open questions is in itself a philosophical question that qualifies as open, thus answering the very question from which it stems.[14] Questioning is a stepping-up process that sooner or later ends up trespassing on philosophy. This is good progress because a more precise way of under-

---

[14] As Uygur (1964) states: "'What is a philosophical question?' is a genuine philosophical question."

standing the crucial, self-reflective nature of philosophical questions is to realize that philosophical questions are open in terms of disagreement but 'closed' under questioning. Let me explain.

Closure is a simple but very powerful concept in mathematics, where a set is said to be closed under an operation if carrying out that operation on members of that set always produces a member of that set. For example, the set of positive integers 1, 2, 3,... is closed under addition: if one adds any two positive integers one always obtains another positive integer. Yet the same set is not closed (i.e. it is *open*) under subtraction: if one subtracts a larger positive integer, say 3, from a smaller positive integer, say 2, one moves out of the positive integers and enters into the set of negative integers, by obtaining in this case -1.

Now, the set of philosophical questions is such that if you question such questions, you obtain one more philosophical question. The set of empirical or logico-mathematical questions, instead, is not closed but open under questioning: carry on the questioning long enough, or by carefully choosing the right questions, and sooner or later you will end up 'outside' the set of those questions and inside the set of philosophical ones, which then you can no longer escape by further questioning the questions themselves. Think, for example, of questions about the nature of causality in everyday life and in scientific explanations. The problem with the first objection and with obituary positions à la Hawking is not just that they are merely mistaken but that they are self-contradictory, because bad philosophy is still philosophy.

In light of the first objection, we can refine our definition by saying that philosophical questions are in principle *open* questions, *closed* under further questioning. This is better, but unfortunately the new definition still fails to deal with a second difficulty: *inflation*. We just saw this above, when talking about Alice and Bob and their marriage. I wrote that all those questions are philosophical. But if we accept that philosophical questions are open questions, in the disagreement-based sense, and closed questions, in the set-theoretic sense, this may include way too much. We should consider as philosophical questions what to wear when going to Alice and Bob's party, whether one should accept their invitation, whether to bring a bottle of wine or some flowers, or why one was invited even if one is only an acquaintance. The space of philosophical questions would explode, and such an inflation would be evidence that something is wrong with the definition itself. This is the second objection.

7. Second Objection: There are Too Many Open Questions

It may seem that we jumped out of the frying pan into the fire: too many questions now count as philosophical because they are open. A vast variety of mundane uncertainties generates plenty of informed, rational, and honest disagreement. Will there be a financial crisis next year? In whichever way one may consider this question, it would be hard to catalogue it as philosophical, and yet it seems open. The concern is sensible, but, in the end, it can be dispelled, for two reasons.

First, uncertainties are not necessarily linked to open questions. Whether there will be a financial crisis next year (or a battle tomorrow, for Aristotle) is a closed question not because we have an answer—we do not by definition, and if we did, we could simply change the example—nor because disagreement, while lacking a definite answer, is unreasonable. It is closed because we understand that our lack of a definite answer, and hence our disagreement, is based precisely on insufficient empirical or logico-mathematical resources. Had we more empirical or logico-mathematical information, we would have a definite answer, on which it would then be unreasonable to disagree. So much so that by the end of next year (or tomorrow, for Aristotle), we will see that the question was closed. This is why, in section 2, I specified 'in principle'. Given boundless empirical and logico-mathematical information, *in principle* Alice and Bob could still honestly, informatively, rationally disagree on how they should go (or indeed should have gone) about organizing their party, but not about how many people attended it yesterday. The 'in principle' clause does an important job.

The second reason concerns the nature or topic of genuinely open questions. Recall that we decided not to pursue such an approach. I have just mentioned the question about the party. It is an open question. Is it also a philosophical one? The answer is yes, but in the same, uninteresting sense in which '2 + 2 = 4?' is a mathematical question. Questions do not have to be highbrow to qualify as philosophical. This is just a cultural prejudice. Philosophical questions, like empirical and logico-mathematical ones, come in a whole variety of degrees of value, importance, relevance, seriousness, difficulty, and so forth. We should approach them without chauvinism. Having said this, it is true that when dealing with philosophical questions we tend to concentrate on more significant and consequential problems than whether we should wear brown or black shoes at the party, no matter how much someone may agonize over this choice. But so do mathematicians and experimental scientists. The conclusion is that, yes, there are plenty of philosophical questions that are rather silly, frivolous, and hence negligible. But sometimes they are the starting point for a full escalation to big philosophical problems. And there are also plenty of empirical or logico-mathematical questions that share the same nature. They too, sometimes, lead to huge scientific problems. Why did the apple fall? Why is 1 + 1 = 2? It took two *Principia* to answer such questions. Philosophy tends to deal with the heavy side of the spectrum, but not necessarily, as some ordinary language analysis shows. On the whole, this is why, I take it, Russell added 'ultimate' after 'such'. In order to grasp better the meaning of this qualification, we need to see how questions are connected.

Questions (and their answers) may lead forwards to further questions. For example, 'Did you buy six bottles of wine?' may lead to the question 'Are you having a party?' which in turn may lead to 'Are you celebrating something?' When this happens, one may say that Q_1 poses Q_2, which poses Q_3, and so forth. But questions (and their answers) may also lead backwards, to previous questions: 'Did you buy six bottles of wine?' may lead to 'Did you buy any wine?' which in turn may lead to 'Did you go shopping?' When this happens, one may say that Q_1 presupposes Q_{-1}, which presupposes Q_{-2}, and so forth. More formally, erotetic implication—the logical relation interpreting the linguistic relations of 'posing' and 'presupposing' or of 'arising from', in the vocabulary of Wiśniewski (1994)—may be as formally stringent as that of ordinary implication. In the long run, it gives rise to a network, sufficiently loose to admit different topologies but not, for that reason, less robust. It follows that it is a mistake to think that ultimate questions are questions that come first or last in time, or at the beginning or the end of a chain of questions. Given the network of questions that mutually pose or presuppose each other, ultimate questions are those questions whose answers are most influential in terms of a cascade of further questions and answers to other related questions within that network. With an analogy, one may say that they are like key pieces in a jigsaw puzzle: once they are placed, it is much easier to locate the other pieces. For example, how one answers the question about the existence of God, or what is a morally good life worth living, has immensely more influence—in terms of how one answers other questions within one's own network—than how one answers the questions about the choice between black or brown shoes, or whether the party should be organized at all. Kant spends so much time discussing the question about causality because that is one of the cornerstones of our understanding of the world. Answer that, and a whole wave of consequences follows, leading to other questions. Ultimate questions are therefore attractors, in terms of systems theory: (answers to) less important questions within the system of questions tend to evolve towards (answers to) them over time. In terms of visual metaphors, it is better to imagine philosophical questions at the main nodes of our set of questions, big roundabouts in life's roads.

In light of the second objection, we can further refine our definition by saying that philosophical questions are in principle *open* and *ultimate* questions, *closed under further questioning*. This is even better, but unfortunately the new definition still fails to deal with a third difficulty: scepticism about the available resources. What if philosophical questions, as defined above, cannot be answered because of an inescapable lack of the right kind of information? This is the third objection.

8. Third Objection: Open Questions are Unanswerable

Philosophical questions may be philosophical doubts (see the quotation from Russell in section 1). When they are, they still preserve the features of being open to reasonable disagreement and closed under further doubting. So, one can follow Descartes, rely on closure, and deploy doubt to reach certainty about the doubting process itself: radical doubts generate more doubts, but at least this much is certain. The problem, even in a Cartesian-friendly scenario, is not so much that certainty is unreachable in this way but that a purely formal, that is, content-empty, status is all that one can reach safely.

The *Cogito* is like a geometrical point: it has a location in space and time but has no informational extent, that is, it is content-empty.[15] If it were not, its informational content could be successfully subject to further doubting, that is, in such a way as to shift further the source of one's own certainty. It is not, and so one can stop there, and use it as an Archimedean point, to step back into the content-full, but doubtable, extension of empirical and logico-mathematical information. In Descartes, that means adopting the clear and distinct features, shown by the content-empty certainty of the *Cogito*, as a bridge to re-acquire at least some of the empirical and logico-mathematical true contents (information) whose epistemic status was suspended during the doubting process. Philosophers disagree on the soundness of the process (see the so-called Cartesian circle problem) and the reliability of the outcome. The difficulty, in our case, is similar: a sort of stalemate. A sceptic like Sextus Empiricus would not argue against the value of our philosophical questions as defined so far, but he may agree with our definition of philosophical questions exactly in order to object that, given their nature, such open questions remain unanswerable in principle. The only resources we have available are declared by definition insufficient (not unnecessary, more on this presently) to provide an answer. Like Descartes' *Cogito*—the sceptic may continue—we have reached a safe point of no exit. Thus, the fact that this much is granted is not the beginning but the end of the story. So-called ineffabilist interpretations of the *Tractatus* reach similar conclusions. Or, to use a more Kantian example, we cannot answer questions about the nature of the *Ding an sich*, because we do not have access to God's database. The conclusion is that philosophical questions remain open not because of the ineliminable possibility of reasonable disagreement in principle, but because there is no way in principle of answering them, and that is because we lack the appropriate informational resources in the first place. The 'anything goes' is simply a relativist variant of the same objection: open questions are unanswerable because any answer will do, so no answer really fits. If a lock can be opened by any key, then there is something wrong with the lock.

If you draw the limits of your resources too closely to the questions whose answers need them for the questions to become answerable, you are left only with the questions themselves unanswerable. There are supporters of such a scorched earth objection, but I am not one of them, for a series of concatenated reasons. Before exposing them, let me make one point clear: carefully understood, when this third objection does not reduce to a version of the previous two, in itself it is an objection not against the value of the definition of philosophical questions adopted so far, but rather against the ambitions of a philosophy that seeks to answer them. It needs to be embedded within a *reductio* in order to work as an objection, somewhat along the following lines: if philosophical questions were so and so, then philosophy would be impossible, but philosophy is possible, so its questions are not so and so. This is usually deployed in order to sever the first half of philosophy's work, the analysis of the questions, from the second half, the synthesis of answers. The objection as a *reductio* logically leads to a

---

[15] I articulated and defended this thesis in Floridi (1996).

proposal for a different conception of philosophy, in terms of only the first half, described as conceptual analysis and clarification. All that is left is then Wittgenstein's view of philosophy as an activity, not a theory. As Dummett (2010) puts it:

[In philosophical debates] the matter is not one to be settled by empirical means: scientific theory may bear on it.... But science could not resolve the dispute: no observation could establish that one or the other side was right. A philosopher will seek either to show that one of the disputants is right and the other wrong, perhaps after some further clarification of the two views, or else to dissolve the dispute by showing both sides to be victims of some conceptual confusion. Philosophy is indeed concerned with reality, but not to discover new facts about it: it seeks to improve our understanding of what we already know. It does not seek to observe more, but to clarify our vision of what we see. Its aim is, in Wittgenstein's phrase, to help us to see the world aright.   (Dummett 2010, p. 10)

Dummett is right, but note how there is something mysterious in what he suggests: where do the two views come from, if not from philosophy itself? Philosophy so impoverished as to be only analysis without synthesis must implicitly, quietly, silently delegate to others the task of producing the *analysanda*. It is only a critical and never a constructive enterprise. In this sense, analytic philosophy shares the same pessimism that characterizes continental deconstructionism: someone else does the job of building conceptual artefacts required to make sense of the world, not philosophers, whose parasitic task extracts value from other intellectual enterprises. This seems to be historically incorrect and conceptually disappointing. It is also morally dangerous, as I shall clarify in the Conclusion. Admittedly, it does remain a viable option. But let me show you why the objection that leads to such a conclusion may be less convincing than it looks, and so why it may be unnecessary to drop the classic conception of philosophy as analysis of questions and synthesis of answers, still endorsed by Russell himself in 1912 (recall: 'philosophy is merely the attempt to answer such ultimate questions', not just to clarify them).

To begin with, the objection is based on a suspicious divide between two alleged sets of open questions: those for which we do have, at least in principle, the required resources to provide an answer, and those for which, allegedly, we do not, not even in principle. That the objection presupposes such a divide becomes clear once one realizes that, when dealing with the second objection, we acknowledged the fact that there are plenty of simple, ordinary questions that qualify as open—such as whether one should accept Alice's invitation to her party. With respect to them, it would be very difficult to argue that we do not have any resources to help us in reaching an intelligent, reasoned answer. Whatever the resources that we use to answer such mundane open questions are—and I shall say more on this presently—they are sufficient to provide a reasonable ground for deliberation and possible, reasonable disagreement. It follows that the objection must mean something else, and this 'else' is the divide to which I just pointed above: the objection must apply not to all open questions, declared unanswerable—for this would be factually mistaken—but only to those that we have defined as in principle open, ultimate questions, closed under further questioning—in short, to the *philosophical* ones in a more interesting sense of the qualification. This divide is very controversial, but suppose such a preparatory move, assumed by the objection, is acceptable. The restriction in scope is not inconceivable, but it does underestimate two factors quite seriously, and hence very implausibly.

First, we saw in the previous section that questions do not occur in isolation. To put it in more Quinean terms, we always deal with a web of questions, posing or presupposing each other. In such a web or network, we saw that philosophical questions as ultimate, open questions, closed under questioning, do have a privileged role because of their influence, but they are not detached from other questions. This is important in terms of two kinds of constraint. Non-ultimate, open questions as well as empirical and logico-mathematical questions receive answers that constrain the space available for answering philosophical questions of an ultimate kind, the philosophical ones declared unanswerable by the objection. As in a Sudoku puzzle, once the easiest answers start piling up, constraints facilitate answering more difficult questions, and so forth. This is why we actually live our lives with our philosophical questions answered by default, perhaps only implicitly and uncritically, through our practices, choices, lifestyles, belief presuppositions, and so forth. We do not usually keep a stack of ultimate questions in a state of suspension. Living is living philosophically, no matter how bad is both the living and the philosophy. So much so that philosophy often begins by challenging our default answers.

Second, the way in which we go about answering mundane, simple, indeed even trivial, open questions points in the right direction when it comes to identifying what resources we can use to deal with ultimate, open questions. Empirical and logico-mathematical resources are likely to be necessary constraints, but they are insufficient. The kind of resource missing has many names in philosophy, and it is here that misunderstanding may occur quite easily. If I were to speak of myths, stories, or narratives, readers would justifiably raise their eyebrows, for this is too vague. In section 4, we saw that Uygur referred to 'discourses embodying these concepts', and indeed, in modern terminology, one could speak of ideas and conceptions, judgements or considerations, but still be found wanting, for this is too restricted. Referring to thoughts, mental states, intuitions, common sense, language-games, semantic practices, or some post-Gettier doxastic vocabulary would mean being even more short-sighted. Cassirer's symbolic forms are perhaps too grandiose, as *Weltanschauung* and cultural *milieu* are. The suggestion by (Dummett 2010) that 'the philosopher's only resource is the analysis of concepts we already possess' seems to approach the problem correctly (resource orientation) but fails to be sufficiently inclusive. Yet I hope that these examples start delineating a profile with which the reader is *de facto* well acquainted.

The resources to which I am referring do include Alice's beliefs, what Bob reads on the web, their cultural background, their language, religion, and art, their social practices, their memories of what was, and their expectations about what will be, their social and emotional intelligence, their past experiences, and so forth. It is the world of mental contents, conceptual frameworks, intellectual creations, intelligent insights, dialectical reasonings. I do not know a word that captures this resource very well. In other contexts, I have spoken about it in terms of *semantic artefacts*: the totality of the outcome of our creative semanticization (giving meaning to and making sense of) and conceptual design of reality. Yet this will not do in this chapter, where we need an inclusive adjective, comparable to 'empirical' and 'logico-mathematical' in terms of scope and *level of abstraction* (more on the latter in the next section). Therfore, let me suggest we opt for *noetic*.[16] It is because of the noetic nature of the resources required to answer philosophical problems that the latter have always tended to be seen more akin to logico-mathematical problems than to empirical ones. Let me quote Dummett one more time:

Philosophy shares with mathematics the peculiarity that it does not appeal to any new sources of [empirical (my addition)] information but relies solely upon reasoning on the basis of what we already know.   (Dummett 2010, p. 10)

Dummett's 'what we already know' is part of what I have called *noetic resources*. Philosophical questioning, as I wish to present it in this chapter, begins by acknowledging one irreducible fact: the permanent nature of informed, rational, and honest disagreement about significant questions, relevant to our lives. These are the questions that I have defined as open to reasonable disagreement, closed under questioning, and ultimate in terms of influence on other questions when it comes to answering them. We have just seen that they are the ones that may be constrained by empirical and logico-mathematical resources, but require noetic resources to be answered. Critics fail to grasp that philosophy is not in the business of discovering solutions but in that of *designing* them. It is *conceptual design* not formal logic that lies at the heart of philosophical thinking, as I shall argue in Chapter 10 more extensively. We rely on semantic artefacts to formulate, discuss, and make sense of open questions, such as the ones Russell and Hawking list, and then to design and assess answers for them. And since the world is becoming more complicated not less, the philosophical space between the empirical and the logico-mathematical is growing, not shrinking. This is why the need for philosophy is actually increasing, not decreasing.

   In light of the third objection, we can now refine even further the last version of our definition by saying that philosophical questions are in principle *open, ultimate, closed under further questioning*, and possibly *constrained* by empirical and logico-mathematical resources, which require *noetic resources* to be answered. This is an improvement, but we have not yet completed our task. There is one last objection that needs to be taken seriously, because the analysis developed so far fails to provide any

---

[16] As in the case of logico-mathematical information, the careful reader may wonder what kind of information is (noetic) information. I take it to satisfy at least the definition provided in Floridi (2011c): well-formed, meaningful, and truthful data. Note that truthful, however, needs to be understood in the realist, constructionist, but "correctness" sense defended in Floridi (2010c and 2011c), as any realist, representationalist, but correspondentist theory will probably not work. Moore seems to adopt a similar approach in his *Principia*; see now Moore (1993a).

means to discriminate between good and bad philosophical questions. This is what we shall see in the next section.

9. Fourth Objection: Open Questions are Indiscriminate

We saw that questions (and answers) never occur in a vacuum but are always embedded in a network of other questions (and answers).[17] Likewise, they do not occur out of any context, without any purpose, or independently of any particular perspective, what I have called above a *level of abstraction* (LoA). So open questions may be 'bad' questions when they are asked in the wrong context or for the wrong purpose. In both cases, philosophers tend to be social bores or gadflies, but such a *faux pas* has nothing to do yet with the answerable nature of open questions. What does matter here is whether an open question, assuming it is a valid question, that is, properly formulated,[18] is asked at the right LoA. This difficulty requires a short diversion in order to introduce the very idea of an LoA.[19] It will play a crucial role in Chapter 2, where I shall explain it more extensively. For the time being, a quick sketch will do.

Imagine the following scenario. Alice asks Bob the price of an item, let's say a second-hand car. Bob gives her the following answer: 5,000. The question concerned a *variable*, namely the price x of the car in question, and Alice received an exact numerical value for the variable, yet something is missing. She still has no idea about the price, because she does not know the *type* of the variable: is it British pounds, US dollars, euros...? Of course, the context usually helps. If Alice is in England and Bob is a local car dealer, her question should be understood as concerning the price in British pounds, and so should the answer. This is trivial, one may think. Grice's conversational rules obviously apply (Grice 1989). It is, and they do. But this is also a crucial assumption, easily forgotten. In November 1999, NASA lost the $125m Mars Climate Orbiter (MCO) because the Lockheed Martin engineering team used British (also known as Imperial) units of measurement, while the agency's team used the metric system for a key spacecraft operation. As a result, the MCO crashed into Mars.[20] Assuming that contexts will always disambiguate the types of your variables paves the way to costly mistakes. This is why the idea of a 'level of abstraction' plays an absolutely crucial role in how we handle any information process carefully, and so in how we negotiate our interactions with the world, and therefore in how we develop our philosophy and

---

[17] The erotetic implication, when answers are also included, covers the three cases analysed in Wiśniewski (1994): the relation of implication of a question by a question and a set of declarative sentences, namely, answers or questions and answers; the relation of implication of a question by a question; and the relation of strong implication of a question by a question and a set of declarative sentences (ditto).

[18] Cohen (1929) provides an early analysis of invalid questions, such as "Who discovered America in 1491?"

[19] The interested reader is referred to Floridi (2008b, 2011c).

[20] "Mars Climate Orbiter Mishap Investigation Board Phase I Report" (Press release). NASA: ftp://ftp.hq.nasa.gov/pub/pao/reports/1999/MCO_report.pdf.

ethics of information. This is so even when a specific LoA is wrong or left implicit, as in the MCO example.

So, what has all this got to do with bad open questions? Quite a lot, as it turns out: bad open questions are absolute questions, that is, questions that are formulated with no regard for the kind of LoA at which their possible answers become sensible. They are like questions asking for the absolute or 'real' price of a car, impatient for any specification of any currency. The following two examples should help to clarify the mistake.

Consider Kant's classic discussion of the 'antinomies of pure reason'. As is well known, each of the four antinomies comprises a thesis and an antithesis, which are supposed to be both reasonable and irreconcilable. I list them here by slightly adapting their formulation from Kant's *Critique of Pure Reason* (Kant 1998):

1) *Thesis:* the world is finite; it has a beginning in time and is limited in space.

Antithesis: the world is infinite; it has no beginning in time and no limit in space (A 426–27/B 454–55).

2) *Thesis:* the world is discrete; everything in the world consists of elements that are ultimately simple and hence indivisible.

Antithesis: the world is continuous; nothing in the world is simple, but everything is composite and hence infinitely divisible (A 434–35/B 462–63).

3) *Thesis:* there is freedom; to explain causal events in the world it is necessary to refer both to the laws of nature and to freedom.

Antithesis: there is no freedom; everything that happens in the world occurs only in accordance with natural causation (A 444–45/B 462–63).

4) *Thesis:* there is in the world an absolutely necessary Being.

Antithesis: there is nothing necessary in the world, but everything is contingent (A 452–53/B 480–81).

One may take each thesis and antithesis as an answer to the corresponding question. As Kant argues, the conflict is not between empirical experience and logical analysis. Rather, the four antinomies are generated by an unconstrained request (recall: we are treating philosophical questions as queries, that is, genuine requests for information) for *unconditioned* answers to fundamental problems concerning (1) time and space, (2) complexity/granularity, (3) causality and freedom, and (4) modality. And this is where Kant's transcendental method and the method of LoAs converge: the attempt to strive for something unconditioned is equivalent to the natural, yet profoundly mistaken, endeavour to analyse a system (reality in itself, for Kant, but it could also be a more limited domain) independently of any (specification of) the LoA at which the analysis is being conducted, the questions are being posed, and the answers are being offered, for a specified purpose. In other words, bad open questions are questions that try to avoid, or overstep, the limits set by any relevant LoA.

Second example. Closer to our time, Turing is probably the first to have introduced the *method of levels of abstraction* in philosophy, at least in terms of influence

(Floridi 2012c). He made clear, for the first time, how philosophical questions could be answered only by fixing the LoA at which it would then make sense to receive an answer. This is one of the greatest and lasting contributions of his famous test (Turing 1950), far more important than the incorrect predictions about when machines would pass it, or what consequences one should draw if they did pass it (Floridi, Taddeo, and Turilli 2009). It is sometimes forgotten that Turing refused even to try to provide an answer to the question 'Can a machine think?' because he considered it a problem 'too meaningless to deserve discussion' (Turing 1950, p. 442). Recall what Uygur said about the question 'Is consciousness a mechanism or organism?' Using our simple example, in both cases it would be like asking the price of the second-hand car in absolute figures, insisting that no currency is used in order to express it. Nonsense. Likewise, Turing objected that the question involved vague concepts such as 'machine' and 'thinking'. In other words, it was an open question that lacked a clear LoA. So Turing suggested replacing it with the Imitation Game, which is exactly more manageable and less demanding because it fixes a rule-based scenario easily implementable and controllable (Moor 2003). By so doing, he specified an LoA—the 'currency' he chose for the game was human intelligence, but it could have been something else, from animal intelligence to human creativity, as many other versions of the Turing imitation game have shown—and asked a new open question, which may be summed up thus: 'May one conclude that a machine is thinking, at the Level of Abstraction represented by the imitation game?' This is an open question well formulated.

After half a century, philosophy is still learning that absolute, open questions are bad philosophical questions not worth asking, as the following quotation from Quine indicates:

The very notion of an object at all, concrete or abstract, is a human contribution, a feature of our inherited apparatus for organizing the amorphous welter of neural input....Science ventures its tentative answers in man-made concepts, perforce, couched in man-made language, but we can ask no better. The very notion of object, or of one and many, is indeed as parochially human as the parts of speech; to ask what reality is really like, however, apart from human categories, is self-stultifying. It is like asking how long the Nile really is, apart from parochial matters of miles or meters.   (Quine 1992b, see now 2008, p. 403)

Too often, philosophical debates seem to be caused by a lack of, or misconception about, the right LoA at which the open questions should be addressed. Absolute (i.e. not properly LoA-constrained) questions generate absolute messes. Many pseudo-philosophical puzzles can be dismissed as mere muddles caused by a lack of LoA. This is not to say that the method of LoA represents a panacea. Disagreement is often genuine and not based on confusion, but chances of resolving or overcoming it, or at least of identifying a disagreement as irreducible, may be enhanced if one is first of all careful about specifying the LoA at which the open question is being formulated and therefore what answers it is sensible to expect in the first place.[21]

---

[21] The careful reader will have understood that this whole chapter is an attempt to set the right LoA at which to answer the question about the nature of philosophical questions.

We are now ready for the final version of the definition: philosophical questions are in principle open, ultimate, but not absolute questions, closed under further questioning, and possibly constrained by empirical and logico-mathematical resources, which require noetic resources to be answered.

All that remains to do now is to look at some of the consequences of this definition for the conception of philosophy applied in the second part.

Conclusion: Philosophy as Conceptual Design

The definition of philosophical questions at which we have arrived by adopting a resource-oriented approach has several advantages. I shall outline some of them here rather briefly. I suspect they may be more easily appreciated by doing some philosophy in such an informational way in the second part. And I hope they will become clearer as the reader goes through the following chapters.

To begin with, approaching philosophical problems as open questions helps to explain the development of philosophy itself. Through time, philosophy outsources questions whose answers turn out to require not noetic but empirical or logico-mathematical resources. I am oversimplifying, of course, since usually many questions tend to require all three kinds of resources anyway, but I hope the point is sufficiently clear: there was a time when many questions we consider nowadays scientific, that is, closed, were taken to be philosophical, that is, open, from astronomy to medicine, from psychology to zoology. At the same time, philosophy insources new or renewed open questions, generated by the history of humankind, its development, discoveries, inventions, new semantic artefacts, new answers to empirical or logico-mathematical questions, new intellectual challenges, and so forth. It is, in other words, a two-way trade between open and closed questions. The geographical discoveries and their cultural impact, the scientific revolution, the Enlightenment, new social, political, and economic conflicts, the debate on the foundations of mathematics and physics, the energy and environmental crises, and the information revolution are all significant examples of macroscopic sources of new open questions (that should be) addressed by philosophy.[22] Like a living heart, philosophy goes through a cycle of systole and diastole, contraction and dilation, outsourcing and insourcing of problems and solutions. Of course, looking at only half the cycle, like a sort of long and agonizing contraction, leads people to declare such a heart dead or at best dying. The mistake should now be obvious. Because philosophy works in cycles and does not move in a straight line, it is preferable to see the history of philosophy as a matter of *evolution* of the semantic artefacts we develop to deal with open questions, rather than a matter of *progress*. In the long run, regardless of how many ups and downs, steps forward and steps back, revolutions and counter-revolutions, progress in science is measured in terms of the accumulation of answers to closed questions, answers that are no longer genuinely open to informed, rational, and honest disagreement. Here is how Schlick summarized the same point:

[22] I have argued in favour of this point in Floridi (2011c, 2014a).

[R]eal questions … can always be shown by proper analysis that they are capable of being solved by the methods of science, although we may not be able to apply these methods at present for merely technical reasons. We can at least say what would have to be done in order to answer the question even if we cannot actually do it with the means at our disposal. In other words: problems of this kind have no special 'philosophical' character, but are simply scientific questions. They are always answerable in principle, if not in practice, and the answer can be given only by scientific investigation.   (Originally Schlick 1932, see now 1979, vol. 2 p. 221)

Still, in the long run, evolution in philosophy is measured in terms of accumulation of answers to open questions, answers that remain, by the very nature of the questions they address, open to reasonable disagreement. So those jesting that philosophy has never 'solved' any problem but remains forever stuck in endless debates, that there is no real progress in philosophy, clearly have no idea of what philosophy is about. They may as well complain that their favourite restaurant is constantly refining and expanding its menu. They should be served a piece of raw mammoth.

The cyclical, progressive nature of philosophy leads to a further consideration. Because philosophy formulates new open questions and designs new answers, or revises old open questions and redesigns their answers, by being in a two-way interaction with its time, it is better to understand philosophy as a *timely* rather than a *timeless* study of open questions.[23] This is not an invitation to follow intellectual fashions but a reminder that living philosophy needs to interact with open problems by being careful not to lose sight of their long-term relevance (context) and purposefulness (human interest). Anything else is historical curation: the preservation, maintenance, and study of the noetic assets accumulated by humanity to answer open questions. It is a vital task, given that arsonist vandalism seems a constant temptation, but it should not be confused with the actual production of such assets. Only the latter qualifies philosophy as the source of conceptual innovation. Of course, there remains one sense in which philosophy, understood as the study of open questions, is, at its best, everlasting. This is when philosophy is not disconnected from its time (timeless) but is so well connected (timely) to human interests as to withstand its own outdating. After all, philosophy as the study of open questions is eschatological by nature: we saw that the open questions that matter most are the *ultimate* ones. A classic in philosophy offers answers that retain their value long after they have been articulated, and can be repurposed in new contexts. *Philosophia perennis* means philosophy you can hack (more on this in Chapter 4). Otherwise, we would not be reading the *Republic*, the *Nicomachean Ethics*, the *Meditations*, the *Critique of Pure Reason*, or Russell's *The Problems of Philosophy*.

Once we realize that philosophical questions are those open to reasonable disagreement, it is a simple act of humble rationality to admit the possibility that other

---

[23] "If by *philosophia perennis* we are to understand the permanence of questions of philosophy, then philosophy is the very reverse of *perennis*; it possesses no fixed framework because it is constantly renewed through fresh questions" (Uygur 1964).

answers may be equally acceptable, sometimes preferable. This is not relativism, for it is perfectly feasible to assess the value of different answers and to deliberate on their respective merits. Recall the example of the restaurant above. It is rather a matter of tolerance. Yet such tolerance is not boundless. For we have seen that empirical and logico-mathematical resources as well as other answers in the networks of questions make philosophy, as the 'science' of open questions, respectful of the empirically true, the mathematically proved, and the logically valid. It is a very bad philosophy indeed that disregards or even disparages some of the highest achievements of human intellect. Here, I fully subscribe to the conclusions reached by Mulligan, Simons, and Smith in their 'What's Wrong with Contemporary Philosophy?' Let me take the liberty to quote their splendid text extensively:

> The honest pioneering spirit of the early and constructive phase of AP [analytic philosophy] had its close parallels also in the early phenomenologists, so much so that a century ago there existed no gulf between them. And it is precisely this spirit that must be rekindled. Philosophers should learn and practice their analytical skills. They should prize the theoretical virtues of consistency, analytic clarity, explanatory adequacy, and constrained simplicity, be aware of the historical depth and pitfalls of the ideas they are manipulating, and be wary of the assumption that everything new is better. They should trust to common sense, avoid bullshit, and beware celebrity. But above all they should lift their heads above philosophy: study and respect good science and good practice, and try to understand their implications. Like scientists, they should cooperate with one another and with other disciplines, and seek funding for cooperative research, aiming at theoretical comprehensiveness, using topic-neutral skills and knowledge to bridge compartments in knowledge. They should learn how to present ideas clearly to all kinds of audiences, and not just to fellow aficionados of the fake barn. Above all, philosophers should be humble, in the face of the manifest complexity of the world, the acumen of their philosophical predecessors and non-philosophical contemporaries, and their own fallibility. But with this humility they should be unwaveringly resolved to discover, however complex, frustrating and unlovely it may be, the truth.   (Mulligan, Simons, and Smith 2006, p. 67)

'They should be unwaveringly resolved to discover . . . the truth', that is, to give answers to the open questions we find so pressing. The overall picture of philosophy that emerges from this chapter is one of a constructive enterprise, in which the identification and analysis of open questions is not the whole task but the preparatory stage for the design (not invention, not discovery) of satisfactory answers. In the past, philosophers had to take care of the whole chain of knowledge production, from raw data to scientific theories, as it were. Throughout its history, philosophy has progressively identified classes of empirical and logico-mathematical problems and closed questions, and has outsourced their investigations to new disciplines. It has then returned to these disciplines and their findings for controls, clarifications, constraints, methods, tools, and insights but, *pace* Carnap (1935; see especially the chapter entitled 'The Rejection of Metaphysics') and Reichenbach (see especially Reichenbach 1951), philosophy itself consists of conceptual investigations whose essential nature is neither empirical nor logico-mathematical. In philosophy, one neither tests nor calculates.

Recall what Dummett, quoted above, suggests: philosophy 'does not make any observations or conduct any experiments of its own'. I agreed. But philosophy is not a conceptual aspirin, a super-science, or the manicure of language either. Its method is *conceptual design*, that is, the art of identifying and clarifying open questions and of devising, refining, proposing, and evaluating explanatory answers. It is in this (scholarly incorrect but more interesting)[24] sense that I like to interpret Schlick's distinction between science, as the pursuit of truth, and philosophy, as the pursuit of meaning. Philosophy is, after all, the last stage of reflection, where the semanticization of Being is pursued and kept open (Russell 1912). Its critical and creative investigations identify, formulate, evaluate, clarify, interpret, explain but above all answer questions that are intrinsically capable of different and possibly irreconcilable treatments, questions that are genuinely open to informed, rational, and honest disagreement, even in principle. It is a constructive enterprise, whose investigations are often entwined with empirical and logico-mathematical issues, and so scientifically constrained, but, in themselves, they are neither. They constitute a space of inquiry broadly definable as *normative*. It is an open space: anyone can step into it, no matter what the starting point is, and disagreement is always possible. It is also a dynamic space, for when its cultural environment changes, philosophy follows suit and evolves.

It matters enormously whether a culture, a civilization, or a society is friendly towards philosophy as 'the attempt to answer such ultimate questions', that is, as the study of open questions, which designs conceptual artefacts to answer them. One way of understanding the *incipit* of Aristotle's *Metaphysics*, that 'All men by nature desire to know', is to realize that we all wish to have our open questions answered. Humanity cannot bear such a semantic vacuum. The serious risk is that, if philosophy does not address such open questions, someone else will. Those who oppose philosophy are consigning to a bad philosophical treatment all the ultimate, open questions whose answers guide most of our lives. They should realize that dubious gurus, religious fundamentalists, impostors, and charlatans of all kinds will step in. The fight against philosophy is a fight for obscurantism.[25] If you play with Hume's fire, you will get burned.

---

[24] (Schlick 1932). Of course, Schlick ends up interpreting philosophy as a semantic activity, a conclusion I tried to show to be evitable.

[25] This is lucidly argued in Wood (2006). I agree with Wood that philosophy should closely collaborate with science, society, and its own history in its fight against the dark forces of stupidity.

2

Philosophy as Conceptual Design

Summary

Previously, in Chapter 1, I provided an updated interpretation of the nature of philosophical questions, based on the kind of informational resources required to answer them. I suggested we should consider philosophical questions to be in principle open to informed and reasonable debate, ultimate in terms of consequences but not absolute in terms of being free from any Level of Abstraction, closed under further questioning, possibly constrained by empirical and logico-mathematical resources, and requiring noetic resources to be answered. Several consequences follow from this analysis. Three are more significant for the following chapters. Philosophy, now understood as the study or science of open questions and their answers, becomes primarily a form of *conceptual design*. This is what we are going to see in this chapter, where I offer an account and a defence of *constructionism*, both as a metaphilosophical approach and as a philosophical methodology, with some references to the philosophical tradition that has inspired it, the so-called 'maker's knowledge' tradition, a topic to which I shall return for a detailed discussion in Chapter 9. Here, we shall see that such *constructionism* needs to be reconciled with *naturalism* (recall that philosophy as conceptual design may be critical but also respectful of the best knowledge and reasonings we may have). This is the topic of Chapter 3. And at the end of the book, in Chapter 10, I shall return to the constructionist issue to understand what difference it makes in terms of a *poietic* (constructive) rather than a *mimetic* (representational) epistemology of the knowing subject.

The main thesis I shall defend in this chapter is that Plato's 'user's knowledge tradition' should be complemented, if not replaced, by a constructionist approach to philosophical problems in general and to knowledge in particular. Epistemic agents know something when they are able to build (reproduce, simulate, model, construct etc.) that something and plug the obtained information in the correct network of relations that account for it. Or, in even more intuitive terms, an agent qualifies as an epistemic agent not when she is a passive user of some information, but when she is a critical producer of it. Her epistemic expertise increases in relation to the scope and depth of the questions that she is able to ask and answer on a particular topic. The maker's knowledge is knowledge of the ontology of the semantic artefact and this is a fundamental epistemological lesson we can learn from poietic disciplines such as computer science, economics, engineering, architecture, or law. So, constructionism shifts the focus away from the *mimetic, passive, and declarative knowledge that* something is the case, in order to concentrate more on the *poietic, interactive, and practical knowledge of* something being the case, that is, of semantic artefacts. Once applied to the interpretation of philosophy itself, constructionism suggests adding *conceptual design* to *conceptual analysis* as a fundamental method.

1. Introduction: From the User's Knowledge to the Maker's Knowledge

There are critical crossroads, in the history of philosophy, when a small conceptual step in one direction has immense consequences for the kind of further investigations it encourages, and the potential alternatives it obliterates. Plato took one of those influential steps when he endorsed the distinction between *episteme* and *techne*, and insisted on grounding our understanding of human knowledge on a user-oriented approach, favouring a passive and mimetic reception of semantic information. Section 2 is largely devoted to the analysis of that crucial step, which ended up influencing twenty-five centuries of epistemological work.

As we shall see, it would be incorrect to suggest that nobody ever questioned 'the user's knowledge' approach, what I shall call the *Platonic dogma*. One may even argue that the historical Plato himself never quite endorsed the Platonic dogma in the way I shall describe below. Perhaps. But it is the Plato that we find in the history books that I have in mind. And along the same line, it is fair to state that, in the same books, the Aristotelian tradition *partially* (on this qualification see section 3) reinforced the Platonic dogma—recall the piece of wax passively taking on the impress of a signet-ring—while Christian philosophy never radically challenged it, attributing to God, like Plato, the only creative intellect in the universe. Alternative views, clustered under the 'maker's knowledge' approach, amounted to a minority report at most; witness contemporary epistemology textbooks, which hardly even mention it. Nowadays, despite some attempts to promote a more nuanced, if not an opposing view about the interactive, constructive, and creative (henceforth *poietic*) origins and nature of our knowledge of the world (e.g. by the American Pragmatists), we still find our academic culture and its philosophers accepting, by default, the priority of knowledge-that over knowledge-of and knowledge-how, of theory over practice, of thinking over doing, of representations as copies and reproductions over representations as models and constructs.

The difficulty lies partly in the fact that the Platonic dogma has its strongest ally in the unquestionable success of our commonsensical dealings with everyday reality—what might be called the 'What You See Is What You Get' experience of the world—partly in the fact that, together, the Platonic dogma and the commonsensical naïve realism shape the very framework within which any further reflection on the nature of knowledge is critically developed.

Given the deep entrenchment and far-reaching roots of the Platonic dogma, pessimism with regards to its overturning may seem fully justified. And yet, some room for hope is offered by the increasing discrepancy between Plato's epistemological orthodoxy and many of our actual epistemic practices. The scientific revolution was made possible by the abstraction and mathematization of phenomena, and the pervasive technologization of science: *episteme* and *techne* may not have entered into philosophical marriage yet, but they have been bedfellows for centuries now, in any lab. The information societies in which we live are neo-manufacturing systems in which the expert and intelligent handling of data and information is the primary value-adding occupation of the majority of the working population. Any child who learnt by doing, any person aware of the fact that understanding requires much more than passive observation, any student trained in a lab or in a field, any engineer who ever designed an artefact, any scientist who ever ran an experiment or devised a simulation, any user who ever felt the need to know more about a technology than just how to enjoy it, any academic who has realized that teaching is a great way of learning, and, in general, anyone involved in the business of information creation, refinement, transmission, and acquisition must have perceived, at some point, that our ever richer insights into the nature of reality have their foundation in our practical and creative interactions with it. We do things with information, to paraphrase Austin (1962). It is because we *know how* to do this and that creatively, interactively, and collectively that we can rightly report to *know that* such and such is the case passively and individually. Propositional knowledge is the glorious conclusion of the informational process, not its humble beginning.

The intellectual divide between epistemic practices and epistemological theorization is widening, not least because the pressure coming from the immense amount of information we are exponentially generating is pushing us towards developing new techniques and technologies to handle them, and new epistemic ways to exploit them. We should be very suspicious of the increasing pedagogical insignificance of our epistemology based on the user's knowledge approach.[1] It seems clear that, if epistemology wishes to be more than just an intellectual game, utterly divorced from the actual dynamics of human knowledge, and hence irrelevant to its understanding and furtherance, it must retrace Plato's steps, and take a different direction. The risk is to foster an epistemological culture of passive information receivers and consumers, rather than of critical and proactive information producers and designers. The time has come to be epistemologically heretical, to abandon a passive, mimetic, user-oriented perspective as to how we generate our knowledge of the world, and join forces with some of the less orthodox thinkers in our philosophical tradition, in favour of a maker-oriented

---

[1] The philosophical constructionism defended in this chapter goes hand in hand with constructionist learning theory (Harel and Papert 1991), according to which learners understand the world by building mental models, and the view that this practice is facilitated by the actual handling of physical objects (see also Piaget's experiential learning theory).

approach. Knowledge is not about getting the message from the world; it is first and foremost about negotiating the right sort of communication with it.

It would be easy to be radical, yet such temptation would also be naïve. For it would mean failing to appreciate the true difficulty of our task. Merely moving in the direction opposite to the one taken by Plato and classic epistemology after him would be difficult, yet simple. This is the unsuccessful strategy adopted by Romantic idealism and post-modern *constructivism* (with a *v*, not an *on*). Both have ended up as friendly fire for the sort of *constructionism* I suggest we should develop. For if the choice is mistakenly reduced to be between denying

(i) either any poietic value to our epistemic activities,

(ii) or any existence, or at least ontological independence, to the external world,

then you only need to miss the train once, or spill some coffee in the morning, to regain some sanity and make up your mind about who is right and who must be wrong. Various forms of constructivism are nothing more than *haute couture*, made possible precisely by that excessive reliance on the propositionalization of our knowledge of the world that they then seek to criticize. At best, they are innocuous parasites that live in a symbiotic relation with the culture they criticize but on which they entirely depend for their survival. They are the best enemy that a conservative, user-oriented epistemology may wish to have, for they pose no credible challenge, since their position is even less tenable than the Platonic dogma they seek to overthrow.

It follows that our difficulty is complex, because it consists in being radically moderate: we need to identify and follow the middle course, represented by the *design* of the world. This hardly thrills young minds, smacks of compromise to older ones, and, worst of all, cannot escape the constant risk of being confused with either Scylla or Charybdis, *discovery* or *invention*. During an arm-wrestling event, you neither expect nor look forward to a balanced draw between the two wrestlers. That is not the exciting outcome of the competition. Likewise, in philosophy we seek clear-cut alternatives and resolutions. In epistemology, we wish either knowledge or reality to pin the other's arm onto the surface of a conclusive answer over primacy once and for all. We can hardly hold firm the view that *constructionism* is neither *realism* nor *constructivism*, because knowledge neither *describes* nor *prescribes* how the world is, but *inscribes* it. The powerful and intuitive polarization between realism and idealism, discovery and invention, naturalism and anti-naturalism, represents the intellectual temptation that makes our difficult task so delicate. For we need to ensure that what we appreciate as the highest and most cherished form of knowledge—our increasingly successful capacity to capture the world in a network of propositional contents and relevant accounts—maintains its deserved high status, keeps flourishing, and remains open to further progress, while replacing the foundations that make it so reliable. We wish to be friendlier to truth, without becoming enemies to Plato. With a political analogy, our revolution will not consist in dethroning classic epistemology as the philosophical Queen, but in transforming her kingdom into a constitutional monarchy. Or think of the difficult but simple task of removing, piece by piece, a fragile dinner service from a table, compared to the difficult and very complex task of pulling a tablecloth from under the same dinner service at once. At the end of the process, if we are successful, what will have changed is what the items are placed on, not their positions.

A change as radical and yet complex and delicate as the one outlined above is not achievable by an individual, let alone by a single book or chapter. So, in the following pages, I intend only to contribute to what I hope may be a larger movement, in which I enlist Kant's transcendental epistemology and Peirce's pragmatism as being among its best expressions. I shall do so by gathering supporters and defending a constructionist philosophy of information. Here is the line of reasoning in synthesis.

In section 1, I shall describe briefly the Platonic step and why it was not a necessary step, and one that could have been recovered. The Platonic dogma left us with some problems and, in section 2, I shall argue that the maker's knowledge tradition, from Bacon to the philosophy of information, may provide a viable alternative to their solution. The rest of the chapter is devoted to outlining a constructionist philosophy (section 3), by discussing minimalist principles (section 4), the method of levels of abstraction (section 5), and constructionism itself (section 6). The chapter ends with a brief conclusion (section 7) that introduces Chapter 3.

2. Plato's Wrong Step

Who really knows an artefact? Plato addresses this question several times in his dialogues. His answers are *largely* (more on this qualification later) consistent, despite being provided at different stages of his intellectual development.

In the *Cratylus*, a dialogue traditionally attributed to the so-called transitional or middle period, Plato argues (390b–d) that the *user* of an artefact (in this case a weaver using a shuttle) knows it better than its *maker* (the carpenter who makes the shuttle). The argument is at best controversial. Allegedly, it is the user who knows whether the proper form (the blueprint) is correctly given to the artefact. Today, we would say that it is up to the user to determine the (or at least up to the maker to guess the user's) functional requirements and the usability features of an artefact first, and then assess how far the actual product satisfies both. Yet, why the maker is supposed to lack (and indeed the user possess) such knowledge of the form remains unexplained, even in the best scenario in which Plato might be talking only of the functional requirements and usability features. Equally puzzling is how the maker could actually produce a good artefact in the first place without a solid grasp of its blueprint.

A later and more famous statement of the 'user's knowledge' dogma fails to be more convincing. The first half of the tenth book of the *Republic* is dedicated to the issue. At the beginning, we find the famous argument of the three couches (597b): the ideal couch is produced by God, the physical couch is made by the carpenter, and then the 'fake' one results from the painter's imitation. The imitator gets bashed, as expected, but the interesting point here is to note that God has intrinsic knowledge of the couch because he is the source of its blueprint, the designer of the perfect exemplar. Intriguingly, no user is mentioned. Later, however, the tripartite distinction shifts into the familiar pattern we have already encountered in the *Cratylus*. In 601c–d, the new example involves reins and bit; the painter fails to know their real nature, since he merely imitates them, and the makers, the cobbler and the smith, have no real knowledge of them but only justified beliefs about their nature, a lower kind of knowledge. The genuine knower is the horseman, who understands how to use them and is truly acquainted with their nature. Plato uses the three-way distinction between *imitating*, *making*, and *using*, in order to argue now (all translations are from Plato 1989):

That there are some three arts concerned with everything, the user's art, the maker's, and the imitator's … [and] the user of everything is the one who knows most of it by experience, and that he reports to the maker the good or bad effects in use of the thing he uses.
(Plato 1989: *Republic* 601–d)

The user now provides the benchmark in the artefact's evaluation, in view of functional requirements and usability features. The maker is merely reduced to a first-class imitator, the imitator of God's creations. Plato has forgotten the real maker, God the Ur-maker, who is the master of a fourth, poietic art, not mentioned. The user becomes the judge, who evaluates how closely the human maker is able to reproduce the blueprint provided by the divine maker.

Historically, Plato might have been motivated by cultural and social biases to degrade the maker's knowledge to mere true belief. Perhaps the artisan must be seen as a mere living tool, a slave, in the hands of the user. As he writes:

the work of the carpenter is to make a rudder, and the pilot has to direct him, if the rudder is to be well made.   (Plato 1989: *Cratylus*, 390d)

Plato might have been unaware of such biases: for he seems to write as if it were utterly obvious and uncontroversial that an artisan could never possibly qualify as a knower with respect to its artefacts. Philosophically, it is important to note that, in both dialogues, the primary targets of Plato's arguments are not the makers (the legislators in the *Cratylus*, and the artisans in the *Republic*), but the imitators (the sophists and the artists, respectively). In both cases, the dismissal of the maker's knowledge as second-rate appears to be collateral damage, in a battle fought against more dangerous and worthier foes. That this is so becomes clearer once we look at another transitional or middle-period dialogue, the *Euthydemus*.

In the *Euthydemus*, Plato defends a more complex interpretation of the relationship between maker's and user's knowledge, not entirely coherent in itself, as we shall see presently, and less consistent with the conclusions reached in the other two dialogues, but much more interesting. Initially, the basic argument looks similar. However, perhaps because the context is not immediately represented by the controversy against potentially competing sources of knowledge such as rhetoric (the sophists) and traditional culture (poets and artists), Plato seems willing to endorse for a moment a more balanced view. Here are the important passages in question:

[288e–289a] ... even if we knew how to turn all the stones into gold, the knowledge would be worth nothing to us; for unless we know *also* how to use the gold, we saw there was no benefit in it. ... In the same way, it seems there is no benefit in any other knowledge, of business or of physics for example, or anything else which *knows how to make something but not how to use what it makes* (ποιεῖν τι ἐπίσταται, χρῆσθαι δὲ μὴ ᾧ ἂν ποιήσῃ). ... [289b] Even if there is a knowledge how to make men immortal, without the knowledge how to use immortality even this seems to bring no benefit. ... Then ... we need such a knowledge (ἐπιστήμης) as *combines* both how to make something (ποιεῖν) and how to use what is made.   (Plato 1989: *Euthydemus*)

The Greek word translated as *combines* is συμπέπτωκεν, literally 'falls along with'. The conciliatory tone could not be more explicit: user's and maker's knowledge are complementary types of know-how, which must be joined together in order to reach full and useful *episteme*. This is the crucial crossroad where Plato could have taken a different path. He does not, because he immediately recalls the specific makers he wishes to attack, the speechmakers, and more generally the sophists. And like someone who, running away from danger, decides to take not the path that leads in the right direction, which he acknowledges to be the closest, but rather the path which is diametrically opposite to where the danger emanates, out of fear rather than reason, so Plato cannot resist the temptation to revise the relationship between the two complementary kinds of knowledge into an opposition, as soon as the old foes reappear. He simply overreacts and, quite astonishingly, in the following passage, which comes immediately after the one quoted above, he completely undermines what he just defended:

[289b] Then we must be *nothing at all* like those who make harps, for instance; we do *not want to become masters of knowledge like that*; [289c] for there the making art is one thing, the using art quite another, and each art deals separately with the harp. For the arts of harp making and harp playing are very different.   (Plato 1989: *Euthydemus*)

One would have expected an appeal to multidisciplinarity, to use a buzzword of our times. Plato could have taken the direction of a more complex education of the philosopher both as a maker and as a user, as a knowledge 'produmer' (producer and consumer).[2] Instead, he prefers to contradict the complementary thesis he just supported, and establish a dichotomy between the user's superior and the maker's inferior knowledge of an artefact. In this way, he can build a stark contrast between the good

---

[2] In his book *The Third Wave*, Alvin Toffler coined the term 'prosumer' to refer to the blurring and merging of the role of producers and consumers (Toffler 1980). Toffler attributed this trend to a highly saturated marketplace and the mass production of standardized products, prompting a process of mass customization, and hence an increasing involvement of consumers as producers of their own customized products. The idea had been anticipated by Marshall McLuhan and Barrington Nevitt (McLuhan and Nevitt 1972), who attributed the phenomenon to electricity-based technologies. Unaware of these precedents, almost twenty years after Toffler, I introduced the word 'produmer' to capture this phenomenon in Floridi (1999). Later, I used it to refer to the consumption of information produced by the same population of producers, for example on YouTube.

and the bad guys, the philosophers and the sophists. The step is taken; maker's and user's knowledge, *techne* and *episteme*, and hence practical and theoretical knowledge start moving apart; the dogma has entered our epistemology. It immediately shows its power: a few lines after the passage quoted above, Plato compares hunters to makers, who do not know well enough what they have hunted and must hand it over to the cooks, the users; he tells us that generals, like hunters, capture cities and armies, but they must then hand them over to politicians, the users who know better, and finally, he writes

[290c] Geometers and astronomers and calculators—for these are sort of hunters too, since they are not mere makers of diagrams, but they try to find out the real meanings—so because they do not know how to use them, but only how to hunt, they hand over their discoveries, I take it, to the dialecticians to use up, at least all of them hand over who are not quite without sense. (Plato 1989: *Euthydemus*)

Something seems to have gone badly awry. Some sort of ideology of power and control, together with the philosophical agenda to cast the highest level of discredit on those wordsmiths and makers of discourses that are the poets and the sophists, pushes Plato in a direction that is practically untenable and philosophically implausible. Who, if not a philosopher, could believe and argue that the maker of an artefact knows it less well than its user? Try that next time your car breaks down and needs to be repaired. Plato was right in stressing the importance of both kinds of knowledge, and he was wrong (and for the wrong reasons) to argue that the user's knowledge should be preferred to the maker's.

The last quotation from the *Euthydemus* introduces a further complication. Geometers, astronomers, and calculators are makers of a special kind of artefact. Today, they would be called knowledge workers, who produce and manage information. This is something that we, as epistemic agents, create, share, and transmit among ourselves and across generations, and accumulate and refine through time. It is difficult to follow Plato when he holds that users know their iPhone better than Apple, at least without adding several qualifications. And it is impossible to agree with him when Wikipedia users are said to know the information they access better than those who actually generated it in the first place. This is a *reductio*. Unless what we are supposed to have in mind is the equation producer = reproducer; that is, unless we hold the view, as Plato seems to, that the ultimate knowledge of things is something we can at most access (reminiscence), but that we do not build. If there is an ultimate, ideal Wikipedia, which producers of the entries of the actual, human Wikipedia are only gradually approximating, then those producers do not have better knowledge of the contents they are conveying, no more than a policeman knows a crime scene better than the criminal. What counts is the exposure to the truth and how you handle it (user's knowledge), not how you construct it in the first place (maker's knowledge). In Plato, geometers, astronomers, and calculators are not co-workers in the scientific enterprise, but mere communication channels through which pre-existing information reaches the dialecticians. Research is reduced to uncovering and reporting. This is disappointing, not least because it prevents understanding the contraposition between dialectic (διαλέγεσθαι) and eristic (ἐρίζειν) in terms of two procedures to engineer semantic artefacts, to be judged on the quality of their products. If sophists and ignoramuses are mere imitators, like painters, and if philosophers or scientists are not the makers with whom we should compare them, then one may argue that none of them is closer to knowing the genuine nature of the semantic artefacts in question. Charlatans of all sorts, in all ages and societies, can feed irresponsibly human cultures with irrationalism, obscurity, dogmatism and relativism, fake news, and 'alternative truths', as one would write these days, at least by claiming to be no worse than their opponents. Such charlatans are disgraceful not because they sell us conceptual replica—as Plato argues—but because they sell us conceptual lemons. Since in Plato it seems that

(i)   all that matters is how you use some information and assess it against the actual, genuine referent,

then the user's knowledge dogma further requires

(ii)   a form of external realism about information (the ideal Wikipedia out there), and

(iii)   some theory explaining our potentially noiseless access to it (recollection is perfectly suited).

Very coherently, Plato defended all three positions. Yet each of them seems to be highly questionable and has been subject to endless criticisms. Is there an alternative to a Platonic philosophy of information? How can information, as a conceptual/semantic artefact, be (better) known by its makers? For a full epistemological answer the reader will have to skip to Chapter 10. What follows is a metatheoretical analysis.

3. The Maker's Knowledge Tradition

The alternative approach to Plato's is a *constructionist* philosophy of information. This is based on the maker's knowledge tradition, which in turn has its roots in some strands of the Aristotelian-Scholastic philosophy. If genuine knowledge is knowledge of the intrinsic nature of the object known (knowledge of the ontology of the known), and if there is no innate acquisition of such blueprint, then knowing a phenomenon, an artefact—or, in our case, gaining information and being able to account for it—means being able to produce it and reproduce it, to assemble and disassemble it, to build and dismantle it, to improve it, and answer questions about it, and all this for the right reasons. For knowledge to be possible, *mimesis* must be replaced by *poiesis*. A similar thesis can be found in the Aristotelian-Scholastic tradition, which holds that knowing something means having a full understanding of the causes that bring about the known. From a Christian but non-Greek perspective, God the Ur-maker is the only artisan that creates *ex nihilo*. This is how God the maker may be seen to be omniscient— recall how Plato himself had to acknowledge the superior nature of the Ur-maker's knowledge in the *Republic*—and how humanity, by partaking in God's nature, may have some epistemic access to the created universe. Nowadays, as I shall argue in Chapter 10,[3] we may be better off by analysing knowledge in terms of holding the information that such and such is the case and being able to provide the correct account of why this is so (Floridi 2012b). The user's knowledge approach can easily be atemporal and single-agent: it does not really matter how many people are looking at the wall, or how many get out of the cave. The maker's knowledge approach, on the contrary, requires trial and error and time-consuming processes of accumulation, so knowledge becomes a collaborative enterprise of growth and refinements in a multi-agent system (humanity) across generations. It is based on man-hours. As Aristotle writes:

... each thinker makes some statement about the natural world, and as an individual contributes little or nothing to the inquiry; but a combination of all conjectures results in something considerable.   (*Metaphysics* II,[α], 1, 993b, 1–5)

Of course, the Aristotelian-Scholastic tradition does not hold a constructionist epistemology yet, for the view of knowing as a passive process of discovery and acknowledgement of the state of the world in itself is still predominant; witness the very history of the word 'information' (Floridi 1994). But when Francis Bacon writes, in the *Novum Organum*, that 'Vere scire, esse per causas scire' (To know truly is to know through causes) he is more than just paraphrasing an Aristotelian maxim: he is pointing us in a new, anti-Platonic direction, according to which we, as epistemic agents, can only know what we make as Ur-makers. This is a major transformation in perspective brought about by Bacon and later on by the scientific revolution. *Constructionism* holds that knowledge is acquired through the creation of the right sort of *semantic artefacts*; information modelling, in other words. We are the builders of the infosphere we inhabit, Bacon's 'intellectual globe'. Thus, both the philosophy of language and the philosophy of mind should be at least equally concerned with creative rather than reproductive capacities, as I shall indicate in Chapter 4. The obsessive emphasis on mimetic representations and propositional knowledge is misplaced. We do not and cannot gain knowledge by passively recording reality in declarative sentences, as if we were baskets ready to be filled (a metaphor used by Descartes and criticized by Popper); instead we must handle it interactively.

A constructionist philosophy might be cause for concern. Even from a historical point of view, the maker's knowledge tradition has often been suspected of sceptical sympathies. Kant himself was accused of being a sceptic. So Hintikka was right in arguing that

[I]n many respects pessimistic conclusions [from the *verum ipsum factum* thesis] should have been as close at hand in Bacon's time as the optimistic ones. ... It is a sobering thought that

---

[3] See also Floridi (2011c).

[in the maker's knowledge approach] the leading idea of the intellectual background of modern applied science and scientific technology can be traced back to sceptical and theological principles calculated to extol the superiority of the Divine practical reason over the human one.

(Hintikka 1974, pp. 85–6)

Yet such concern overlooks the fundamental task of modern constructionism, which is that of soldering together the Platonic dichotomy between human and divine making and hence between the two different epistemological 'arts', by reinterpreting the dualism between human and divine knowledge in ontological terms, between *noumena* and *phenomena*, between the reality of data in themselves and the world of information as we know it.

This is not scepticism, and it is not relativism either. It would be difficult to over-stress how realistically oriented such constructivism is. Since the beginning, it has been based on a new understanding of technological production and control (e.g. in Bacon) and perceptual cognition (e.g. in Locke). Recall the 'false friends' mentioned in the previous section. Bacon was certainly no idealist. Locke has been interpreted—rightly in my view—as a supporter of a maker's knowledge epistemology (Tully 1980; Jacovides 2002). And I am certainly not advocating a *constructivist* epistemology. But just in case some readers were still suspicious about the empirical pedigree of the maker's knowledge approach, and hence of the corresponding *constructionist* philosophy of information, here is how Hobbes aptly sums up the view that the only true knowledge is knowledge possessed by the maker of his creation:

Of arts some are demonstrable, others indemonstrable; and demonstrable are those construction of the subject whereof is in the power of the artist himself, who, in his demonstration, does no more but deduce the consequences of his own operation. The reason whereof is this, that the science of every subject is derived from a precognition of the causes, generation, and construction of the same; and consequently, where the causes are known, there is place for demonstration, but not where the causes are to seek for. Geometry therefore is demonstrable, for the lines and figures from which we reason are drawn and described by ourselves; and civil philosophy is demonstrable, because we make the commonwealth ourselves. But because of natural bodies we know not the construction, but seek it from the effects, there lies no demonstration of what the causes be we seek for, but only of what they may be.   (Hobbes 1656, Epistle Dedicatory; EW, VIII, 183–4)

Hobbes still lacks a view of science as a poietic activity, and of perception as a way of interpreting data, but he is on the right track: in the mathematical as well as in the human sciences we can acquire full knowledge because we can come to know the causes of our objects of investigation. After all, you know a theorem if you know how to prove it, not if you can merely state its result, and experiments do not imitate the world, they shape it in controllable ways, as Galileo understood.

So far I have described the new theoretical outlook. We have a new direction towards which *constructionism* might develop. The question is how. One way to answer this question would be by embarking on a thorough historical exploration.[4] Unearthing the various intellectual stages through which the maker's knowledge tradition developed, as one of the important epistemological undercurrents of modern philosophy, into a contemporary constructionist movement, would be both fascinating and enlightening. Yet this is not what I intend to do in the rest of this book. Another alternative would be to show how empirical knowledge itself develops through the constructions of our information about the world. This is how I interpret Kant's epistemological project, and in Floridi (2011c) I have tried to show how Kant's transcendentalism might be combined with a constructionist philosophy of information. Chapter 10 will provide further details on such a constructionist epistemology. Here, I wish to keep the dialogue with Plato open, and hence still work at the same metalevel of reflection, applying the reflective lesson endorsed in Chapter 1. If the user's knowledge approach is joined by that of a maker's knowledge, as a viable way of making sense of human knowledge, can it be applied to itself, and hence be used to make sense of a constructionist methodology? In other words, could the maker's knowledge approach be coherently applied to the very theorization of its value? Can we make sense of the possibility that it might be constructionism all the way up, and hence include philosophy as well? We saw in Chapter 1 that the short answer is yes: by interpreting philosophy in general and the philosophy of information in particular as conceptual design. The long answer will keep us busy for the rest of this chapter.

4. A Constructionist Methodology

Too much ink has been spilt on philosophy as conceptual analysis. The alternative view, that philosophy is at least as much, if not actually more, engaged with creating, refining, and fitting together our conceptual artefacts in order to answer open questions, that is, questions that are not answerable in principle empirically or mathematically,[5] has received too little attention.[6] Clearly, much work lies ahead, and what I shall highlight here is no more than a contribution to such a large project. I shall divide the overview into three parts: *minimalism*, the *method of levels of abstraction* (LoAs), and *constructionism*. Together, they flesh out a constructionist methodology, that is, a philosophy that takes seriously the view that the maker's knowledge is the right approach from which to interpret all expressions of human knowledge, from our empirical interactions with the world to the self-reflective interpretation of our own epistemology and philosophy. This means that I take *minimalism*, the *method of levels of abstraction*, and *constructionism* as providing the core of a constructionist philosophy

---

⁴ On the history of the knowledge maker's tradition see Child (1953) and Pérez-Ramos (1988). I read Rorty (2009) as a criticism of the user's tradition.

⁵ I discuss the nature of open questions and of erotetic foundationalism in Floridi (2011c).

⁶ For an interesting exception, of course coming from two non-analytic philosophers, see Deleuze and Guattari (1994).

of information. However, I am also aware that other philosophers of information may wish to endorse only *minimalism* and the *method of levels of abstraction*, but not a full constructionist philosophy. I suspect Dretske might have been one of them, for example.[7] For this reason, I shall restrict the use of that label to refer only to the third part, instead of the whole. If you are a constructionist, you are likely to be better served in your philosophy by a minimalist approach and the method of LoAs. But you might wish to help yourself with the latter two tools and stop short of accepting a maker's knowledge perspective.

5. Minimalism

Minimalism is an erotetic principle. The view is simple: philosophical questions often pose multi-faceted problems, which can form a problem space, which, in turn, following Descartes, can be decomposed and dealt with by means of a divide-and-conquer approach (Raftopoulos 2003). The outcome is a set of more approachable sub-problems, interconnected in a sort of Quinean web of dependencies (Quine 1951). We saw in Chapter 1 that, when dealing with a philosophical question, the starting problem often presupposes other open problems. The strength of the answer depends on the strength of the corresponding assumptions. A minimalist starting problem relies as little as possible on other open problems, thereby strengthening the final answer to the philosophical question. Very often, one may improve the tractability of a problem space by choosing a model with which to study it. *Minimalism* outlines three criteria to orientate this choice: *controllability*, *implementability*, and *predictability*.

A model is controllable when its features can be modified purposefully. Given this flexibility, the model can be used as a case study to test different solutions for the problem space.

The second criterion recommends that models be implementable, usually through the description of conceptual mechanisms (e.g. thought experiments, analogies, logic constructs, ideal models, counterexamples, etc.), sometimes through virtual simulations (also known as experiments *in silico* (Grim 2003)), and seldom through physical realizations. The more transparent a model becomes, that is, the more its mechanism and dynamics move from making it a black to making it a white box, the better. Metaphorically, the maker of the model is a Platonic 'demiurge', fully cognizant of its components and of its state transition rules. The model can therefore be used as a conceptual laboratory to test specific constraints on the problem space.

The third criterion follows from the previous two: ideally, the chosen model should be such that its behaviour should be foreseeable, at least in principle. The demiurge can forecast the model's behaviour in that she can infer the correct consequences

---

[7] I have learnt much from Dretske in general, and I agree with him in several ways, but I believe that, because of Dretske (1994) and some later conversations we had, he would not have welcomed the sort of synthetic (as opposed to naturalized) constructionism I defend in this chapter.

from her explanations of the model. The model outcomes then become the benchmarks of the tested solutions.

Given the previous three criteria, three properties further characterize *minimalism* as I am advocating it here. First, *minimalism* is *relational*. Problems and models are never absolutely minimalist, but always connected with the problem space posed by the philosophical question. Such a relational nature percolates through the approach, making it easier to understand that, often, a conceptual difficulty lies in the innate temptation to see only Boolean solutions. I have already referred to this tendency above, when mentioning the difficult task of steering a middle course between extremes that work as very powerful attractors. For example, as soon as a particular issue is framed in terms of *internalism* vs. *externalism*, we lose the possibility of opting for a third, *liminalist* solution. Imagine being forced to define the concept of 'food' either in externalist terms, only as physical nutrients in the world, or in internalist terms, only as dietary requirements for a specific biological species. The debate could easily be endless, since food is a relational concept. Recall my early warning: *relationalism* or, as I prefer to call it, *liminalism*, is most emphatically *not* to be confused with *relativism*. It is simply false to say that something is food independently of the nature of the feeder, but it is also obviously false to say that, therefore, it just depends on the eater, and hence that anything might qualify as food. Relativists should be made to eat their hats. Semantic information is another useful example, for it is neither only in the environment nor only in the mind, but arises from the interactions of specific agents within their environment. The relational nature of *minimalism* further clarifies the need to *triangulate* our basic concepts: it is often easier to start with a Boolean dichotomy, but it is equally often essential to treat the dichotomy as providing, as in geometry, the two known points at either end of a distinction which can help to determine the third point that provides the right perspective on the issue under examination. The reader might rightly perceive traces of a Hegelian logic in this.

Second, *minimalism* provides a way to choose critically the most fruitful starting problem for the analysis of a problem space, thus enhancing the strength of the next step forward in the process of answering the philosophical question. According to a minimalist approach, the tractability of a philosophical problem is a function of the three criteria outlined above. They allow the use of dynamic models to test possible solutions and to derive properties of the problem space.

Finally, *minimalism* is a matter of inferential relations between a problem and its space, but it is not a way to privilege simple or elementary problems. Minimalist problems may be difficult or complex. *Minimalism* is an economic method related to, but not to be confused with, Ockham's razor. The two methods are of course compatible and indeed complementary. However, whilst Ockham's razor increases clarity and elegance and avoids inconsistencies and ambiguities by eliminating redundant, explicative, or ontological elements in a theory, *minimalism* offers criteria for choosing problems and models relative to a given specific question. Moreover, Ockham's principle of parsimony is absolute and is applied to any theoretical element, while *minimalism's* main maxims of strength and tractability are always relative to a given problem space. Thus, a quick and dirty way of defining *minimalism* is by describing it as the erotetic version of Ockham's razor.

The definition of *minimalism* is based on two main assumptions. One concerns the existence of a problem space. *Minimalism* does not give an account of the decomposition process of the problem space to which it applies. The other is that a dynamic model, whether conceptual, virtual, or physical, is useful in finding the answer to the investigated question. *Minimalism* does not explain why and how this approach works. In the next sections, two other methods are presented to ground both assumptions: the *method of levels of abstraction* and *constructionism*. We already saw that the *method of levels of abstraction* is used to describe the observables that compose the problem space and how they are related. *Minimalism* is always relative to a given Level of Abstraction, because the structure of the problem space depends on the LoA assumed by the investigator. *Constructionism* clarifies how to devise the model and how to use it in order to investigate the set of minimalist problems that will lead to the required answer.

6. The Method of Levels of Abstraction

The *method of levels of abstraction* (henceforth *method of abstraction*) has been formalized in Floridi (2008b).[8] The terminology has been influenced by an area of computer science, called *Formal Methods* (Zeigler 1976; Boca et al. 2010), in which discrete mathematics is used to specify and analyse the behaviour of information systems. Despite that heritage, the idea is not at all technical and, for the purposes of this chapter, no mathematics is required.[9] We already saw in Chapter 1 a couple of examples: the price of a car, and NASA's Mars Climate Orbiter disaster. Let us consider another everyday example.

Suppose we join Alice, Bob, and Carol at a party. They are in the middle of a conversation. Alice is a collector and potential buyer; Bob tinkers in his spare time; and Carol is an economist. We do not know the subject of their conversation, but we are able to hear this much:

- Alice observes that *it* (whatever the reference of 'it' is) has an anti-theft device installed, is kept garaged when not in use, and has had only a single owner;
- Bob observes that its engine is not the original one, that its body has been recently re-painted, but that all leather parts are very worn;
- Carol observes that the old engine consumed too much, that it has a stable market value, but that its spare parts are expensive.

---

[8] The reader interested in a more technical treatment and further applications may wish to consult Hoare (1972) and Floridi (2008b, 2010a, 2011c, 2013b). I am grateful to Hoare for pointing out the relevance of that text.

[9] For a recent, mathematical implementation of the method of abstraction see in particular Le Goc and Vilar (2017).

The participants view the 'it' according to their own interests, which teleologically orient the choice of their conceptual interfaces or, more precisely, of their own *levels of abstraction* (imagine a computer interface; more on this presently). We may guess that they are probably talking about the second-hand car we already met in the first chapter, but, if you check carefully, although it is not true that 'it' could be anything—it could not be a cat—there is enough scope for it to be a motorcycle, or even an airplane, since any of these three artefacts would satisfy the descriptions provided above by A, B, and C. Whatever the reference is, it provides the source of information under discussion. We shall call this 'it' the *system*. An LoA consists of a collection of observables, each with a well-defined possible set of values or outcomes. For the sake of simplicity, let us assume that Alice's LoA matches that of an owner, Bob's that of a mechanic, and Carol's that of an insurer. Each LoA makes possible a determinate analysis of the system. We shall call the result or output of such analysis a *model* of the system. Evidently, a system may be described at a range of LoAs and so one can have a range of models. We are now ready for a more formal definition.

When discussing the price of the car, in the example in Chapter 1, we saw that a 'typed variable' is understood as a variable qualified to hold only a declared kind of data. For example, if Bob asks Alice for her telephone number, whatever the latter is (variables), he expects natural numbers to be the type of the variables she will provide. Since the system investigated may be entirely abstract or fictional the term 'observable' should not be confused here with 'empirically perceivable'. Historically, it might be an unfortunate terminological choice, but, theoretically, an *observable* is just an *interpreted typed variable*; that is, a typed variable together with a statement of what feature of the system under consideration it represents. For example, a set of data could have natural numbers as a type and *telephone number* as a feature of the system. A level of abstraction is a finite but non-empty set of observables, which are expected to be the building blocks in a theory characterized by their very choice.

From the previous example and definition, the reader might have guessed that an *interface* is a specific kind of LoA, one that is placed between systems and transforms the outputs of a source (call it system S) into the inputs of a target (call it system T), producing a change in data types. LoAs share with interfaces the following features:

1. they are networks of observables;
2. the observables are related by behaviours that moderate the LoA and can be expressed in terms of transition rules;
3. they are conceptually positioned between data and the agents' information spaces;
4. they are the place where (diverse) independent systems meet, act on, or communicate with each other.

An interface is used in analysing some system from varying points of view or at varying LoAs. The only difference is that an interface consists of a collection of LoAs, that is, it is technically a *gradient of abstractions*.

Models are the outcome of the analysis of a system developed at some LoA(s). The *method of abstraction* consists in formalizing the model. This often happens implicitly, and only in *qualitative* rather than *quantitative* terms, by using the concepts just introduced (and others relating to system behaviour which we do not need here). In the previous example, Alice's LoA might consist of observables for SECURITY, METHOD OF STORAGE, and OWNER HISTORY; Bob's might consist of observables for ENGINE CONDITION, EXTERNAL BODY CONDITION, and INTERNAL CONDITION; and Carol's might consist of observables for RUNNING COST, MARKET VALUE, and MAINTENANCE COST. For the purposes of discussion, the interface might consist of the set of all three LoAs. In this case, the LoAs happen to be *disjoint*, but in general they do not have to be. LoAs can be *nested*, *disjoint*, or *overlapping* and may, but do not have to, be *hierarchically related*, or ordered in some scale of priority, or support some *syntactic compositionality*. A particularly important case is that in which one LoA includes another. Suppose, for example, that Dave joins the discussion and analyses the system using an LoA that includes those of Alice and Bob. Dave's LoA might match that of a buyer. Then Dave's LoA is said to be more concrete, finely grained, or lower than Alice's or Bob's, each of which is said to be more abstract, more coarsely grained, or higher; for both Alice's and Bob's LoAs abstract some observables that are available at Dave's. Basically, Dave can obtain all the information about the system that Alice and Bob might have, for example the name of the previous owner, and that it is rather expensive to maintain, and so he can obtain some information that is, in principle, unavailable to one or the other of them, since Alice does not know about running costs and Bob has no clue about the ownership history.

An LoA qualifies the level at which a system is considered. One should rely on the *method of abstraction* in order to refer to the LoA at which the properties of the system under analysis can sensibly be discussed. In general, it seems that many uninteresting disagreements might be clarified, if the various interlocutors could make their LoAs explicit and precise. Yet a crucial clarification is in order. It must be stressed that a clear indication of the LoA at which a system is being analysed allows *pluralism* without endorsing *relativism*. I already referred to this middle-ground position as *relationism*. When one criticizes a position as *relativistic*, or when one objects to *relativism*, one should not equate such positions to non-absolutist, as if there were only two alternatives, for example as if either moral values were absolute or relative, or truths were either absolute or relative, objective or subjective, observer-independent or observer-dependent. The *method of abstraction* enables one to avoid exactly such false dichotomies, by showing that a subjectivist position, for example, need not be relativistic, but only relational. To use a simple example: Alice may be tall when compared to Bob, but not when compared to someone in the basketball team. It does not mean that her height changes, but only that she is or is not tall depending on the frame of reference, that is, on the LoA. Relativism is really the equivalent of an 'anything goes' position. Now, it is a mistake to think that 'anything goes' as long as one makes explicit the LoA, because LoAs are mutually comparable and assessable. Consider again the example of Alice's telephone number. There might be some significant differences in the way in which Alice communicates it to Bob. She might add a plus and the relevant country code at the beginning, thus modifying the overall type of the information provided. She might omit the plus, the country code, and the city code, if it is a local number. So, there is quite a lot of 'relationism' ('it depends on...') but no 'relativism': it would be silly to conclude that any LoA would do. Because a string of letters would not work, nor would a mix of letters and numbers, or numbers and non-alphanumeric symbols, or an endless string. Using a different example, when we are asked to provide the number of our credit card, the type is (a finite number of) NATURAL NUMBERS. This is why an interface can easily constrain the sort of input required. In general, only some LoAs are possible and, among those, some are better than others. Relativism, as a position about the interchangeability of LoAs at no epistemic cost, is simply mistaken because, crucially, the assessment and corresponding preference is usually dictated by the *purpose* driving the original request for information. Deciding whether Alice is tall depends on the purpose for which we are asking the question in the first place. The implicit LoA may easily be the average population height. She may be a tall child. Or it may be an old army parameter according to which someone below a specific height cannot be recruited. This is clearly not relativism, because one may challenge the appropriateness of the LoAs in question on perfectly reasonable and justifiable grounds.

Introducing an explicit reference to the LoA clarifies that:

(i) the model of a system is a function of the available observables;
(ii) different interfaces may be correctly ranked depending on how well they satisfy modelling specifications (e.g. informativeness, coherence, elegance, explanatory power, consistency with the data, etc.) and the *purpose* orienting the choice of the LoA (LoAs are teleologically oriented);
(iii) different analyses can be correctly compared provided that they share the same LoA.

Let us now agree that a system is characterized at a given LoA by the properties it satisfies at that LoA. Systems are often dynamic: they change, and this means that some of those properties change value. The evolution of a changing system is captured at a given LoA and at any instant by the values of its observables (the attributes of the system). Thus, a system can be thought of as having states, determined by the value of the properties that hold at any instant of its evolution, for then any change in the system corresponds to a state change and *vice versa*. Generalizing, this enables one to view any system as having states and transitions. The lower the LoA, the more detailed the observed changes and the greater the number of state components required to capture the change. Each change corresponds to a transition from one state to another. A transition may be non-deterministic. Indeed, it will typically be the case that the

LoA under consideration abstracts the observables required to make the transition deterministic. As a result, the transition might lead from a given initial state to one of several possible subsequent states.

We have now moved from a static to a dynamic observation of a system, analysed as a transition system. The notion of a 'transition system' provides a convenient means to support the identification of the necessary and sufficient criteria for agency, being general enough to embrace the usual notions like automaton and process.[10]

A *transition system* comprises a (non-empty) set S of states and a family of operations, called the *transitions* on S. Each transition may take input and may yield output, but, at any rate, it takes the system from one state to another and in that way forms a relation on S. If the transition does take input or yields output, then it models an interaction between the system and its environment and so is called an *external* transition; otherwise the transition lies beyond the influence of the environment (at the given LoA) and is called *internal*. It is to be emphasized that inputs and outputs are, like states, observed at a given LoA. Thus, the transitions that model a system are dependent on the chosen LoA. At a lower LoA, an internal transition may appear external; at a higher LoA an external transition may appear internal.

Returning to our example, the system being discussed by Alice might be further qualified by state components for location, whether in-use, whether turned-on, whether the anti-theft device is engaged, history of owners, and energy output. The operation of garaging the system might take as input a driver, have the effect of placing the system in the garage with the engine off and the anti-theft device engaged, leaving the history of owners unchanged, and outputting a specific amount of energy. The 'in-use' state component could non-deterministically take either value, depending on the particular instantiation of the transition. Perhaps the system is not in use, being garaged for the night; or perhaps the driver is listening to a programme broadcast on its radio in the quiet solitude of the garage. The precise definition depends on the LoA. Alternatively, if speed were observed but time, accelerator position, and petrol consumption abstracted, then accelerating to 60 miles per hour would appear as an internal transition.

We can now use the *method of abstraction* and the concept of LoA to make explicit the ontological commitment of a theory, in the following way.

A theory comprises at least an LoA and a model. The LoA allows the theory to analyse a given system and to elaborate a model that identifies some properties of the system at the chosen LoA (see Figure 1).

The ontological commitment of a theory—the grey triangle—can be clearly understood by distinguishing between a *committing* and a *committed* component within the scheme. On the one hand, a theory commits itself ontologically by opting for a

---

[10] For a formal treatment of much more than is required in this context, the reader might wish to consult Arnold and Plaice (1994).

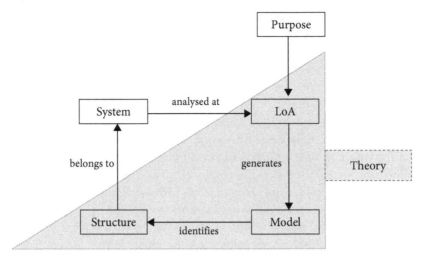

Figure 1 The scheme of a theory

specific LoA. Compare this to the case in which one has chosen a specific kind of car (say a Volkswagen Polo) but has not yet bought one. On the other hand, a theory is ontologically committed in full by its model, which is therefore the bearer of the specific commitment. The analogy here is with the specific car one has actually bought (that blue, four-wheeled, etc. specific vehicle in the car park that one owns). To summarize, by adopting an LoA, a theory commits itself to the existence of some specific types of observables characterizing the system and constituting the LoA (by deciding to buy a Volkswagen Polo one shows one's commitment to the existence of that kind of car), while, by adopting the ensuing models, the theory commits itself to the corresponding tokens (by buying that particular vehicle, which is a physical token of the type Volkswagen Polo, one commits oneself to that token, for example one has to insure it). Figure 2 summarizes this distinction.

By making explicit the ontological commitment of a theory, it is clear that the *method of abstraction* plays an absolutely crucial role in philosophy, especially if the latter is understood as conceptual design. The reader may recall the quotation from Quine in Chapter 1. If not, let me repeat it here for the sake of simplicity:

The very notion of an object at all, concrete or abstract, is a human contribution, a feature of our inherited apparatus for organizing the amorphous welter of neural input.... Science ventures its tentative answers in man-made concepts, perforce, couched in man-made language, but we can ask no better. The very notion of object, or of one and many, is indeed as parochially human as the parts of speech; to ask what reality is really like, however, apart from *human categories* [my italics], is self-stultifying. It is like asking how long the Nile really is, apart from parochial matters of miles or meters. (Quine 1992b, see now 2008, p. 403)

This section may be read as an attempt to clarify what 'human categories' in the first quotation above means, in terms of a less parochial method of LoA.

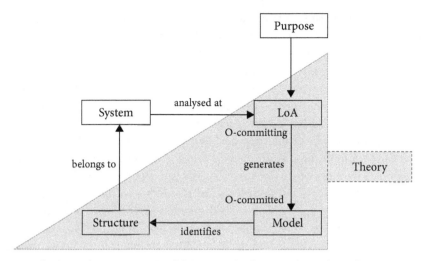

Figure 2 The SLMS (System-LoA-Model-Structure) scheme with ontological commitment

7. Constructionism

Providing the guidelines for choosing a problem and supplying a method for observing and analysing it are two of the fundamental steps in the information-theoretical, constructionist treatment of philosophical problems. In order to be complete and sound, the general methodology must also give an account of how the problem must be investigated once it has been fully delineated. I shall refer to this method as *constructionism*.

Constructionism is at the core of the maker's knowledge approach and of the kind of philosophy of information that I advocate in Floridi (2011c). As for *minimalism* and the *method of abstraction, constructionism* too finds its roots in both the philosophical tradition and in computational theories and practices. We have seen that a black box is a system whose internal structure, rules, and composition remain opaque to the observer. A white box is a system about which the observer knows everything, because the observer is actually its maker. This perspective, well known in Computer Science and Artificial Intelligence, lies in the wake of the so-called maker's knowledge tradition, according to which:

1. one can only know what one makes, and therefore
2. one cannot know the genuine nature of reality in itself.

Like Vico[11] and Hobbes, philosophers who hold (2) argue that, since any attempt to know the intrinsic nature of reality will inevitably fail, it is better to concentrate on

---

[11] Vico famously argued that *verum ipsum factum* or *verum et factum convertuntur* (what is true and what is made are interchangeable). Zagorin (1984) provides an insightful discussion of Vico's epistemology in the more general context of the maker's knowledge tradition. For a critical assessment see Gaukroger (1986).

those sciences whose subject is created by us, such as politics and social sciences. Philosophers who hold (1) argue that it is possible to improve our knowledge of reality through the development, application, and improvement (of our knowledge) of the techniques by which reality is investigated. We saw that this tradition finds its champion in Francis Bacon's philosophy of technology and it is related to Kantism. Following Bacon, technological mediations—which should be seen as including language as well, as Plato rightly perceived; see section 2 for the discussion about the dialectic method— become a crucial subject of philosophical enquiry because they are both a human product and the means through which the world is conceptualized, appropriated, and investigated. Likewise, when Kant stresses the importance of understanding the conditions of possibility of our knowledge, he is working within the constructionist tradition. One can investigate scientifically the phenomena one experiences only insofar as one is epistemically responsible for them. Combining the Baconian and the Kantian lesson, Friedrich Dessauer argued convincingly that technology establishes a positive, poietic contact with noumena.[12]

The constructionist method consists of the following six principles:

1. The Principle of Knowledge: only what is constructible can be known. Anything that cannot be constructed at least conceptually could be subject, at most, to working hypotheses.
2. The Principle of Constructability: working hypotheses are investigated by conceptual models (including simulations) based on them (Humphreys 2004).
3. The Principle of Controllability: models must be controllable.
4. The Principle of Confirmation: any confirmation or refutation of the hypothesis concerns the model, not the modelled system.
5. The Principle of Economy: the fewer the conceptual resources used in the conceptual models the better. In any case, the resources used must be fewer than the results accomplished.

Constructionism suggests that, given a theory, one implements and tests it in a model. Because one constructs the model, one can also control it. As Newell and Simon remarked:

neither machines nor programs are black boxes; they are artefacts that have been designed, both hardware and software, and we can open them up and look inside.

(Newell and Simon 1976, p. 113)

Suppose that a robot that Alice has built behaves like the ant she observed. The Principle of Confirmation prevents Alice from generalizing the working hypotheses, as if they were the real cause (or internal structure) of the modelled. It is obviously possible to provide an endless number of models with different internal structures whilst still obtaining the same behaviour. From this, the Principle of Context-dependency is derived:

---

[12] Dessauer (1958). I owe this insight to Mitcham (1994).

1. The Principle of Context-dependency: isomorphism between the simulated and simulation is only local, not global.

In the previous example, the robot accounts for the behaviour of the ant only under the constraints specified by the model. If the constraints change, so does the evaluation of the hypotheses.

Constructionism is in plain contrast to any mimetic approach in epistemology and the philosophy of information, according to which reality is approached through some reproductive or representational mechanism. Ideas, mental images, corresponding pictures, concepts, and so forth are supposed to be mere copies or portraits of some otherwise mysterious reality in itself. From a constructionist point of view, on the contrary, knowledge is a modelling process, which shapes and edits reality to make it intelligible. It therefore rejects more 'mimetic' theories such as Plato's, Aristotle's, or Descartes', in favour of a more Kantian approach. The Principle of Economy refers to the careful management of resources. On the one hand, in defining knowledge pro-cesses, mimetic theories are ontologically very wasteful, for they use a large amount of resources. Assuming that there is a transparent reality, that it works in some particular ways, and that such ways are fully knowable means making a heavy ontological com-mitment. On the other hand, *constructionism* does not state anything about reality in itself. This more modest and cautious commitment makes errors less likely. As in the case of *minimalism*, the constructionist Principle of Economy differs from Ockham's razor too. While the latter is a post-production revision tool, for it provides a criterion for choosing among theories already produced, the former is a pre-design planning norm, for it requires the designer to be fully aware of the initial assumptions before she undertakes the investigation process and it binds the construction of any explanatory model to the conceptual resources available. Because in philosophy we always deal with intrinsically open questions, most of the conceptual costs supported in reaching plausible answers are hidden in the starting assumptions. The more powerful the latter are, the easier it will be to reach the wanted conclusions, yet the costlier the initial investment will be. In philosophy, as in life, free lunches are not available, and what we do not pay at the end, we pay upfront. The real difficulty, in a conceptual cost–benefit analysis, is balancing resources employed and results obtained. Cost-free conclusions are a chimera.

Conclusion: Against Degenerate Epistemology

Science, especially physics, has taught us to be very cautious about our naïve certain-ties ('that's the way it is!'), everyday intuitions ('it must be that way!'), and commonsen-sical rejections ('that's impossible!'). While reading this book, just recall that we are all travelling at about 100,000 km/h around the sun. Indeed, we are getting so used to contemporary science supporting extraordinary claims that abrasively clash with what we would consider plausible that we might overreact, and be inclined to believe almost anything. If tomorrow some credible source tells us that unicorns have been biologically engineered in some lab, how many of us would be utterly incredulous? When scientists come up with some incredible results, what should we believe? The problem is exacerbated by the fact that these days experiments churn gazillions of data. The Large Hadron Collider, currently the largest and highest-energy particle accelerator, pumps out approximately 15 petabytes of data per year, which require a dedicated computational grid to be refined, analysed, and put to proper use. The more data and analysis we need, the more likely it is that something might go wrong in the process. Quality Standards and Safety Measures are serious issues in the knowledge industry too.

The problem is widely felt, not just by insecure philosophers in search of Cartesian reassurance. This is why scientists require very high levels of probability when it comes to deciding whether we are witnessing an amazing discovery or just some weird glitch in our systems. Have some neutrinos really travelled faster than light (http://www.bbc.co.uk/news/science-environment-15017484)? Enter statistics.

We know that, in statistics, a result is increasingly significant the more unlikely it is that it might have occurred just by chance. To pass the test of a genuine discovery, the threshold is very high: a result must be five-sigma unlikely. As the expression indicates, the sigma notation conveys the statistical significance of an event (standard deviation) in units of 'σ'. If a result reaches a five-sigma level of reliability this means that obtaining it by chance would be like getting twenty times heads when tossing an allegedly fair coin. Not impossible, but so unlikely that other explanations (including a biased coin) become much more plausible. Clearly, statistical analyses, and the computers that run them, do not provide certainties in the same way as logic and mathematics do. They cannot. For we could ask for higher sigma values and still be dealing with likelihoods. At the roots of our philosophy of information there is a kind of uncertainty principle: if a result R is mathematically certain then R is not empirical but rather a matter of logic (the negation of R is a contradiction), and if R is empirical then it remains in principle uncertain. Luckily, there is plenty of room between the two alternatives, and a combination of data, software, machines, and intelligence helps us to identify the negligible and opt for the best compromise. Knowledge is a balance between improbabilities. This is both reassuring and humbling. Classic epistemology loves to concentrate on what are describable, to borrow a technical term from mathematics, 'degenerate cases': Alice is usually a single, disembodied, epistemic agent, isolated, not embedded in any environment, rational, unbiased, open-minded, well informed, in full control of her language, capable of having access to all her doxastic content reduced to a set of beliefs, in search for certainty ... This is not an idealization. It is more like reducing the study of ellipses to the study of circles (degenerate ellipses with eccentricity 0), and then the study of circles to the study of points (degenerate circles with radius 0). Doable, but we are left with very little that resembles epistemic practices in the real world, where chances that we might be brains in a vat, or avatars in some futuristic software experiments, are ludicrously negligible and should keep nobody awake (I shall return to this point in Chapter 6, when arguing against radical scepticism). There is of course a price to pay for our most likely but still uncertain empirical information. This is that we cannot hold on to naïve views about some epistemologically immediate contact with things in themselves. Some forms of realism also become negligible as 'degenerate'. If knowledge must be Cartesianly certain, then we really cannot know the world in itself. We can only be more or less confident on the statistical significance of our data analyses about the world, whether naturally implemented in our sensory and nervous apparatus (see Chapter 4) or in our computers. The aforementioned uncertainty principle holds true not just at the CERN, but at the supermarket; not only for science, but also for the ordinary knowledge we enjoy when crossing the road. It was also the view of the founding father of statistics, Karl Pearson. In his classic *The Grammar of Science* (Pearson 1900) he supported a Kantian epistemology. It makes sense. As I shall argue in Chapter 4, reality provides the data that we manipulate and interpret statistically, as organisms, epistemic agents, and scientists, in order to construct the phenomenal world in which we live. Reality in itself is the source of our knowledge, yet knowledge is of the message, not of the sender. Reality as we experience it is a semantic artefact. Any talk of things in themselves is just metaphysics, of which there is a rampant resurgence these days (just google 'causal powers' or the explanations of why unicorns are metaphysically impossible, despite the lab mentioned at the beginning of this article). Interestingly, *The Grammar of Science* influenced the young Einstein so deeply that he recommended it as the very first reading for the Olympia Academy. The issuing history is complex, but the story is not: Kant's conditions of possibility of knowledge (see Chapter 10) became statistical conditions of significance, which in turn went hand in hand with the crucial importance of frames of reference, and it all ended up with the development of Russell's theory of types and the method of levels of abstraction in computer science, where both (types and abstractions) are needed to build systems that can deal successfully with the data we are accumulating in our scientific experiments. Computers later caused an information revolution, and here we are today talking about minimalism, the application of levels of abstraction, and a constructionist methodology in our philosophical understanding of what science tells us about our knowledge of the world. It takes a while to understand what it means to know that we *probably* know, although not quite certainly, and not quite so 'realistically'.

We have come to the end of this chapter. In the previous pages, I argued that a constructionist approach in philosophy, in line with the maker's knowledge tradition (see Chapter 9), is both viable and fruitful. It also seems badly needed. Constructionism is a very common and unproblematic approach in all those disciplines and sciences that have a poietic attitude towards their subject, which they tend not only to study but also to build, like computer science and economics. They could teach some important methodological lessons to philosophy, once the latter is seen as the highest expression of conceptual design. Plato was right in defining someone who knows (the dialectician) as the person 'who knows how to ask and answer questions' (*Cratylus* 390c). I will come back to this quotation more than once in the following pages. But he was wrong in identifying such a knower as the information user rather than its maker. I am embarrassingly aware that much more work lies ahead, not only in order to develop and refine the constructionist approach in more detail, but also, and perhaps more importantly, in order to apply it to philosophical problems, both old and new.[13] This should not be discouraging. The world in which we live seems in great need of all the possible help we can give it, and a constructionist philosophy capable of devising the required concepts that will enhance our understanding may definitely lend a hand, if we can manage to develop it. Thus, in Chapter 3, I hope to contribute to such effort by outlining the relationship between constructionism and naturalism. It is the last chapter of the first, metatheoretical part.

[13] An important example is provided by the question what kind of understanding a constructionist philosophy of information both supports and requires; see Kuorikoski (2009).

3

Constructionism as Non-naturalism

Summary

Previously, in Chapter 2, I argued that philosophical constructionism is far from being relativistic. In this chapter, I shall argue that it does not have to be naturalistic either. This metatheoretical conclusion will require some theoretical unpacking in Chapters 4 and 5, where I shall discuss perception and testimony as the sources of the material of our conceptual constructions, and then information quality. This means that I shall ask the reader to wait until Chapter 6 before embarking on a close analysis of how an anti-relativistic and non-naturalistic constructionism can deal with the most theoretical doubts successfully to be also anti-sceptical. I shall begin the discussion by looking first at a strange predicament in which contemporary science seems to be caught.

On the one hand, science holds a firm and reasonable commitment to a healthy naturalistic methodology, according to which explanations of natural phenomena should never overstep the limits of the natural itself. On the other hand, contemporary science is also inextricably and now inevitably dependent on ever more complex technologies, especially Information and Communication Technologies, which it exploits as well as fosters. Yet such technologies are increasingly 'artificializing' or 'denaturalizing' the world, human experiences, and interactions, as well as what qualifies as real. The search for the ultimate explanation of the natural seems to rely upon, and promote, the development of the artificial, seen here as an instantiation of the non-natural. In this chapter, I shall try and find a way out of this apparently strange predicament. I shall argue that the naturalization of our knowledge of the world is either philosophically trivial (naturalism as *anti-supernaturalism* and *anti-preternaturalism*), or mistaken (naturalism as *anti-constructionism*). First, I shall distinguish between different kinds of naturalism. Second, I shall remind the reader that the kinds of naturalism that are justified today need to be protected and supported pragmatically, but they are no longer very interesting conceptually. We know how to win the argument. We just have to keep winning it. Not a small or worthless task, yet not something about which we are unclear either. Meanwhile, the kind of naturalism that is still interesting today is now in need of revision in order to remain acceptable. Such naturalism may be revised on the basis of a *realistic* (not just realist) philosophy of information, introduced in Chapters 1 and 2, according to which knowing is a constructive activity, through which we do not merely represent the phenomena we investigate passively, but create more or less correct (correctness can be a matter of degrees) informational models (semantic artefacts) of them, proactively and interactively. I shall conclude that the *natural* is in itself *artefactual* (a semantic construction), and that the information revolution is disclosing a tension not between the natural and the non-natural, but a deeper one between a user's and a producer's interpretation of knowledge. The outcome is a constructionist view of knowledge and science in the information age and a revival of philosophy as a classic, foundationalist enterprise. How such constructionism works in terms of a logic of design will be discussed only in the last chapter of the book.

1. Introduction: A Plea for Non-naturalism

This chapter is a plea for non-naturalism, not an argument for it, let alone a proof or demonstration of it. If you are a naturalist, I am afraid I believe you are mistaken, but I shall not try to convince you that you are, and that you should change your mind. Naturalism is not a bad position to hold. It is a dominating *Ur*-philosophical thesis— call it a Kuhnian paradigm, at least in contemporary, English-speaking philosophy departments[1]—and a widespread faith (I shall specify later exactly in what), which ultimately can withstand any objection or counter-evidence. In this, I agree with Jack Ritchie (a naturalist himself):

There is no clever philosophical argument that can force you to make this naturalist move [that is, as Ritchie writes just before: 'start with our well-developed science and build our philosophy from there']. There is no argument to show that other approaches to philosophy will not succeed. Naturalism is a position that can claim at best only *motivations* [my italics].

(Ritchie 2008, p. 196)

The dialogue between the best forms of naturalism and the best forms of non-naturalism remains open.[2] Following the logic of open questions presented in Chapter 1, I think this very openness, an empirical fact that any naturalist should acknowledge, is also a very significant reflective reason in favour of non-naturalism, but more on this later in the chapter. For the moment, I would like to clarify that I am a non-naturalist because I find naturalism's *motivations* unsatisfactory. Serious naturalism is called science. And serious naturalization is the reduction of some philosophical area of investigation to a scientific one, in terms of what resources are required to answer the questions under investigation. In both cases, a specific philosophical enterprise ends and a new scientific one begins, and that is the end of the story. Quine was right:

---

[1] De Caro and Macarthur (2010, p. 3).
[2] See for example the attempt made by De Caro and Macarthur (2010) to develop a form of 'liberal naturalism'.

Naturalism does not repudiate epistemology, but *assimilates* [my italics] it to empirical psychology. (Quine 1981, p. 72)

This holds true for all sorts of philosophical naturalisms, which do not repudiate their correspondent naturalized branches of philosophy. But make no mistake: *assimilation* is a matter of absorption, incorporation, conversion, and ultimately disappearance of the assimilated in favour of the assimilating. In Quine's version, naturalism is just a euphemism for the end of epistemology. The same seems to apply to similar programmes such as the one presented in Maddy (2007). And once assimilation is expanded to all areas of philosophy, from metaphysics to ethics, naturalism becomes another way of talking about the death of philosophy, as seen in Chapter 1. Now, I do not disagree on the logic but, as will become clearer below, I do differ on the premises. I argued in the previous chapters that philosophy deals with ultimate questions that are intrinsically open to reasonable and informed disagreement. And these are not 'assimilable' to scientific enquiries. True, whenever such questions are discovered to be 'closed' in principle, then their answering moves out of the scope of philosophy and is (and indeed should be) naturalized. Western philosophy has been outsourcing 'closed' questions since the Pre-Socratics. If one wants to know the nature of colours, for example, the best thing to do is to engage in some serious cognitive science or neuro-science, and to stop tinkering conceptually and pretending that the investigation has got anything to do with epistemology. The pretence generates only an internal 'discourse' among equally minded philosophers, who are going to be ignored by science and society alike; what I have called 'scholasticism' (more on it in the Afterword). The same holds true for the study of linguistic meaning, human psychological motivations, the nature of animal reasoning, or the relation between physical space (not spatiality) and physical time (not temporality). Of course, philosophy should be critically conversant and consistent with the best of our knowledge and understanding, and hence with science. And of course, anyone is free to call any very abstract scientific investigation 'philosophy'; most of the philosophy of quantum physics seems to be just very theoretical physics, for example. The same holds true in areas such as the philosophy of mathematics or the philosophy of biology. All this is perfectly fine. And if this is naturalism, then good philosophy has always been naturalist, and bad philosophy is merely anti-scientific nonsense. However, at least since Quine, naturalism means much more than just science-friendly philosophy or abstractly rarefied science. We saw that it means 'assimilation'. And it is this 'assimilation' that I find both unconvincing and irresponsible, as I shall clarify in the following pages.

Withstanding scientific assimilation is not the only motivation for my plea in this chapter, which is also partly due to a strange predicament in which contemporary science seems to be caught today, as I anticipated in the summary.

On the one hand, science holds a firm and reasonable commitment to a healthy nat-uralistic methodology, according to which explanations of natural phenomena should never overstep the limits of the natural itself. Such a 'closure' (we already encountered this mathematical concept in Chapter 1) also applies, as it should, to social and human phenomena, from economics and sociology to neuroscience and psychology.

On the other hand, contemporary science is also inextricably and now inevitably dependent on ever more complex technologies, especially Information and Communication Technologies, which it exploits as well as fosters. Yet such technologies are increasingly 'artificializing' or 'denaturalizing' (no evaluation implied here) the world, human experiences, and interactions, as well as what qualifies as real, and what may be epistemically accessible. One only needs to recall the data-based and software-driven nature of contemporary research in the physics of particles, in neuroscience, or in the social sciences.

The outcome is that the search for the ultimate explanation of the natural seems to rely upon, and promote, the development of the artificial, seen here as an instantiation of the non-natural. I call it a 'predicament' and not a 'contradiction' because science and technology are allies, on the same (and right) side of the naturalist vs. anti-naturalist divide. But I also qualify it as 'strange' because the increasing and profound technologization of science is creating a tension between what we try to explain, namely all sorts of realities, and how we explain it, through the highly artificial constructs and devices that frame and support our investigations. Naturalistic explanations are increasingly dependent on non-natural means to reach such explanations. In this chapter, I would like to try and find a way out of this apparently strange predicament, hence my plea. I shall argue that the naturalization of our knowledge of reality is either philosophically trivial (naturalism as *anti-supernaturalism* and *anti-preternaturalism*), or mistaken (naturalism as *anti-constructionism*). I shall do so through the following steps. First, I shall distinguish between different kinds of naturalism. Second, I shall remind the reader that the kinds of naturalism that are justified today need to be protected and supported pragmatically, for example in terms of educational policies (think of the attempt to reject evolution in favour of creationism, or the whole debate about 'post-truth'), but they are no longer very interesting conceptually. It is a battle won once and for all in theory, even if it still needs to be fought very hard in practice, again and again, to avoid the complacency of reason. Meanwhile, the kind of naturalism that is still interesting today is now in need of revision in order to remain acceptable. Such a kind of naturalism may be revised on the basis of a realistic philosophy of information, according to which knowing is a constructive activity, through which we do not merely represent the phenomena we investigate passively, but create more or less correct informational models (semantic artefacts) of them, interactively. This latter point will be defended in the next two chapters. At the moment, it is worth stressing that this is a thesis about both philosophy and science or, more precisely, it is a thesis about the nature of knowing, affecting both philosophy and science. When Quine defended his version of naturalism as scientific assimilation (see previous quote) he asserted that

Science itself tells us that our information about the world is limited to irritations of our sensory surfaces, and then the epistemological question is in turn a question within science:

the question how we human animals have managed to arrive at science from such limited information.   (Quine 1981, p. 72)

He was mistaken on several counts. The 'irritations of our sensory surfaces' may be limited, but this is an irrelevant distraction: by the same reasoning, one should then try to answer the question how Beethoven managed to arrive at his *Ode to Joy* from the seven-note diatonic musical scale, Leonardo to his *Mona Lisa* from the three colours in the RGB model, Orson Welles to his *Citizen Kane* from just black and white, and today any computer multimedia from just zeros and ones. Quine's question is no longer a mystery as soon as one drops a *representationalist* interpretation of knowledge—an unquestioned *Ur*-philosophical thesis in most English-speaking philosophy depart-ments, which we saw has Platonic roots—and acknowledges that science tells us that our information about the world is also based very significantly on our abilities to combine and repurpose data and re-use them to help us make sense of the world. With an analogy, we are not the customers in reality's restaurant; we are the chefs, as I shall argue in Chapter 4. Kant was right: we construct the world that we experience as we experience it; we do not mirror it. Thus, Quine's previous quote is actually a *reductio ad absurdum*. This is why he was also wrong in his description of epistemological ques-tions, which are not descriptive or scientific, but rather semantic and normative (e.g. 'should this count as a case of knowledge?'), as Barry Stroud already objected very convincingly in the 1980s.[3]

For all these reasons, I shall conclude that the natural is in itself artefactual (a seman-tic construction), and that the information revolution is disclosing a tension not between the natural and the non-natural, but a deeper one between a user's and a pro-ducer's interpretation of knowledge.[4] The outcome is a constructionist view of knowledge and science in the information age, and a revival of a classic, foundational-ist role for philosophy itself.

2. The Nature of Naturalism

'Naturalization', broadly understood as a family of positions defending philosophical *naturalism* (more on the latter presently), used to be a popular strategy in philosophical analysis. Figures 3 and 4 show the Ngrams for 'epistemology naturalized' and 'naturalization'.[5]

Apparently it all started in the late 1960s (Rysiew 2016), with Quine's famous and influential article on 'Epistemology Naturalized' (Quine 1969). 'Naturalization' then

---

[3] See Stroud (1981) revised in Stroud (1984).

[4] For a realist, non-correspondentist but 'correctness-based' theory of truth see Floridi (2010c).

[5] Note the American spelling, which I preferred in these two Ngrams because of Quine's article and because it seems more influential than the British English, where the 'z' is replaced by the 's'. It is also the spelling preferred by OUP, and hence used in this book. The results are robust, as the reader may check by testing different variants at https://books.google.com/ngrams.

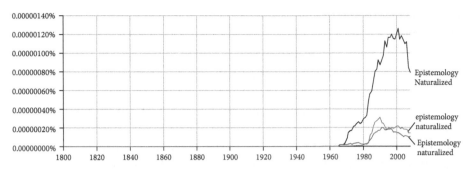

Figure 3 Ngram of 'epistemology naturalized'; case-insensitive; year-range = 1800–2008; Corpus = Google Books in English; smoothing = 3

Figure 4 Ngram of 'naturalization'; case-insensitive; year-range = 1800–2008; Corpus = Google Books in English; smoothing = 3

spread to other areas, such as the philosophy of mind, the philosophy of language, the philosophy of mathematics, and metaphysics. Today, its popularity seems to have peaked. The two Ngrams lend a bit[6] of statistical credibility to the anecdotal impression that the 1980s and 1990s were the two decades when naturalization became mainstream in philosophy, especially in English-speaking departments. Naturalizing philosophical areas of investigation seemed less fashionable at the end of the millennium. Perhaps the debate has been exhausted, with all the main positions clarified, and only minor adjustments and personal positioning still adding to the literature. Or maybe other fashions have become predominant in philosophy, such as the recent trend concerning 'grounding' analyses. Whatever the reasons, the decline in the popularity of 'naturalization' seems real. It certainly makes it reasonable to explore whether some version of non-naturalism may now be plausible even for supporters of 'naturalization' strategies. The heat of the debate is probably over, and a calm assessment of non-naturalism may be due.

---

[6] This 'bit' should be taken with a pinch of salt because of course this is a very coarse analysis. For example, 'naturalization' also refers to the legal process by which a person acquires a new nationality.

'Naturalism'—as the goal, if not the outcome, of naturalization—may mean different things to different philosophers.[7] Perhaps the most famous statement about naturalism is to be found in Heidegger, in terms of a:

desideratum which philosophy has long found disturbing but has continually refused to achieve: *to work out the idea of a 'natural conception of the world'*
(originally Heidegger 1927; Eng. Tr. in Heidegger 1962, p. 76)

It seems that a clarification of how I shall use this concept in this chapter is overdue. I shall start from the entry in *The Oxford Philosophy Dictionary*, not as an appeal to authority, nor as a naïve endorsement of the questionable view that philosophy is done by checking dictionaries, vocabularies, and Indo-European linguistic habits, but because it is particularly clear, and provides good evidence for what I take to be today's philosophical *vulgata*:[8]

Naturalism. Most generally, a sympathy with the view that ultimately nothing resists explanation by the methods characteristic of the natural sciences.   (Blackburn 2016)

Leaving aside the pointless reference to 'sympathy', I shall follow Blackburn and treat naturalism as a thesis about *explanation* first, and hence about *reality*, that is, about what there is or what entities exist. This priority of *epistemological* naturalism over its *ontological* twin has a Kantian origin: it is more reasonable to decide whether there are fairies in the world depending on what kind of explanation one has for their (alleged) occurrence, rather than evaluate what kind of explanation is acceptable depending on whether it can make sense of the existence of fairies. If this seems obvious and uncontroversial, the reader should consider the fact that it applies also to the existence of God.

Having clarified the kind of naturalism I shall discuss, I shall need three concepts to offer a refined definition of *epistemological naturalism*.

The first one is that of 'explanation' itself. In other contexts, I have interpreted it in terms of 'providing an account' (Floridi 2012b) but here it will be sufficient to treat it as a shortcut to refer to an answer to a why question, in order to include the twofold meaning of explanation/answer as 'causal reason-giving' ('why were you late?' 'because there was traffic') and as 'clarification-giving' ('why did you decide to apply for this job so late?' 'because I was not sure I would qualify'). Note that the distinction is not a dichotomy but a matter of emphasis (hence 'twofold' not 'two'). In one case one is stressing more the causal aspects, in the other one may be looking for a better understanding.

The second concept is 'closure'. We already saw in Chapter 1 that a set is closed under an operation if carrying out that operation on members of that set always

---

[7] Ritchie (2008) provides a valuable introduction although it leaves out a major and most significant debate on normative non-naturalism.

[8] This is common. For example, the same approach is shared by Papineau (2015), even if in terms of 'investigation'. It is roughly what Ritchie (2008) defines as 'methodological naturalism'.

produces a member of that set. The reader may recall that, for example, the natural numbers are closed under addition—if you add any natural number you get another natural number—but not under subtraction, and this is why we need the set of negative numbers.

The third and last concept is that of 'natural phenomena'. I shall leave it at the intuitive level, but any identification in terms of biochemical and physical state or process, subject to causal order in the world, and at least in principle knowable empirically should be fine. Of course, one should also keep in mind the crucial role played by the right level of abstraction.

With the aid of these three concepts, let me suggest the following as a good definition of methodological naturalism (henceforth simply naturalism):

N^*)   Naturalism:$_{def.}$ the philosophical thesis according to which all natural phenomena are closed under explanation (in the sense that every explanation of a natural phenomenon will only have to refer to one or more natural phenomena).

By using NP to refer to the set of natural phenomena and C to indicate 'closed under explanation', one may reformulate N^* more concisely thus:

N)   Naturalism:$_{def.}$ the philosophical thesis according to which $C(NP)$.

Usually, supporters of N have in mind a strong, assimilating version of it *à la* Quine, one that combines N with the following two assumptions:

(A.1)   if a non-natural phenomenon is explainable in terms of natural phenomena, then it is to be re-assigned to the set of natural phenomena;

and

(A.2)   there are no non-natural phenomena that cannot be explained in terms of natural phenomena.

Supporters of (A.1) but not (A.2) may remain agnostic about whether there may be any non-natural phenomenon that is not re-assignable to NP. I shall return to this position later, in section 5. For the moment, I am interested in naturalism as the philosophical thesis that combines N + (A.1) + (A.2), where (A.2) means that all non-natural phenomena can be explained naturalistically, at least in principle, and thus be re-assigned to the set of natural phenomena, and therefore also be forced to close under natural explanation. N + (A.1) + (A.2) is what I think philosophers assume when they talk about naturalism, but let's label this position *strong naturalism* (*SN*) just to be fair to potentially less demanding positions. According to *SN*, all natural phenomena are closed under explanation and non-natural phenomena either do not occur at all—so there is no need for an explanation—or, if they seem to occur, their explanation entirely reduces them to natural ones, hence re-assigns them to NP, and forces them to close under natural explanation. In either case, the set of non-natural phenomena (NNP) is empty *de facto* or can be emptied *de jure*, in short:

SN) Strong Naturalism:$_{def.}$ the philosophical thesis according to which $C(NP) \wedge \neg \exists x$ ($x \in$ NNP), where x may be interpreted as ranging on all phenomena.

One final clarification is in order before discussing *SN*. *SN* assumes that the explanatory *reduction* of non-natural phenomena to natural ones is achievable exhaustively and *non-reductively*. This latter condition may seem contradictory but it is crucial. Reduction is always possible; the question is whether a full reduction fails to include at least some important features of the *explanandum* that are both significant and in need of explanation. The idea of a non-reductive reduction can be made clear and precise by introducing a metaphorical comparison[9] with 'lossless information'. Data compression can be used to reduce the size of a file. When it is lossless, that is, non-reductive, this means that the original data can be perfectly reconstructed from the compressed data (reversibility). When it is lossy, that is, reductive, this means that the data compression allows only an approximate reconstruction of the original data. Important features have been irrecoverably lost. Using this distinction, one can talk of a lossless (i.e. non-reductive) explanatory reduction when the *explanans* leaves no residual information in the *explanandum* unexplained. The reduction is lossy (reductive) if some residual information remains unexplained. Some simple examples in section 3 will illustrate the point more intuitively. What remains to be stressed here is that a good test to check whether the explanation provided is lossy is the fact that—after the natural explanation and the reduction of the non-natural to the natural phenomena has occurred—it is still perfectly legitimate to reiterate the same query: 'yes, this is correct, but why...?'. In ordinary circumstances, assuming that Alice has fully and clearly understood Bob's explanation, it would be unreasonable of Alice to reiterate her request for an explanation, because she could not hope to be better informed by doing so. We already saw in Chapter 1, when discussing the nature of the 'reasonably reiterable query' test (RRQ), that, if it is reasonable to reiterate the query, as a request for the original explanation, then clearly one is asking a question that has not been satisfied by the answer just received. Now this is what happens with lossy or reductive explanations. To re-use the same example already encountered, Alice may ask Bob why they are not organizing a party on Saturday, and all the empirical facts or observations and logico-mathematical proofs or calculations available will not make it unreasonable to keep asking the typical 'yes, but...' question: 'Yes, I understand, but why are we not organizing a party on Saturday?' because Alice may be asking a normative question. I shall say more about the RRQ test presently, but for now we are ready to see how *SN* applies to all non-natural phenomena.

---

[9] The appeal to data compression is potentially misleading if one understands explanation and reduction as concerned with phenomena and not (primarily) with data (Bogen and Woodward 1988). Since the primacy of data over phenomena is not the topic of this chapter, the reference to data compression should be understood here only metaphorically and not as something that can be used to compare phenomena as well.

There are two (compatible) ways in which the set of non-natural phenomena may be populated and therefore, conversely, emptied by *SN*. NNP may comprise phenomena that are non-natural not so much in themselves but because they require non-natural phenomena in order to be explained. I shall analyse these in terms of *supernatural* or *preternatural* phenomena. Or (inclusive or) NNP may comprise phenomena that are non-natural in themselves, quite independently of their non-natural explanations. I shall analyse these in terms of normative and semantic phenomena. I shall illustrate the analysis with some simple examples and argue that the first form of non-naturalism is untenable, while the second remains defendable, and indeed preferable.

A note of warning before moving to the next section. It may seem out of place to argue here in favour of naturalism and naturalization against the supernatural and the preternatural. The objection has some merit. It is true that the fact that billions of people believe in alternative medicine, astrology, bad luck and good fortune, magic, religious miracles, and other similar 'explanations' is disappointing, even disheartening, but this does not mean that this chapter is the right context in which to defend the voice of reason. An op-ed would be a better place, perhaps. However, the objection is not conclusive because the following section should help to achieve two theoretical goals: support the view that naturalism is a perfectly justified position in many circumstances; and show-case how the RRQ test applies in some cases that are less philosophically controversial. And this should clarify the alternative cases when neither condition is satisfied.

3. Two Indefensible Non-naturalisms: The *Supernatural* and the *Preternatural*

Consider first *supernaturalism*, defined here as the view that there are phenomena that are non-natural, not in themselves, but in terms of their explanation, which is supposed to be paranormal, that is, appeal to non-natural phenomena. A great example is provided by the Cottingley Fairies. In 1917, two young girls, the cousins Frances Griffith and Elsie Wright, took a series of photos of fairies while playing in the garden of Elsie's Cottingley village home, in England. Photographic experts initially declared them genuine and they soon became famous. It was only decades later, in the 1980s, that Elsie and Frances admitted that the photographs were faked, made using cardboard cut-outs of fairies copied from a popular children's book of the time.

If something does not exist then you cannot take a photograph of it, so the Cottingley Fairies, which appeared in a series of five photographs, were thought to be real and their existence to require an explanation that had to appeal to phenomena beyond the realm of the natural, that is, *supernatural*. Conan Doyle gave a spiritualistic explanation and made the fortune of the pictures. The reasoning at the time was that ontology—the view that the fairies are real—preceded epistemology (their intelligibility)—and therefore that one needed to find an explanation for their occurrence in ordinary circumstances. Doyle had made Sherlock Holmes utter the famous phrase: 'when you have eliminated the impossible, whatever remains, however improbable, must be the truth'. He thought that the only available explanation for the photographs was non-natural and went for it. However, according to the first assumption (A.1) of strong naturalism, if a phenomenon is explainable naturalistically without any information loss (recall: exhaustively and non-reductively) then it is a natural phenomenon. Now queries such as 'why were there fairies in the Cottingley Fairies photographs?' are fully answered by proving that there weren't any in the first place, and by giving the details of the hoax. All these answers amount to a natural explanation, and there is no information loss, meaning that any reasonable requests of explanation raised by those pictures can be fully satisfied without ever overstepping the realm of natural phenomena. Using our RRQ test, we can check that, asking again, after having received the full explanation, 'yes, all this is correct, but why are there fairies in the Cottingley Fairies photographs?' would simply indicate that one had not understood the explanation in the first place. This holds true for all forms of non-naturalism as supernaturalism (including magic and miraculous phenomena), which are untenable because they are fully reducible to naturalism non-reductively.

Consider next *preternaturalism*, defined here as the view that there are phenomena that are non-natural in terms of their *source* (that is, what gives rise to them), which is supposed to be outside the realm of natural phenomena. If we wish to remain in the context of fairies, a great example is provided by an old app, unfortunately no longer available, called *Fairy Trails*. Fairy Trails was a beautiful augmented reality game for iPhone and iPod touch, created in 2009 by Freeverse, a company that no longer exists. One would shake the device to power the detector and then scan the surroundings for magical creatures (Figure 5). The app used the camera and compass to merge the real world and game world. The user would tap the fairies on the screen to collect them in a jar. The more fairies one captured, the more power one had to detect the special, quicker fairies. Later, in 2016, a vaguely comparable app worked not too differently to catch Pokémon.

In this case too, of course, the fairies do not exist, yet not in the same sense as the Cottingley Fairies did not, because these fairies exist as artefactual phenomena, not as a hoax. They are equally naturalizable because their lossless explanation is entirely natural, in terms of the technology that generates them. To the request of explanation for the occurrence of fairies in one's own environment, the answer would have pointed to the nature of the software involved. In this case too, any further question would betray a lack of understanding. The RRQ works fine.

4. Two Defensible Non-naturalisms: The Normative and the Semantic

There are phenomena that some philosophers,[10] including myself, consider non-natural in themselves, and not just because of the characteristics of their *explanation*

---

[10] If two philosophers need to be chosen as their champions, these are probably E. G. Moore and Paul Grice, respectively. The reader of this chapter is likely to be acquainted with the work of both, so I shall not

Figure 5 Fairy Trails from Freeverse (2009)

or *sources*. These are *normative* and *semantic* phenomena. They are non-natural not
because they work against the ordinary laws of nature or refer to non-natural
domains, but because they do not pass the RRQ test. According to normative (also
known as moral or ethical) and semantic non-naturalism, normative and semantic
phenomena are not naturalizable because their explanation cannot be provided in a
way that appeals exhaustively and non-reductively only to natural phenomena. In
both cases, any naturalistic explanation is lossy, in the sense that it is perfectly reasonable to ask again for an explanation, correctly and informatively. Their failure to pass
the RRQ test shows that the request for an explanation is really a request to change the
Level of Abstraction at which the answer is expected and needs to be given, from a
naturalistic to a non-naturalistic one. Failure to understand such a request of change
and the insistence to use a naturalistic LoA is equivalent to committing a category
mistake in Ryle's sense, or a fallacy of μετάβασις εἰς ἄλλο γένος ('change/shift into
another genus'), to use Aristotle's terminology. This was already very clear to Husserl
(see Reynaert 2015).

For example, suppose one finds pornographic photographs of semi-naked children
dressed like fairies[11] and declares them to be immoral. The question why there are such
pictures is entirely naturalizable. But the question why they are immoral can be asked

---

summarize it here, where I am more interested in addressing the two positions understood as theses about
the nature of explanation.

[11] The example is based on a real story: 'University tutor asked to photograph semi-naked children
convicted of pornography', http://www.telegraph.co.uk/news/uknews/2511121/University-tutor-asked-to-
photograph-semi-naked-children-convicted-of-pornography.html.

again and again, reasonably, correctly, and in an informed manner, for as long as the answer is provided in terms that appeal only to natural phenomena, for example, because that is what a society sanctions, or because some people find them repulsive. This is also the lesson we have learnt from Hume's 'no ought from is' and from Moore's 'naturalistic fallacy'. Similarly, there is no naturalistic way to explain the presence of fairies in Shakespeare's *A Midsummer Night's Dream*, if not by missing the point, for example in terms of a historical account of beliefs in fairies in Shakespeare's time. The request for explanation can only be fully satisfied by referring to the LoA represented by the internal narrative, that is, to the semantic construction to which the fairies belong. In a combined example, one may ask why Romeo and Juliet die. A naturalistic explanation, using a CSI-like LoA, could offer the following reasons: they do not die because they do not exist; or, they die in the tragedy because in the tragedy they are victims of a double accidental suicide due to lack of communication. A non-naturalistic explanation would have to refer to their love, their relations with their families, etc.; in other words, to the internal meanings of the story. The more one asks for an explanation for normative and semantic phenomena ('why…?' sorts of questions), the clearer it becomes that they can be neither eliminated *de facto*, like the Cottingley Fairies, nor forced to close under naturalistic explanation *de jure*, like the fairies in Fairy Trails. The recalcitrant, residual element that remains unexplained is precisely the all-important element that requires an explanation in the first place. In the end, it is the contribution that the mind makes to the world, and it is up to the mind to explain it, not the world. This is the sort of the mind's epistemic responsibility that I find convincing in Descartes' *cogito*, for example. Admittedly, one may object that the recalcitrant, residual elements still in need of explanation may be just the result of our own insipience (understood as the presence of a question without the corresponding relevant and correct answer), perhaps as just a (maybe even only temporary) failure to see that there is merely a false impression of an information deficit (by analogy with a scandal of deduction, D'Agostino and Floridi (2009)). This objection may not be incorrect. But it may not be correct either. For this objection too is open to debate, reasonably, informatively, intrinsically, permanently. And so, it could be used to undermine itself, reflectively: once more, we would have to metatheorize the debate on the tenability of the objection and conclude that there is an openness to the questioning that the questioning itself keeps open, non-naturalistically.

5. In Defence of Non-naturalism

We are amphibian beings, who live partly within natural environments as bodies and mostly within normative and semantic ones as minds. The normative and semantic environment—the *Manifest Image* of the world, to use Sellars' terminology (Sellars 1963a)—is built by our minds, but it is no less real and often robustly constraining than the laws and social rules that regulate our societies, or the money we exchange.

It is also the environment through which we know and semanticize (give meaning to and make sense of) the natural environment, which we know in terms of the *Scientific Image*.[12] Seeking to reduce the natural to the non-natural means misunderstanding both, as well as our own special role within each of them. The previous analysis suggests that a more fruitful way of approaching natural and non-natural phenomena is by interpreting *initially* both as being closed under explanation, but interpreting them independently of each other, in the same way as both the set of positive integers and the set of negative integers are closed under addition and yet neither can be reduced to the other or generate members of the other set through addition. This weaker form of naturalism, to be refined presently, allows the set of non-natural phenomena (NNP) to be explained non-naturally, with closure still applying to both sets respectively. As a *first* step, it makes more sense to acknowledge that the explanation of members of NP leads to other members of NP, and the explanation of members of NNP leads to other members of NNP. If this seems just a fancy philosophical distinction consider that a naturalistic defence of miracles can be based on it: miracles are explained by other miracles, and the non-miracles by other non-miracles. For example, one may argue that the explanation of Alice's recovery from cancer is entirely natural, no magic or miracles involved, and that the explanation of the fact that she should be grateful to those who supported her during her illness may be non-natural. Difficulties arise when the natural and the non-natural intersect, for example when someone argues that Bob's magnetic healing abilities exist, are explainable non-naturally, and in turn explain Alice's recovery from cancer. In order to prevent such forms of supernaturalism from entering surreptitiously into our definition of non-naturalism we need to add the assumption (A.1) formulated above. In this way, we obtain the following definition of non-naturalism:

NN)   Non-Naturalism:$_{def.}$ the philosophical thesis according to which $C(NP) \wedge C(NNP) \wedge (A.1)$

It may now be tempting to see *SN* and *NN* as opposite and irreconcilable. One may see them as the roots of the two-cultures dichotomy—with scientists supporting *SN* and humanists as well as legal scholars supporting *NN*, *positivism* vs. *interpretivism*—or linked to the so-called 'explanatory gap' existing between the external, objective, and naturalized (quantitative and physiological) understanding of mental states and their internal, subjective, and non-naturalized (qualitative and psychological) experience, hence between science and phenomenology. Yet all these kinds of dualism would be a mistake, because one more reflective step needs to be taken: where is the whole preceding analysis taking place? In the space of the natural or in the space of the non-natural? Answering this question means realizing that ultimately the natural

---

[12] The reader should not miss the excellent article by Philipse (2001). Within his framework, given my own theory of levels of abstraction, I am much closer to the epistemological position supported by Peter Strawson in *Skepticism and Naturalism* (Strawson 1985) than the ontological one supported by Nicolai Hartman and defended by Philipse himself.

is artefactual and there is no dichotomy, only articulation, as I shall argue in the conclusion of this chapter.

Conclusion: The Artefactual Nature of the Natural

If the initial distinction between *SN* and *NN* is tenable, it seems clear that, meta-theoretically, its very explanation cannot belong to the set of natural phenomena.[13] A self-reflective understanding of a philosophical analysis of naturalism is partly semantic and partly normative. Even the debate about the tenability of naturalism, and the very view presented at the beginning of this chapter that 'Naturalism is a position that can claim at best only motivations', constitute that normative–semantic residue that escapes naturalization. Questioning it means seeking to explain the difficulty conceptually, not through some combination of empirical data, experiments, or logico-mathematical proofs. This leads to the conclusion that our interpretation of the naturalization of phenomena, including cultural and philosophical ones, is itself a cultural phenomenon, and hence non-naturalistic. It is the non-natural that enables us to create categories such as 'natural', 'naturalized', and 'naturalization'. There is nothing anti-realist or relativistic in such an acknowledgement. It only means that such a construction would not be reducible to a natural process without information loss. We know, semanticize, and explain reality (the system) through the construction, expansion, and refinement of our semantic artefacts about it (the model) by taking as much advantage as possible of realities (data) as constraining affordances. Therefore, either the natural is only a very minimalist and uncontroversial way to refer to data in themselves (noumenal) as constraining affordances, and this is uninteresting; or the natural—as we conceive and perceive it in a rich and multifarious way—is a construction, a model of the noumenal (reality in itself). The naturalization of the non-natural turns out to be an expression of the artefactual nature of the natural. Ironically, naturalization is really a second-order semanticization. This seems to me the same road taken by John McDowell, with the only, profound difference that we need to take the opposite direction: the non-natural is our first nature, and the natural is actually our second nature. And this means that what we need is a genealogy of the natural from the non-natural, not vice versa.[14] We know there is no God's-eye external perspective from which to try to analyse and solve philosophical problems. The mistake is to think that the inevitable internal perspective we must adopt can be naturalistic, when naturalism is actually the philosophical outcome of the very process of re-embedding our perspective in our own non-natural predicament. We cannot stop halfway from heaven, and call at Nature's station; we must go all the way back to the initial point of departure, a fully human constructionism. Philosophy as the ultimate form of first-order semanticization can only be foundational or be 'assimilated', *tertium non datur*.

---

[13] For an early and more elaborated defence of this point see Floridi (1996).

[14] See Bridges (2007) on Gaskin (2006) on McDowell (1996) and more recently De Caro and Macarthur (2010).

All this should help explain why science is increasingly artefactual. It is because its existence and features depend on the mental. As we progress in building ever more complex explanations of what there is (whatever *it* is in itself), we develop models that inevitably rely on more and more artificial forms of understanding. This process is kept honest by the constraints provided by the data. Our methodological mistakes in the advancement of knowledge have not been due to a lack of naturalism for a long time now. For naturalism is rightly taken for granted in any decent scientific endeavour. They are due to our being enchanted by the affordances provided by the data—the sort of information that the data invite us to transform them into—and being forgetful or indeed wilfully negligent towards the constraints provided by the same data, the sort of information that the data intractably resist to become. On this, I believe Lakatos was correct (Lakatos 1978). And this seems to me a crucial and permanent lesson we must learn from Popper's falsificationism (Popper 1968).

Naturalism is a user's philosophy: it endorses a primacy of ontology (the description of the system) over epistemology (the elaboration of the model of the system) and a representationalist/correspondentist interpretation of the knowledge of the system. It is almost irresistible, in its intuitive and common-sensical features. Non-naturalism endorses a primacy of epistemology over ontology and a constructionist/correctness-based interpretation of knowledge. It is counter-intuitive and not in line with common-sense. Yet so are many truths that we have come to accept in science and mathematics. In a world that is increasingly dominated by technology, normative constructs and conventions, artificial products, engineered environments, design, maker's knowledge, and mental *poiesis* of all kinds, strong naturalism seems to be a mere long-term consequence of the modern scientific revolution, a hang-over from modern empiricism. It is what our mammalian brain cannot help assume. But it can no longer provide an appropriate way of approaching our responsibilities, opportunities, and limits as careful and respectful (recall the constraints) creators of our understanding of the world, of ourselves within it, and of the ways in which we shape both. Constructivism is what our human mind is rather suggesting we accept. The conclusion is that it is non-naturalism, interpreted as a realist constructionism, that can claim the best motivations today. This is why our philosophy of information should be both foundationalist and non-naturalist. To be human is to refuse to accept the natural as naturalistic, and to take full responsibility for such a refusal.

PART II

Philosophy as Conceptual Design

Chapter 3 concluded the metatheoretical part of the book. In this second part, the chapters investigate some of the formal issues raised by the logic of open questions, the logic of conceptual design, and the logic of constructionism as non-naturalism. The following quotations provide a good description of what the reader may expect:

> In order to understand the phenomena surrounding a new technology, we must open the question of *design*—the interaction between understanding and creation. In speaking here of design, we are not restricting our concern to the methodology of conscious design.
>
> (Winograd and Flores 1986, p. 4)
>
> ...One cannot understand a technology without having a *functional* understanding of how it is used. (Winograd and Flores 1986, p. 6)

4

Perception and Testimony
as Data Providers

Summary

Previously, in Chapter 3, I defended constructionism and non-naturalism as the correct ways of approaching our philosophy of information. A major question left unanswered was: how does the epistemic construction of our semantic world work? Or, to put it more precisely, if knowledge is accounted information (more on this in this chapter; for a full analysis see Floridi 2011c) how is one supposed (to apply this analysis in order) to understand perceptual knowledge and knowledge by testimony?

In the first part of this chapter, I articulate an answer in terms of a re-interpretation of perception and testimony as data providers rather than full-blown cases of knowledge. But then, if perception and testimony are correctly understood as data providers, how is one supposed (to apply this analysis in order) to understand the semantic value of the data provided by such processes? In the second part of the chapter, I argue in favour of a constructionist hypothesis about how data may become meaningful for human cognitive agents through a process of *repurposing* of natural data/ signals. The conclusion of the chapter is that, from a non-naturalistic, constructionist perspective, human agents are natural-born data hackers.

1. Introduction: The Relationship between Knowledge and Information

What is the relationship between information and knowledge? In previous works (Floridi 2010d, 2011c, 2012b), I answered this question by arguing that information— understood as well-formed, meaningful, and truthful data—upgrades to knowledge if and only if it is correctly accounted for. The basic idea is rather simple and can be quickly summarized here. Each piece of factual, propositional information that p (e.g. 'the dishwasher's yellow light is flashing') can be analysed in terms of a Boolean question and answer ('Is the dishwasher's yellow light flashing?' + 'Yes'), which, as a stand-alone item, does not yet constitute knowledge, but poses further questions about itself. Such further questions require the right sort of information flow in order to be answered correctly, through an appropriate network of relations with some informational source. This network of information flow is what accounts for the information, and upgrades it to knowledge. To see intuitively why information requires such an accounting network, consider that, if all Alice can do—when asked by Bob why she holds the information that the dishwasher's yellow light is flashing—is to repeat that this is what the yellow light is actually doing, the fact that the dishwasher's yellow light is indeed flashing only warrants at most the conclusion that Alice is informed about the state of the dishwasher's yellow light, but nothing else. For all Bob knows, Alice might have uttered 'the dishwasher's yellow light is flashing' as the only English sentence she can master, or she might have dreamed or guessed correctly the state of that particular light. Indeed, in a Gettierized context, the light that Alice reports to Bob to be flashing might have stopped flashing, but then, when Bob goes to the kitchen to check the status of the dishwasher, another dishwasher's light, also yellow but different from the one to which Alice was referring, might have started flashing, making Alice correct, yet only accidentally so. This is all very well known, and frankly not very interesting. The proposal to resolve such difficulties is to analyse knowledge informationally (Floridi 2011c). The result is a definition of knowledge according to which an epistemic agent S knows that p if and only if:

(i) p qualifies as semantic information (it is well-formed, meaningful, and truthful data);
(ii) q accounts for p, that is, $A(q, p)$;
(iii) S is informed that p; and
(iv) S is informed that $A(q, p)$.[1]

The articulation of the informational analysis of knowledge, in terms of a network theory of account, and its defence, especially against a potential Gettierization (Floridi 2004d), are explicit tasks with which I have dealt elsewhere (Floridi 2012b). So, I shall not rehearse the arguments here. Rather, in the following pages I intend to investigate two important consequences of such an analysis:

(a)   if knowledge is accounted information, how are we supposed (to apply this analysis in order) to understand perceptual knowledge and knowledge by testimony?

In the first part of this chapter, I shall articulate an answer to (a) in terms of a re-interpretation of perception and testimony as data providers rather than full-blown cases of knowledge. This, however, leads to a further question:

(b)   if perception and testimony are data providers, how are we supposed (to apply this analysis in order) to understand the semantic value of such data?

In the second part of this chapter, I shall argue in favour of a constructionist hypothesis about how data may become meaningful for cognitive agents like Alice. This will build upon the naturalistic, action-based semantics developed in (Floridi 2011c; Taddeo

---

[1] I take condition (iv) to imply that S is informed that q. The reader who finds this unclear may add a further condition: (iv*) S is informed that q.

and Floridi 2005, 2007), and provide the missing link between that kind of semantics and the richer, more convention-based semantics enjoyed by Alice and Bob when having an ordinary conversation, basically their uniquely human way of generating and managing non-natural meanings.

In the conclusion, I shall outline some of the consequences of the two answers and contextualize them within the wider context of some previous research.

2. A First Potential Difficulty

The first question has actually been asked explicitly, by phrasing it in terms of a 'potential difficulty' by Tommaso Piazza (2010). In an insightful article discussing my proposal for an informational analysis of knowledge, Piazza wrote:

No less clearly, however, the considerations above [about the nature of the informational account of knowledge] also face Floridi's account with a *potential difficulty*, as they seem to sustain a reasonable doubt about the very viability of this strategy: if one believes that *knowledge can be acquired through perception, or by testimony,* and one also believes that *in those cases there is no accounting or explaining information which could explain the epistemic status to which it is upgraded,* one could well be tempted to suggest that *knowledge could not, at least not in general, be analysed as accounted information*; for at least in the cases just envisaged, an explanation of it will have to proceed by taking into account the justificatory role which perception and testimony seem to perform.   (Piazza 2010, p. 79, italics added)

I believe Piazza to be mostly right, but perhaps in a way that may not entirely satisfy him, for I shall argue that his premises can be accepted, indeed strengthened, without accepting his conclusion, but first, let me clarify the background against which the discussion is best understood.

3. Some Background

All the empirical information about the world that we enjoy flows, and keeps flowing, to us through our sensorimotor interactions with the world: *directly*, through our perception of the world, possibly mediated by some technologies; and *indirectly*, through our perception of other (possibly even artificial) epistemic agents' perception of the world. We either saw it or read it somewhere, to put it simply, if slightly incorrectly (for we might have heard it, or tasted it, and reading after all is also a case of seeing etc., but I am sure the point is clear). Thus, Aristotelians and Empiricists of various schools are *largely* correct in holding that *nihil est in intellectu quod non prius fuerit in sensu* ('Nothing is in the understanding that was not earlier in the senses'), if and only if (the biconditional qualifies the 'largely' above) what we are talking about is empirical information about the external world.[2]

---

[2] Of course, Leibniz's qualification 'excipe, nisi ipse intellectus' ('but the intellect itself') remains correct; *New Essays on Human Understanding*, Book II, Ch. 1, § 2. See (Leibniz 1996).

If we distinguish the *direct* and the *indirect perception* of the world by referring to the former as sensorimotor perception or simply *perception*, that is, the first-hand testimony of our senses, and to the latter as *testimony*, that is, the second-hand perception by proxy, we see immediately that the potential difficulty, highlighted by Piazza above, concerns the only two sources of empirical information available to cognitive agents like us. Without any external perception, either direct or indirect, we could not even be brains in a vat, bio-batteries in a *Matrix*-like world, or dreamers in a Cartesian scenario, because, in each of these cases, we could not be fed any data through our senses. The very channels would be missing. Obviously, it is quite important to check how far the potential difficulty affects the proposal to analyse knowledge in a constructionist way, as accounted information. Before doing so, however, let me first clear the ground of a potential misunderstanding.

Knowledge and information states, as well as epistemic, cognitive, and informational processes, are sufficiently similar for our terminology to be interchangeable in most daily circumstances, without any significant loss either in communication or in pragmatic efficacy. This fact reminds us that some tolerance might be sensibly acceptable, even in our technical language. There is an imprecise but still very reasonable sense in which, if Alice sees that such and such is the case, then Alice holds the information that such and such is the case, and *ipso facto* Alice knows that such and such is the case. Thus, if Alice sees a yellow light flashing, then she may rightly claim to know that there is a yellow light flashing in front of her. The same holds true for testimony: if there was a yellow light flashing, and Alice is told by Bob (where Bob could even be a robot or a parrot), who perceived that yellow light flashing, that there was a yellow light flashing, then Alice knows that there was a yellow light flashing. All this I am very happy to concede as uncontroversial in everyday scenarios and parlance.

The value of such a mundane equation—perceiving, or being provided (through testimony) with, well-formed, meaningful, and truthful data amounting to p is equivalent to being informed that p, which is equivalent to knowing that p—is that, by adopting it, we gain much simplicity. The cost is that we lose the possibility of drawing some conceptual distinctions, which become essential once we wish to be precise in our epistemology and philosophy of information, especially in view of a constructionist approach coherent with Helmholtz's Neo-Kantian philosophy of perception and with the most recent lessons we can learn from neuroscience (more on this in section 10). This is partly why some philosophers, including myself, resist the equation's deflationism. 'Partly' because the reluctance is due not only to the cost to be paid (a decrease in our ability to draw finer distinctions), but also to the fact that such cost is philosophically unaffordable once we realize that knowledge that p is a specific kind of information that p, the kind enriched by the capacity for answering relevant questions about p, that about which one is informed, by reference to further information that q, which accounts for p. Perception and testimony may be analysed along the same lines because—in the best (i.e. non-Gettierized, scepticism-free, error-free (Floridi 2004d)) circumstances—they *end up conveying* information about their specific references, but they do not yet represent cases of knowledge: in slightly different ways (to be specified soon) they are our data providers. Let us consider perception first.

4. Perception and the Phaedrus' Test (Plato)

Epistemologically, our bodies are our cognitive interfaces with the world. Their sensory and kinetic apparatus implements hard-wired levels of abstraction (more technically, we are embodied, cognitive gradients of abstraction (Floridi 2008b)), which determine the range and type of data (observables) that can be negotiated, acquired, processed, and even projected. Perception is then a general term that refers to the process of data input through which epistemic agents like us acquire first-hand data about their environments, at the levels of abstraction offered by their bodies. In the best scenarios, such data come *from* the world, and this guarantees their facticity. However, they are not necessarily (in fact hardly ever) *about* the world, and we shall see that this requires some explanation. Suppose Alice sees a yellow light flashing on the panel of her dishwasher at home. Such a process of data input is fallible, but it can be corrected at least through *redundancy* (e.g. Alice sees the yellow light flashing and hears the noise associated with it), *control and/or intervention* (e.g. Alice double-checks that the yellow light is actually flashing by turning on the light in the kitchen and moving closer to the dishwasher), *reasoning* (e.g. Alice infers that it is time for the yellow light to be flashing), and *social interaction* (e.g. Alice notices that Bob too sees the yellow light flashing). The data input can also be *enhanced* (e.g. through a pair of glasses) and *augmented* (e.g. through a remote monitoring system). By itself, such a first-hand, data-gathering process may be considered a case of knowledge acquisition, but then any elementary signal-processing gadget, like Arduino,[3] would qualify as an epistemic agent, and this seems to be a bullet not worth biting. Let me explain.

In some circumstances, we are not much better off than the aforementioned gadget. Suppose that, when Alice sees a yellow light flashing on the panel of her dishwasher at home, she actually hasn't got a clue what it might mean. At this stage, all she has acquired, through such perception, is at most the information (equivalent to the propositional content) that a yellow light on the dishwasher's panel is flashing. If Alice has further background information—for example, about the covariance between the yellow light flashing and the dishwasher running out of salt—then, by perceiving the light flashing, she may also acquire that further information about the low level of salt. All this is uncontroversial. What is notoriously open to debate is whether this yellow-

---

[3] 'Arduino is an open-source electronics prototyping platform based on flexible, easy-to-use hardware and software. It's intended for artists, designers, hobbyists, and anyone interested in creating interactive objects or environments. Arduino can sense the environment by receiving input from a variety of sensors and can affect its surroundings by controlling lights, motors, and other actuators', from the official website, http://www.arduino.cc.

light-flashing-in-front-of-her kind of perception, by itself, may amount to more than just information-gathering at best. I hold that, if we wish to be epistemologically accurate, it does not. It is not enough for Alice to *perceive* a yellow light flashing to *know* that there is a yellow light flashing in front of her, for two sets of reasons.

First, because several complex concepts and experiences must already be in place and at play: light; yellow; flashing; the fact that lights can flash; that flashing lights of any colour on the panel of a white good are normally not decorative features (like on a Christmas tree) but signals; that, as signals, lights being off are less perspicuous and hence conventionally less indicative than lights being on; that lights might not work properly but a flashing light on a dishwasher's panel is normally working well and it is meant to be intermittent; etc.

Second, but equally importantly, because the perceptual data input (to simplify: the stream of photons that turns into a there-is-a-yellow-light-flashing-there), plus the conceptual framework (the yellow light flashing there means . . .) required to formulate and make sense of it, further demand an account (explanation) in order to graduate from information to the higher status of knowledge.

In other words, unless Alice understands and is able to answer (at least potentially, or implicitly) a whole series of 'how come' questions—how come the light is flashing? How come it is the yellow light and not another light that is flashing? How come the light is yellow? etc.—her epistemic status is no better than Arduino's or indeed the dishwasher manual's, where one can read that 'the yellow light flashing indicates that the dishwasher is running out of salt'. Call this the Phaedrus' test: Alice may claim to have more than mere information about the yellow light flashing if she can pass it.

5. Testimony and the Parrot's Test (Descartes)

Let us now turn to testimony. This is the process through which epistemic agents like us *transfer* information to each other. Note that testimony does not *generate* information: the GIGO (garbage in garbage out) rule applies. If Bob tells Alice that *p*—for example that the dishwasher's yellow light was flashing yesterday—then, at most, Alice now holds the information that *p*. Unless we quietly presuppose that Alice, the receiver of *p*, is actually doing *more* than just receiving and registering *p*—for example that Alice is not acting as a simple repository but she is also inferring something that Bob did not, namely that the dishwasher is running out of salt, or that she is evaluating the reliability of Bob as the source of *p*, but then all this 'more' is where a theory of account is hiding—all we have, at the end of a testimony process, is at most the transfer of some information from the original source to the final target, through a network of senders and receivers. What must happen for testimony to work is that the informational baton is passed through the several nodes that are relaying it without being lost or altered.

Luckily for us, testimony is not a Boolean process. The network is *resilient*—nodes can implement information correction procedures, as when a later epistemic agent recovers or reconstructs what was the original information and relays it in its corrected, restored format—and there is often plenty of *redundancy*—as when several epistemic agents act as independent sources, conveying the same information about the same event, or repeatedly sending the same information at different times and through different channels (Bob tells Alice that the yellow light was flashing, and so does Carol). Still, this is information *transfer*, not *yet* information (let alone knowledge) *generation*. The expression 'knowledge by testimony' is really a shortcut not to be taken literally. Receiving *p* can hardly amount to knowing that *p*, for knowledge requires more than true content (or, which is equivalent, well-formed, meaningful, and truthful data). If this were not the case, any database would be very knowledgeable indeed and all medieval scribes who copied Greek manuscripts without speaking much Greek at all would have been very learned. In other words, we would like Alice to pass the parrot test (Descartes' *Discourse on the Method*, Part Five): given that the yellow light was indeed flashing, being told, correctly, by a well-trained source like a parrot that the yellow light was flashing while Alice was not in the kitchen does not yet suffice to ensure that Alice *knows* that the yellow light was flashing. At best, she has now acquired that piece of information. If she cannot do anything else with it, then that is all the epistemic dividends she may enjoy.

6. Data Providers

Let us now put the two threads together. Perception is the process through which Alice acquires data about the world, which need to be made *meaningful* and properly *interpreted (semanticized)* in order to become information. Perception does not generate propositional semantic information in and of itself. Testimony is the process through which Bob transfers to Alice propositional information (also but not only) about the world, but does not yet generate propositional knowledge in and of itself. In both cases, what is missing, in order to gain empirical knowledge of the world in a precise epistemological sense, is the understanding (explanation in a different vocabulary, or account, as I would prefer) of the empirical information acquired. Such understanding (explanation) is obtained through the intelligent accounting of the available propositional semantic information. This is what I have argued in Floridi (2011c). Time to return to the potential difficulty.

It should now be clear that Piazza is right in stating that (first premise):

(P.1)   'knowledge can be acquired through perception, or by testimony',

as long as 'acquired' in (P.1) is understood, as it should, as stating necessary but not yet sufficient conditions. Compare this to '*x* (a mortgage, a passport, a skill, etc.) can be acquired through *y* (a credit evaluation, a full application, the relevant training, etc.)'.

Indeed, in this sense, I have argued for a stronger thesis: empirical knowledge can be acquired *only* through perception or by testimony. If one day we are able to implant Wiki-microchips under our skin, it will still be a case of testimony.

Piazza is also right in stating that (second premise):

(P.2) 'in those cases [perception and testimony] there is no accounting or explaining information which could explain the epistemic status to which it is upgraded',

if we understand by (P.2) that unaccounted perception or testimony do not qualify *yet* as knowledge.

Where he seems to be mistaken is in drawing the following conclusion from the previous two premises:

C) 'one could well be tempted to suggest that knowledge could not, at least not in general, be analysed as accounted information'.

Nobody who understands the previous analysis and the two premises above should be tempted to jump to such a conclusion. Piazza adds that

for at least in the cases just envisaged, an explanation of it will have to proceed by taking into account the justificatory role which perception and testimony seem to perform.

So perhaps the problem lies with the devilish concept of justification. Now, without entering into a lengthy discussion of the nature of justification and its role in epistemic processes (Floridi 1996), there are at least two ways in which perceiving that such and such is the case—for example seeing that the yellow light is flashing—justifies Alice in holding that such and such is the case. One is by interpreting the justification in terms of causal interactions. Reliabilist theories used to like this approach. It seems impossible to disagree with this interpretation: it is the perceptual (visual, in the example) process of data-input that causally makes possible the acquisition of the relevant bits of information about the yellow light flashing. Yet causality is not all that is being invoked here, since we are not looking for a mere descriptive account, but for a normative one (see Chapter 3). The alternative is to use justification to mean exculpation. This, however, adds nothing to our, or Alice's, understanding of the case in question, even if it does add a note on her epistemic conduct in such circumstances. She did not dream it, nor imagine it, she did not project it out of fear, nor carelessly assume it: she saw a yellow light flashing, eyes wide open, double-checking, changing angle and perspective, perhaps asking Bob as well. Alice really did her best to make sure that what she actually saw was indeed a yellow light flashing. She did the right thing. The verdict is: causally sound and epistemologically not guilty. Yet all this is irrelevant to Alice's epistemic state. We still cannot tell whether she *knows* or is merely *informed* that p. As I have argued above and much more extensively and in detail in (Floridi 2011c), being correct about p and having done everything reasonably possible to avoid being mistaken about p does not yet mean that one knows that p. An important part of the epistemic story is still missing. In order to see why, let us first turn to the second question.

7. A Second Potential Difficulty

Suppose the previous analysis is correct, or at least moves in the right direction. Perception and testimony are both to be understood as data providers. In the case of testimony, the suggestion seems less controversial, as long as one understands that testimony is a data-providing process not in the sense that it transfers raw data about the world (think of the photons in the case of the yellow light flashing), but in the sense that it transmits well-formed and meaningful data from sender to receiver. Ultimately, perception deals with the world, testimony with information about the world: it is the difference between cooking with fresh ingredients (perception) and microwaving a pre-cooked meal (testimony). Testimony that conveys empirical information about the world ultimately depends on perception of the world based on data from the world. It is informative when the well-formed and meaningful data it transmits are also truthful, otherwise it is misinformative (unintentionally false) or disinformative (intentionally false). I shall return to such a crucial role at the end of the chapter.

Testimony presupposes the occurrence of data already meaningful. This cannot be said of perception, and this raises a second, potential difficulty. For once perception is stripped of its high epistemological status—once perception no longer counts, philosophically, as a full-blown, genuine instance of knowledge, but rather as a necessary condition of possibility of empirical information and hence of knowledge—one may object that we have swung to the other extreme. For now, it becomes difficult to explain how perception, so epistemologically impoverished, may progress to generate empirical knowledge at all. Recall the example of Arduino: artificial agents are very proficient at collecting, storing, and manipulating data, and yet they do not go on to produce empirical knowledge, not in the sense in which Alice does. If the previous analysis reduces Alice's epistemic state to Arduino's, we have a new potential difficulty.

This second difficulty can be phrased in terms of a dilemma: either perception is *overinterpreted* informationally, but then this fails to explain how it differs from full-blown empirical knowledge (what is the difference between perceiving that such and such is the case and knowing that such and such is the case?) and why it does not require the ability to (explain, justify, or) account for the information it provides; or perception is *underinterpreted* informationally, as the necessary source of the data that go on to constitute empirical knowledge, but then this fails to explain how such data can become full-blown empirical knowledge. We move from an inflated to a deflated view of perception, when what we need is just the right epistemological evaluation in between. As I argued above, working on the first horn of the dilemma looks unpromising. The alternative is to show that the data-based interpretation of perception is not stuck in the impasse of an underinterpretation. This is the task of the next three sections, for which we need more background.

8. More Background

Semantic information is a very slippery topic. If we know the relevant codes, we patently have no difficulty in understanding sentences, maps, formulae, road signs, or other similar instances of well-formed and meaningful data. And yet, scientists and philosophers have struggled to determine what exactly semantic information is and what it means for an agent to elaborate and understand it. One of the sources of the difficulty is known as the 'symbol grounding problem' (SGP):

How can the semantic interpretation of a formal symbol system be made intrinsic to the system, rather than just parasitic on the meanings in our heads? How can the meanings of the meaningless symbol tokens, manipulated solely on the basis of their (arbitrary) shapes, be grounded in anything but other meaningless symbols?   (Harnad 1990, p. 335)

The difficulty in solving the SGP consists in specifying how agents can *begin* to elaborate *autonomously* their own semantics for the data (symbols, signals) that they manipulate, by interacting with their environments and other agents, without begging the question, that is, without relying on more or less hidden forms of *innatism* or *externalism*: semantic resources should be neither presupposed, as already 'pre-installed' in the agents in question, nor merely 'uploaded' from the outside by some other agents already semantically proficient. If they are, we are really addressing a different kind of question.

In Chapters 6 and 7 of Floridi (2011c), I argued that all the main strategies proposed so far in order to solve the SGP fail to satisfy the previous conditions (clustered under the expression *zero semantic commitment condition* or Z condition), but they provide several important lessons to be followed by any new alternative. In light of such critical analysis, I elaborated a constructive proposal for a *praxical* solution to the SGP. There is neither space nor need to outline it here. Suffice it to say that the praxical solution is based on two main components: a theory of meaning—called *Action-based Semantics* (AbS)—and an architecture of agents—which models them as being constituted by at least two modules, M1 and M2. M1 operates at an *object level* (OL), interacting directly with the external environment, for example by navigating, detecting obstacles, avoiding them, etc., thus outputting and inputting actions. M2 operates at a *metalevel* (ML), taking as data the actions at the OL and as the target of its elaborations the internal states of M1. Any action that M1 outputs to, or inputs from, the environment defines a particular internal state (S_n) of M1. Hence actions and internal states are causally coupled: for any different action in M1 there is a different internal state S_n, and for all similar actions in M1 there is the same S_n. Simplifying, M2 uses such states to provide a semantics for the symbols developed by the system. Thanks to their architecture, agents can implement AbS, and this allows them to ground their symbols semantically as well as to develop some fairly advanced semantic abilities, including forms of semantically grounded communication and of elaboration of semantic information about the environment, and hence to overcome the SGP without violating the Z condition. The reader interested in the details (and viability) of the proposal is invited to read Chapters 6–7 in Floridi (2011c). Here, it is important to stress that such a praxical solution points towards a more ambitious and challenging possibility: the elaboration of a theory of meaning that can enable us not to underinterpret perception as a data provider but rather account for its role in the elaboration of empirical knowledge. The hypothesis is that the praxical solution of the SGP provides the seeds for an explanation of how advanced semantic and linguistic skills may develop among higher biological agents in more complex environments when perception and later testimony are in question. This is what we shall see in the next two sections.

9. The Vice Analogy

In trying to show how the analysis of perception as data provider may lead to the elaboration of a meaningful experience of the world, and hence to empirical knowledge of it, two converging strategies may be adopted. They may be quickly introduced as the two jaws of a vice. On the one hand, one may rely on *quantitative* analyses, especially, but not only, through information theory and Shannon information, the algorithmic theory of information and Kolmogorov information, and signalling theory. On the other hand, one may rely on *qualitative* analysis, especially, but not only, through truth-theoretic semantics, inferential role semantics, game-theoretic semantics, and meaning as use.

The limits of such strategies are well known. Quantitative analyses are not meant to deal with semantics, while qualitative analyses offer at most semantic *criteria* (how one can tell whether Alice understands the meaning of *p*), or presuppose meaningful contents (how Alice successfully handles meanings by becoming proficient in a particular perceptual or linguistic game), but are not meant to explain how semantics (including meaningful data) arises in the first place.

When misapplied, both kinds of analyses are a way of cheating. Quantitative analyses do less than they are said (but not meant) to do. When misused, this leads to a *semantics-from-syntax fallacy* so flagrant in the failures of classic AI. Qualitative analyses presuppose (correctly) what they are said (mistakenly) to deliver. When misused, this leads to a *semantics-from-semantics fallacy* and the failures of current solutions to the SGP (see Z condition defined in section 8).

The question is whether there is a way to bridge the physical/syntactic side, addressed by quantitative analyses, and the mental/semantic side, addressed by qualitative ones, in order to explain how perception, and later on testimony, as a data-providing process, may lead to the generation of meaning. The answer is that pragmatics might help. Here is a quick list of some lessons we have learnt from the two kinds of strategies recalled above:

(a) there is an active component dealing with meanings; call this the semantic engine (*agent*);

(b) *interactions* between the environment (*system*) and the agent elicit the data used by the agent as constraining affordances to create semantic information (a *model*) of the system;

(c) *semanticization* (the generation and attribution of meaning to data/signals) is a functional relation between meaningless input and meaningful output;

(d) evolutionarily, models of the system compete with each other on the basis of two quality requirements: *fit for purpose* and *correct* (right) *first time*;

(e) the agent's interactions with the system provide the competitive context within which incorrect models are revised or abandoned (Bayesian learning);

(f) ultimately, semantic information is the outcome of the agent's active and constructive interpretation of the system that is the referent/source of the relevant data, not of its passive representation.

Let me now show how the elements may be put together with a praxical approach (the pragmatic 'bridge' just mentioned) to give rise to a full picture.

10. The Constructionist Interpretation of Perception and Testimony

Imagine a very early stage where there is no difference between agent and system, or sender and receiver, informer and informee. We may assume the presence of only an environment, in which physical structures occur more or less dynamically, that is, there are patterns of physical differences understood as asymmetries or lack of uniformities. There is no specific name for such 'data in the wild'. One may refer to them as *dedomena*, that is, 'data' in Greek (note that our word 'data' comes from the Latin translation of a work by Euclid entitled *Dedomena*). Dedomena are not to be confused with *environmental information*. They are pure data, that is, data before they are interpreted or subject to cognitive processing. They are not experienced directly, but their presence is empirically inferred from, and required by, experience, since they are what has to be there in the world for our information about the world to be possible at all. So dedomena are whatever lack of uniformity in the world is the source of (what looks to an informational agent like Alice) data. Try to imagine the photons that will generate the perception of a yellow light flashing before they are perceived as a yellow light flashing. Such data might be flowing around, but they are not signals yet, as there are no senders or receivers.

Such an initial stage is where there are environmental data and patterns that might be exploitable as information by the right sort of agents for their purposes, before there is any kind of communication. Therefore, it is also the stage (see Figure 6) where

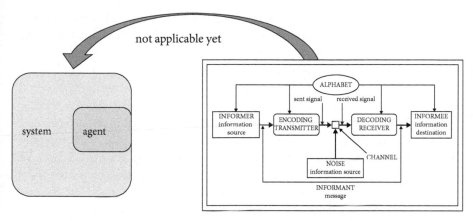

Figure 6 Shannon's model of communication not applicable

Shannon's classic model of communication may easily be misleading, if applied too early. In the relata (sender, receiver) vs. channel and communication process (message), it is the message that comes logically first, in the form of physical data as potentially exploitable constraining affordances.

Once some structures in the environment become encapsulated through a *corporeal membrane*, such encapsulation of part of the environment allows the separation of the interior of an agent from the external world. The ontological function of the membrane is to work as a hardwired divide between the inside, the individual structure or agent, and the outside, now the environment *for* the agent. Its negentropic function is to enable the agent to interact with the environment to its own advantage and withstand, evolutionarily, the second law of thermodynamics, for as long and as well as possible. The epistemological function of the membrane is that of being selectively permeable, thus enabling the agent to have some minimal variety of degrees of inputs and outputs with respect to the environment. At this stage, data are *transduceable* physical patterns, that is, physical signals now seen as *broadcast* by other structures or agents in the environment, which are captured by the permeable membrane of the agent. The body is a barrier that protects the stability of the agent (physical homeostasis). A good example is a sunflower.

We move from pre-cognitive to post-cognitive agents once data become *encodable* resources, exploitable by agents through some language broadly conceived (sounds, visual patterns, gestures, smells, behaviours, etc.). Patterns and flows of data/differences, which were before quantities without direction (scalars), broadcast by (what it is still improper to interpret as) sources not targeting any particular receiver (e.g. the sun generating heat and light, or the earth generating a magnetic field), acquire a direction, from sender to receiver (become vectors), and an interpretation (e.g. noises become sounds interpreted as alarms), thus being exploitable as signals. From now on, latent Shannon information becomes manifest and Shannon's classic communication model applies. This shift requires a *cognitive membrane*, or *bodily interface*, which allows the encapsulation of data (some form of memory) for processing and communication. The body as an interface or cognitive membrane is a semi-hardwired (because configurable through learning) divide between the cognitive agent and its environment, that is, a barrier that further detaches the agent from its surroundings, and allows it to exploit data processing and communication in its struggle against entropy.

At this stage (see Figure 8), sensorimotor interactions through bodily interfaces are best understood as interactions at a given set of levels of abstraction or LoAs (gradient of abstraction (Floridi 2008b)), where LoAs are hardwired as sensory receptors. Note that, according to this reconstruction, there are no signals (let alone information) in the wild: data as signals are elicited by the nomic interactions between types of systems and types of agents. This is not relativism but *relationism* as described in Chapter 2: recall, not everything is food, but food is understandable only relationally, by understanding the nature of both the consumed substance and the consuming agent. Agents are further de-coupled from their environments, with different embodiments determining different types of epistemic agents, which are able to interact informationally with their environments and other agents through their bodily interfaces. Thus, each type of agent is a type of LoA implementation. Same type, same LoAs. Wittgenstein's lion (Wittgenstein 2001) and Nagel's bat (Nagel 1974) are incommensurable LoAs. The stability (cognitive homeostasis) now concerns the internal data within the agent and their codification: memory and language.

The emergence of natural signals as meaningful for an agent is the stage where the praxical solution to the SGP is applicable. To oversimplify, the semantic value (meaning) of the signals is the state in which they put the receiving agent (cf. adverbial theory of perception and Grice's comments below). A good example is a bird on the sunflower.

The elicited data, in Figure 7, understood now as signals, may have both a source *s* (a sender) and a referent *r* that is in some state φ (this is what the data are taken to be 'about'), see Figure 8. Clearly, if there is no referent *r*, then we have a *virtual system*: the model (the interpreted data) generates its referent, as in a computer game. If there is no source *s*, then the agent is in a state of complete ignorance, where 'complete' means that the state of ignorance itself is unknown. If both *r* and *s* are present, then, in most cases of communication, including perception and testimony, *s* ≠ *r*. This simply means that the data come *from* a source interacting with the agent (the photons coming from the

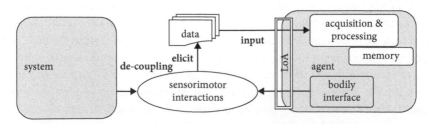

Figure 7   The agent-system interactions elicit data as signals at a bodily LoA

yellow light), but they are not *about* the source (the photons are not 'about' the yellow light), which is not their referent, not least because they are the outcome of the cognitive interactions and negotiations between agent and the data source, although we shall see that there is a plausible sense in which ordinary perception works correctly when it interprets $s = r$. If $s = r$, testimony becomes an unusual case of self-confession. Francis Bacon was perhaps the first to rely on this feature in order to speak metaphorically of the scientific inquiry as a questioning procedure addressed to Nature, an informational interpretation of the logic of discovery that we consider rather common nowadays (Sintonen 1990). However, even conceding that all this, including the praxical solution of the SGP, is correct, it still falls short of providing a full account of Alice's perception of the yellow light flashing as indicating that the dishwasher is running out of salt. For the latter is a conventional meaning, and we saw in Chapter 3 that Grice was right in distinguishing it from natural meaning (Grice 1957). At this stage, the best one can do, without begging the question, is to show how Alice may be 'put in a yellow state', as it were, by a yellow light flashing. According to the praxical solution of the SGP, there is a plausible sense in which Alice may be said to see 'yellowly', to put it *à la* Chisholm, but she cannot be said to see 'salt-in-the-dishwasher-running-outly', not without presupposing what needs to be accounted for.

Pace Skyrms, the naturalist tradition—which seeks to account for non-natural meanings by reducing them entirely to natural ones through signalling or information theory (Skyrms 2010)—provides the right beginning but seems to be unable to deliver the whole story. Using a different example, it struggles to explain why the same sound is perceived as (mind, not merely believed to be) a song by some and as a national anthem by others. Non-natural (conventional, artificial, synthetic) semantics seems to require more than natural semantics to emerge. If this were not the case, we would have already made at least some successful steps in the realization of classic AI, where the frame problem is just a specific instance of the SGP (Harnad 1993). We have not (Floridi et al. 2009). Indeed, the whole project of information or signal processing as sufficient for the development of a full-blown semantics runs into the semantics-from-syntax fallacy, seen in section 9. The usual reply to such an objection consists in asking for more, indefinitely: more time, more complexity, more processing, more 'add your preferred resource'. In AI, this has often and conveniently translated into more funding.

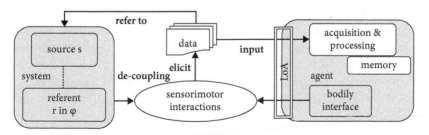

Figure 8 Data source and referent

Yet, in the same way as we are reminded in AI that climbing to the top of a tree is not the first step towards the moon, but the end of the journey, no matter how many more resources may become available, likewise, in naturalistic theories of meaning and of meaningful perception, accounting for the communication procedure among birds, bees, monkeys, or indeed robots is not the first but the last chapter in the book of natural semantics. It is where things start becoming interesting if difficult, not where one may accept an '. . . and so on' clause or some hand-waving.

This is hardly news. More than half a century ago, Grice had already identified and exposed the shortcomings of such a naturalism:

> I want first to consider briefly, and reject, what I might term a causal type of answer to the question, 'What is non-natural meaning? [Grice actually uses the abbreviation meaning$_{NN}$]' We might try to say, for instance, more or less with C. L. Stevenson,[4] that for x to non-naturally mean [mean$_{NN}$] something, x must have (roughly) a tendency to produce in an audience some attitude (cognitive or otherwise) [in the praxical solution this is expressed in terms of putting an agent in the specific, correlated, internal state] and a tendency, in the case of a speaker, to be produced by that attitude, these tendencies being dependent on 'an elaborate process of conditioning attending the use of the sign in communication.'[5] This clearly will not do.
>
> (Grice 1957, p. 379)

Grice goes on to explain several reasons why such a naturalization will 'clearly not do'. They were as clear and hardly refutable then as they are now, but if the reader remains unconvinced, let me add a further consideration. The irreducibility of non-natural meanings to natural ones is not just a matter of scientific results and philosophical arguments. The view that just more data or signals processing, without appeal to any further variable, may somehow lead to the development of higher-level, non-natural semantics—what Grice describes as, at best, a circular reasoning ('We might just as well say, "X has non-natural meaning [meaning$_{NN}$], if it is used in communication," which, though true, is not helpful'), see the fallacy (section 9) of obtaining semantics from semantics—also runs against a specific result in information theory, one that indicates that natural data input and processing is necessary but insufficient to generate the meaning for perceptions and concepts such as 'the dishwasher is running out of salt'. This is the data processing theorem (DPT).

The DPT concerns the quantity of *mutual information* between signals, messages, or data. Mutual information, indicated as $I(X; Y)$, is a measure of how dependent two random variables X and Y are; for example, the dependency between the information X = the dishwasher is running out of salt (that is, the average reduction in uncertainty or the expected reduction in yes/no questions needed to guess X) and the information Y = the low salt yellow light indicator is flashing. The higher the dependence is, the higher the degree of mutual information is. Mutual information satisfies the properties $I(X; Y) = I(Y; X)$; $I(X; Y) \geq 0$; if X and Y are independent, then $I(X; Y) = 0$; highest

---

[4] Grice adds here a footnote to Stevenson (1944, ch. iii).
[5] Grice adds here a footnote to Stevenson (1944, p. 57).

I when $X = Y$ (ideal, noiseless channel). *Mutual information* is, together with the *inverse relation principle*,[6] the *covariance model*,[7] and Shannon's *communication model*, one of the pillars of any information-based project for the full naturalization of semantics. Based on the concept of mutual information, the DPT states that data processing tends to *decrease* information. Here is an informal summary.

Suppose three systems S_1, S_2, and, S_3 are such that X is the output of S_1 and the input of S_2, Y is the output of S_2 and the input of S_3, and Z is the output of S_3, as illustrated in Figure 9, then:

DPT)   if the random variables depend on each other, that is, $[X \Rightarrow Y \Rightarrow Z]$; and if $[X \Rightarrow Y \Rightarrow Z]$ is a Markov chain; then the mutual information I satisfies the following condition: $I(X; Y) \geq I(X; Z)$.

This means that the average amount of information that Z conveys about X is usually less than, and at most equal to, the average amount of information that Y conveys about X. Of course, larger degrees of mutual information correspond to greater degrees of statistical dependence between a system's input and output, in our example between X and Z. Indeed, we shall see later in this section that such mutual information can reach total equivalence between variables. But the introduction of further n stages of data processing can never increase the statistical dependence between the variables, and is likely to decrease it. In short, if one does not have such and such information at the input, data processing, as formulated above, is not going to generate it. If one obtains it at the end of it, either it was already there since the beginning (see above Grice's comment about the true but unhelpful solution, or the fallacy of semantics-from-semantics), or it has been surreptitiously introduced by something other than the data

if X ⟹ Y ⟹ Z is a Markov Chain
and if I = mutual information
then: I (X; Y) ≥ I (X; Z).

Figure 9 The data processing theorem

---

[6] The principle states that there is an inverse relation between the probability of p—where p may be a proposition, a sentence of a given language, a situation, or a possible world—and the amount of semantic information carried by p. Thus, a biased coin provides increasingly less information the more likely one of its outcomes is. The principle, though very plausible, runs into two problems, the 'scandal of deduction' (Hintikka 1973; D'Agostino and Floridi 2009) and the 'Bar-Hillel-Carnap Paradox' (Floridi 2005b).

[7] The model states that if two systems a and b are coupled in such a way that a's being (of type, or in state) F is correlated to b being (of type, or in state) G, then such correlation carries for the observer of a the information that b is G. For example, the dishwasher's yellow light (a) flashing (F) is triggered by, and hence is informative about, the dishwasher (b) running out of salt (G) for an observer O, like Alice, informed about the correlation. See Barwise and Seligman (1997), Dretske (1999), Floridi (2010a).

processing itself. For example, the Markov chain has been broken[8] (for a classic example of such a 'break' in human communication consider the 'crying wolf' scenario).[9]

Intuitively, the reader may recall the game of Chinese Whispers, in which a first player in a line whispers a message to the player next in line, who whispers it as accurately as possible to the next player, and so on, until the last player communicates the message to the whole group. The players are the equivalent of S_1, S_2, S_3, and so forth, and their whispered messages are X, Y, Z, and so forth. The longer the chain of speakers is, the less likely it becomes that the final message will resemble the initial one. With a slogan more memorable but less accurate: data processing tends to destroy information; it certainly cannot increase it. Asking for more signal processing is not going to solve the problem of escalating natural semantics to non-natural semantics. At best, it can only deliver more natural semantics. Some other factor must be at play.

Let us take stock. We saw that, if perception is a data-providing process, then we need to be able to explain how such data become meaningful and hence suitable for generating information (well-formed, meaningful, and truthful data) and then knowledge (accounted information). There are ways, such as the praxical solution to the SGP, to show how the meaning of some perceptual data may be naturalized. However, many, if not most, of our perceptions deal with non-natural meanings. There was a time when Alice saw a piece of cloth with some coloured patterns on it, but it is now impossible for her not to see the Union Jack, or Old Glory, or the Tricolore, etc. In this case, signalling, the agent's data processing and internal states, and the memory of such states are necessary but insufficient conditions to account for the emergence of non-natural semantics. We also saw that the development of cognitive agents should be interpreted in terms of an increasing distance from their environment. Despite this—and despite the fact that data as signals are elicited by the interactions between the agent and the system, and hence should be taken as negotiations with, rather than representations of, the system—we usually correctly assume that, in the best (but also very common) circumstances, even when non-natural meanings are in question, the end-product of the agent's perception of the system is a faithful grasp of the state of the system by that agent. When Alice sees the yellow light flashing and perceives that the dishwasher is running out of salt, that is normally the case: she is correct and the dishwasher is indeed running out of salt. The same holds true for her perception of the national anthem, the flag of her country, the red traffic light at the crossroads, and so forth. Mistakes are the exception in Alice's cognitive life. She would not be here as a species, if they were the rule. Or, to put it in more Davidsonian or Dennettian terms, the more mistakes she made the

---

[8] This has been suggested as a solution to the problem of enriching the semantic value of computer visualizations, in Chen and Floridi (2013). For a simple and balanced introduction to the limits of Markov Chains in animal communication see Bregman and Gentner (2010, pp. 370–1).

[9] This is Aesop's famous tale: a young shepherd repeatedly raises a false alarm (by crying wolf) in order to trick nearby villagers into thinking that a wolf is attacking his flock. When a wolf actually does attack it, his signal goes unnoticed because the villagers, who *remember* all the times this was a false alarm, no longer believe him, and the flock is destroyed.

less she would be interpretable as a cognitive agent.[10] In order to solve this strange predicament—according to which perception as data provider both decouples the agent from her environment through more and more non-natural meanings and couples her to it successfully and indeed in a way that is cognitively superior to any other species—we need to adopt a different perspective and move from a naturalistic to a constructionist view (Floridi 2011a). Here is how we may do it.

It seems incontrovertible that human agents do not merely use natural meanings but constantly *repurpose* them for other epistemic, communicative, and semanticizing goals. Alice not only sees the yellow light flashing, she also repurposes it to mean, in the kitchen appliance context, that the dishwasher is running out of salt. Conventional or non-natural meanings are the outcome of such repurposing. The cognitive strategy of using, converting, or modifying data/signals for a purpose or function other than their original, natural one, to fit a new use—think of Peirce's distinction between icon, index, and symbol—is very cost-effective and can be reiterated endlessly: a cloth becomes a flag, which becomes a country, which becomes a foe to burn, or something to be proud of and wear as qualifying one's identity, and so forth. By repurposing perceptual data, human agents like Alice actually use them as resources to interact with the world, with themselves (see narrative theories of the self (Floridi 2011b)) and among themselves more richly, innovatively, inventively, indeed more intelligently, than any other kind of agents we know, which are unable to go beyond natural semantics. And since 'repurpose' may be just another word for 'hacking', a simple and more colourful way of putting the previous point is by saying that *humans are natural-born data hackers* (see Figure 10; the arrow top-right indicates the 'hacking' place).

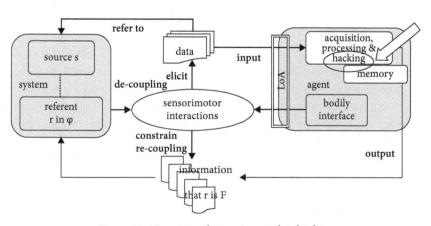

Figure 10 Non-natural meanings as data hacking

---

[10] I owe this point to one of the anonymous referees of the manuscript, who actually remarked: 'Of course the more Dennettian or Davidsonian view is that "she wouldn't be [interpretable as] cognitive at all, if mistakes were the rule". I agree, but I think it would be a matter of degrees rather than threshold.

A conception of Alice as a cognitive mirror, a basket (Descartes endorsed this analogy), a bucket (Popper criticized this analogy), or a representationalist mechanism is simply wrong. It is certainly inconsistent with our best neuroscience:

Increasingly, the brain reveals itself proactive in its interface with external reality. In the past, our conception of the brain changed from that of a mirror to that of an interpreter. Several current lines of research—in fields such as memory, motivation and attentional orienting—now begin to cast the brain as a predictor. The results of experience are integrated over various timescales in order to anticipate events relevant to the current task goals and motivational state of the individual and to tune the relevant perceptual and motor machinery accordingly. In particular, research on attentional orienting has shown how signals coding predictions about the location, identity or simple features of relevant events can influence several stages of neural processing. Recent evidence shows that these predictions are not restricted simply to the contents of events but also extend to their anticipated timing.   (Nobre et al. 2007, p. 465)

The philosophical hypothesis about repurposing—the view that humans are natural-born data hackers—may be convincing, but there is a final problem. For unless Alice's repurposing of natural data and signals is somehow successfully constrained, its outcome could be indistinguishable from the delusions or hallucinations of a mentally ill person. The similarity between semantic repurposing and mental disorder is an important point, to which I shall return in the conclusion. At the moment, it is clear that, while the hypothesis of a data hacking process may solve the problem of understanding how the data acquired through perception may move from natural to non-natural meanings, it does not, in itself, say anything about the fact that, through perception, human agents interact very successfully with each other and their environments, and are re-coupled to the world in the most realistic, indubitable, 'what you see is what you get' kind of way. What does re-couple Alice to the world, once she is decoupled from it by her data hacking? Recall that, normally, outside Hume's studio, Alice has no doubts whatsoever about the fact that the yellow light flashing is exactly what the world is like, and that the world is such that it now contains her dishwasher running out of salt. She is right, and her successful interactions with the world show her to be right, but this is a problem because, at the moment, the creativity offered by data hacking fails to explain the cognitive and pragmatic success of her naïve and commonsensical realism. Indeed, it works counter to it.

What seems to be required is a re-interpretation of the representational correspondence between (i) Alice's perception of the world and (ii) the way the world is, as (iii) *retro-fitness*, in the following sense. In normal and common circumstances, say in Alice's kitchen, data/signals (the yellow light flashing) sent by, and referring to, system r (the dishwasher) in state φ (running out of salt) become the information (model) that r is F (the dishwasher is running out of salt) by being processed in such a way that the mutual information $I(\varphi(r); F(r)) = \text{MAX}$. This ensures complete correlation between the perception and the perceived, which Alice enjoys cognitively and on which her actions are successfully based practically. However, such a complete correlation seems possible only if

(a) either: s (the source) = r (referent), $F(r)$ is a faithful representation of $\varphi(r)$, and there is a noiseless ideal channel between the system-referent and the agent;
(b) or: $F(r)$ constitutes $\varphi(r)$.

None of the three conditions in (a) seems really satisfiable, so (b) remains the only option, but this means that perceptual information is the *output* of the perceptual data processing/hacking not the input (see Figure 11; the arrow bottom-left indicates I $(\varphi(r); F(r)) = \text{MAX}$.

Such output—the models of the world that the data (constraining affordances) hacking generates—competes for success on the basis of *fit for purpose* and *correct* (right) *first time*. Given her constraining affordances (data), Alice generates an endless amount of interpretations of the world: some of them are correct because they respect and make the most of her data and are evolutionarily selected to ground and improve her interactions with her environment and other agents ('the dishwasher needs more salt'), some are simply mistaken ('the dishwasher is not getting enough water'), and many are simply innocuous and unrestrained by the available data ('the yellow light flashing means I will not get the job'). Following the inverse relation principle, Alice will be in no state of surprisal (Shannon's term) with regard to her perceptions: she cannot be informed *about* them (mind, not *by* them) because to her the probability P of her perception ($F(r)$) is 1. New information, of the kind exemplified by the yellow light flashing, is the exception, certainly not the norm. To put it in Kantian terms, perceptual information about the world is the world, and the world-information by default has probability 1 for those who perceive it. The system is the source/referent of the data, but the interpreted data, properly understood as semanticized constraining affordances, do not represent the system, no more than radio signals represent the

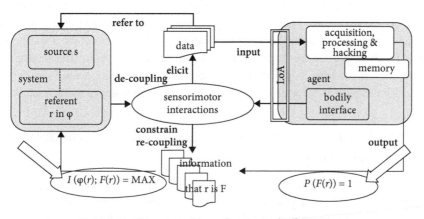

Figure 11 The construction of perceptual information

radio sending it. To a realist this may sound a bit suspicious, so let me hasten to add that we are standing on the shoulder of a gigantic champion of realism, Helmholtz. Here is how he put it:

Our sensations are effects brought forth in our organs by means of exterior causes, and how such an effect manifests itself depends of course quite essentially on the nature of the apparatus on which the cause operates. Insofar as the quality of our sensations gives us *information* about the peculiarities of the exterior process that excites it, it can count as a *sign* of that process, *but not as a picture*. For one expects of a picture some sort of similarity with the pictured object.... But a sign need have no similarity of any sort whatever with that of which it is the sign. The relation between them is only that the same object, working its effects in the same way, produces the same sign, and that unequal signs always correspond to unequal causes. To the popular view, which naively and complacently assumes the full truth of the pictures that our senses give us of things, this remainder of similarity that we recognise may seem rather paltry. In truth it is not; with its aid something of the greatest significance can be achieved: the representation of the regularities in the processes of the real world.... So even if our sense impressions in their qualities are only signs, whose special nature depends wholly on our internal organisation, they are nonetheless not to be dismissed as empty appearance, but are in fact a sign of something, whether this is something existing or something occurring; and what is most important, they can picture the law of this occurring.

(Helmholtz 1995, pp. 347–8, cited by Carus 2007, pp. 117–18)

Helmholtz published this in 1878. Had he written it after Shannon, he would have spoken of data providers.

In all this, testimony as information transmission, not yet generation, and as a by-product of perception, which allows further semantic hacking, plays a final and crucial role. So far, the analysis has been developed by considering only a single agent. Of course, this is an untenable simplification. Alice is part of a community of speakers and epistemic agents. Most of the semantics she enjoys and controls is inherited. She read in the manual that the yellow light flashing non-naturally means (or, to put it *à la* Grice, means$_{NN}$) that the dishwasher is running out of salt. It is here that testimony—understood as the main mechanism through which agents learn and share a language as well as information and hence can constitute a multiagent system (a community of speakers)—plays a fundamental role (see Figure 12). For testimony is what enables the development of language as the main cognitive tool to hack natural meanings, thus allowing the Lamarckian evolution of hacked data through generations (cumulative learning).

11. Informational Realism: Structures, Interactions, and Causality

The previous analysis leads to the development of an informational interpretation of structural realism. I developed the latter in volume one (Floridi 2011c), so I shall not rehearse it here. However, for the sake of completion, it may be worth giving a quick overview by focusing on three key concepts: *structures*, *interactions*, and *causality*.

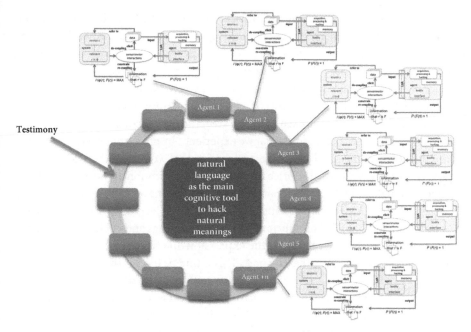

Testimony

Figure 12 Perception, testimony, and language

Structures have been increasingly important in the history and the philosophy of logic and mathematics. They are now crucial in almost any branch of knowledge and hence in epistemology and philosophy of science. Understood as systematic patterns of differences—like a black circle on a white surface, the set of all points whose Cartesian coordinates satisfy the equation $x^2 + y^2 = 2^2$, thus identifying a circle of radius 2, or the set of natural numbers—structures shift our ontological focus, from the substantial nature of mathematical entities as *things*, to their underlining relational essence as *patterns*. This is a crucial lesson I learnt from Cassirer and his masterly essay dedicated to the replacement of the concept of substance by that of function in the philosophy of mathematics (1910, now Cassirer 1953). Just a decade before its publication, Hilbert had elegantly and famously explained such structuralism at the beginning of his *Grundlagen der Geometrie* (1899, see now Hilbert 1971):

We think of these points, straight lines, and planes [in Geometry] as having certain mutual relations, which we indicate by means of such words as 'are situated,' 'between,' 'parallel,' 'congruent,' 'continuous,' etc. The complete and exact description of these relations follows as a consequence of the axioms of geometry. These axioms may be arranged in five groups. Each of these groups expresses, by itself, certain related fundamental facts of our intuition.   (Hilbert 1971, p. 1)

Replace in the quotation 'as *having* certain mutual relations' with 'as *being constituted* by certain mutual relations', and you obtain a structuralist ontology of geometrical elements. A similar analysis can be provided for arithmetical structures. Mathematical as well as physical *objects* are what we, as specific informational structures (cognitive systems, in an equivalent vocabulary), find easier to handle logically, mentally, and empirically. However, there are good philosophical, mathematical, and scientific reasons[11] to commit ourselves to a structuralist/informationalist ontology according to which *mathematical* as well as *physical* objects do not play the role of ultimate *realia*. Like icons on a computer screen, they are user-friendly, but they should not be confused with what lies behind them and constitutes their nature. Recall that we are, to the best of our knowledge, the only semantically structuring structures in the infosphere. As such, we give and make sense of what we experience by objectifying it (hypostatization). The detachment and distance from the noumenal world, which makes our rich cognitive life possible, is also the price imposed by the reification of the noumenal into the phenomenal world. We freeze changes into state- or phase-transitions and modular events, and transform patterns and structures into objects and properties, finally privileging a naïve ontology of sufficiently permanent things and qualities. How many times do we hear philosophers using the expression 'the furniture of the world'? We deal with Being by forgetting the -ing part. This is fine, as long as the task is to survive and reproduce in a hostile environment, which promotes fast reactions and punishes slow reflection, but it is much less satisfactory if the goal is to understand the ultimate nature of reality philosophically. From this unifying perspective, it is reasonable to presume that we are always dealing with dynamic structures in flux, whether empirically or mathematically reified as objects. Structures are not second-class citizens of our ontology, with first-class citizens represented by material things, the usual chairs and horses, kicked stones and white snow, co-referential stars, chariots and trolleys, hammers and thalers, and so forth. They are the *ipokeimena*, what lies below the surface of the world as we experience it.

The sketch I have just provided is in line with what Shapiro (1997) has defined and defended as the *ante rem* approach to mathematical structuralism. The difference is that the *whole ontology* is *ante rem*, not just the ontology of mathematical objects. An informational approach to structuralism helps to prevent (rather than solve) the problem of why mathematics is so readily applicable to the empirical world: it is a matter of structures all the way down.

Let me now turn to the concept of interaction. Mathematical structures interplay and interlock with each other in various ways. Such *internal* interactions (Hilbert's more static 'certain mutual relations') are what an informational structural realist qualifies as primarily necessary, not the mathematical objects that they end up constituting. Yet interactive is also our relationship with such structures. Such *external interactions* give us a metaphysical *criterion* of existence: a yardstick to check whether x exists, not what it means for x to exist, or what kind of existence x enjoys. To put it simply, ghosts do not exist not because you cannot touch them, but because there is no LoA at which you can interact with them. That is why subatomic particles exist, and so do non-Euclidean triangles, even if you cannot touch or smell them. True, *whether* and

---

[11] See Floridi (2008a, 2011c), Shapiro (2000), French and Ladyman (2003).

how we can interact with certain structures depends on the adopted LoA. You may not consider functions of the kind x^y among your observables, or, once they are admitted by your LoA, you may work with them differently, depending on whether you make the x and the y range only on the natural numbers (so that, for example, you obtain $3^2 = 9$) or on the integers as well (so that $3^{-2} = 1/3^2$). Once the observables are admitted and specified, their dynamics is often a matter of acknowledgement and discovery, not construction or invention. This is where I take a more Platonist route.[12]

Finally, causality. The clarification of this concept in this context requires a long premise. One of the most abstract observations possible of a population is its *size* or cardinality as a set, that is, the number of its members. In the terminology of the *method of abstraction* (see Chapter 2), that is an observable of type WHOLE NUMBER and it is well typed provided that the population is finite and well defined. At this LoA, a population provides no more information than its *size*. There is no distinction between live populations, artificial populations, and, for that matter, any ordinary set. In order to gain more information, one may then add one more observable; call it *generation number of each member*. Its type is FUNCTION FROM MEMBERS OF THE POPULATION TO WHOLE NUMBERS: the argument of the function is the member of the population and the result is its generation number. If the original members of the population were observable, then some convention would be necessary for their generation number; a reasonable choice would be 0. More details can easily be added. A more general alternative, always well typed, is obtained by assuming time (rather than generation number) to be observable and observing the *size of the population at any time*. The result is of type FUNCTION FROM TIMES TO WHOLE NUMBERS. An LoA containing such observables, though simple, would be sufficient to support the well-known Fibonacci model of population size per generation. At this LoA, a population provides no more information than its growth. However, this might be already of some interest if we include additional observables such as the rates of birth, mortality, migration, or harvesting. It is sufficient, for example, to discuss age distribution across the population, for the management of pest populations, for the harvesting of natural populations, for the modelling of insect outbreaks, of interacting populations, and so on. One further step, in revealing information about the population, is to investigate aspects of the state of its members, perhaps the simplest being position in space. Thus, one may consider *spatial distribution* as a further observable. If the population consists of cellular automata, then the distribution is a subset of automaton positions, namely those positions at which automata are located. If it consists of a population of

---

[12] This Platonism is a bit Popperian. In *Scepticism and the Foundation of Epistemology* (Floridi 1996), see especially ch. 7) I discussed at length Popper's World 3 hypothesis as well as his arguments in favour of an 'epistemology without a knowing subject'. The latter especially was very influential in my understanding of the philosophy of information. It is easy to see this in my admittedly qualified support for Mark Notturno's interpretation, according to which 'Popper's concept of subjectless knowledge is a legitimate use of the word "knowledge". It corresponds to the sense of "knowledge" as *information* or a branch of learning [my emphasis]' (Notturno 1985, p. 153).

animals then the observable's type is some mathematical representation of the domain inhabited by the animals, for example a map with a point on it for each animal. In the case of bird flocks, it may be interesting to observe *spatial distribution at time t*, whose type is FUNCTION FROM TIMES TO SPATIAL DISTRIBUTIONS. This LoA is sufficient for many studies of population dynamics, both in biological and in artificial contexts. One may, for example, consider the population of 'bicycles in Oxford'. They arrive in Oxford, move around, sometimes in correlated ways or at specific times (e.g. according to the lecturing schedule), and even leave. The story is that they are stolen and sold in Cambridge, and vice versa, thus giving the impression of a sort of two-way migration pattern. At this LoA, they appear to be equivalent to entities that are born, graze, possibly migrate, and die. In terms of recycling of parts, they might even be seen as reproducing. Alternatively, for a system of cellular automata *spatial distribution* can be seen as a special case of *individual state*, in which state contains just one bit of information: dead or alive. In all these examples, the population forms a dynamical system whose next state is a function of just the current state, and at least (part of) the current state is observed. This important setting characterizes most modelling in applied mathematics and computer science. It implicitly endorses a very strong assumption: the *Markovian nature* of the transfer function. We already saw that this means that state transitions (both continuous and discrete) are treated as a process in which the probability of the system to be in state X at time $t + 1$ is dependent only upon the state (and hence the properties) Y of the system at the immediately preceding time t. Intuitively, this is why you can join a chess game at any time and still follow what is happening, or become an expert in chess endings: the state of the chessboard at $t + 1$ depends only on the state of the chessboard at t.

We have finally reached the end of the premise. Such a Markovian approach (the causal version is known as the causal Markov condition), interpreted from the perspective of a philosophy of information and a *method of abstraction*, does not seem to be a case of discovery, since the world often appears to be more inextricably complex and intertwined than a chess game. But it does not seem to be a case of mere invention either, since the successful nature of our epistemic efforts based on Markov analyses hardly justifies a complete form of scepticism, as if Markov conditions were artificially and externally imposed on a recalcitrant world. It seems more a case of design features: our *method of abstraction*, both theoretically and empirically (e.g. whenever it makes sense to talk of algorithms, the actual software programs and the resulting simulations), naturally leads to a Markovian approach and, at the same time, it privileges and makes more salient those features and aspects of the systems under observation that are Markov-friendly. And this points in the direction of a more metaphysical lesson about causality. Differential equations, state transitions, Bayesian networks, Markov chains, and so forth can all be interpreted as ways of *re-structuring* the targeted systems (structures), after they have been *de-structured* (articulated) in figures, states, nodes, or events. The reifying nature of our cognitive approach is such that we first of all look at a billiard game (the structure) as divided (de-structured) into sequences of well-formed events, in which well-formed and independent objects, with specific properties, behave in such a way as to generate transformations. We then find such a dismembered (de-structured) system in need of re-composition, or reconstruction (re-structuring). As in the case of a vase which we have first shattered into pieces—or like a Humean philosopher thinking that there are actually two events in the world, one consisting of a stone flying against the window, and the second consisting of the window breaking—we are then left with the task of gluing together what was intact and in one piece in the first place. Such re-structuring of a de-structured structure cannot restore the pristine state. To put it in Humean terms, causing is not necessitating; there is no necessity linking the de-structured event A and event B, for the simple fact that, if there were, we would not be able to split the two events in A and B. The broken glass will not be fully restored, yet it is crucial to realize that this is not a problem at all. For the re-structuring follows normative rules (how the modelling should be done), like the Markov condition, which are not meant to ensure that the re-structured model is indistinguishable from the original un-de-structured system. Their goal is epistemic and pragmatic—for example in terms of understanding, prediction, explanation, evaluation, control, modification, construction, reproducibility—not metaphysical (grasping as far as possible the essential nature of the system), and this is what both justifies the de-structuring in the first place and what guides the re-structuring afterwards. Causality is an epistemic glue and it works well when it re-structures (more hacking) the de-structured structures efficaciously.

Conclusion: The Beautiful Glitch

Much more could and should be said about the two answers I provided in this chapter to the questions outlined in section 1. The data hacking hypothesis is only the beginning. In order to facilitate further steps ahead, and especially the development of a constructionist logic of information in Chapter 9, in this conclusion I shall only summarize a few salient points we will need to keep in mind when reading the next chapters.

We saw that perception is a complex process through which constraining affordances (data) are negotiated, acquired, elaborated, and repurposed by epistemic and semantic agents like Alice and Bob in order to make sense of, and interact successfully with, their environments both naturally and non-naturally. The interpretation of perception as a decoupling and then re-coupling process of the cognitive agent is coherent with the development of language, through testimony, as mainly a cognitive tool (Deacon 1997; Schilhab et al. 2012) rather than just a communication medium, and with the emergence of *consciousness* (Floridi 2005a) and the construction of a sense of *personal identity* (Floridi 2011b) as part of a progressive detachment of the agent from the world. Mentally healthy humans differ from animals because they are non-naturally de-coupled from the here-and-now by their data hacking. And they differ from the mentally ill because the same data hacking re-couples them to the here-and-now inventively, purposefully, teleologically, and often successfully. Contrary to animals, we construct increasingly complex, semantic artefacts. Contrary to the mentally ill, our semantic artefacts work *correctly*.[13] From an evolutionary perspective, we are uniquely different from, and more successful than, other species not because of a plus but because of a minus; namely the (both perceptual and linguistic) semantic incapacity of being absolutely and inseparably present, cognitively, where we are located, bodily. We cannot help experiencing the world *as*. This gap, this detachment or decoupling, this initial incapacity of being thoroughly absorbed by the world—which our intelligence and mental life then has to bridge through the development of language and our knowledge of the world—is what makes us special. Looking for our semantic, linguistic, mental, conscious *quid* is looking for an absence, for a gap, for a fissure. Indeed, it has been controversially argued in psychiatry[14] that the same evolutionary causes lie behind our capacities to develop both language and mental illness. It seems that the price to be paid to be *Homo sapiens sapiens* is that of being potentially the schizophrenic species as well. The fissure is double-edged, as it were.

Some 50,000 years ago, the *Homo* species finally snapped and began regularly, widely, and consistently to distance itself from its environment through the development of a culture of tool- and weapon-making, art (sculpture, cave painting, body ornaments), travelling, long-distance trade, and burial rituals (Diamond 2006). We are not evolution's finest moment, the peak of the process, some kind of *Über*-animal, but Nature's *beautiful glitch*. We are the oddball in the natural set. It is because we are a bit less that we are so much more. And in the same way as a broken mechanism that manages to survive and evolve by repurposing itself is perfectly natural, and yet unlikely to be reproducible, it remains an open question whether we might ever be able to 'break' our syntactic machines in such a way as to make them intelligent like us. Real, old-fashioned artificial intelligence as we know it may remain unachievable not because it is physically impossible—Nature managed the trick with us—but because some mistakes may be perfectly natural and yet be forever unique. The beautiful glitch may well be Nature's *hapax legomenon*.

Philosophically, the accidental and yet resilient balance between informational decoupling and re-coupling, detachment and engagement, is better understood from a constructionist and non-representationalist perspective than from a naturalistic and representationalist one. This means understanding our informational, linguistic, and cognitive activities as part of our creative manipulation of the data/signals (the cognitive constraining affordances) negotiated with the world. Epistemologically, this leads to the acknowledgement that knowledge by acquaintance is more fundamental, in terms

---

[13] For a theory of truth as correctness see Floridi (2010c).

[14] The theory that schizophrenia might be a consequence of the human evolution of language is scientifically associated with the research of Tim Crow, a professor of psychiatry at Oxford University. A close view, according to which schizophrenia contributed to the evolution of *Homo sapiens*, was popularized, rather controversially, by David Horrobin (2001). More recently, the publication of Faulks (2005), a novel in which the theory is presented in a fictional scenario, 'sparked an academic feud' (Thorpe 2005).

of input, than know-how, and this, in turn, is more fundamental than knowledge-that, to rely on a useful but slightly inadequate Russellian terminology. The opposite is true when it comes to creativity and repurposing. It also means that we should be able to find a middle ground between naïve realism—which is not a philosophical position but really the final outcome of a complex process of successful construction—and relativism, reinforcing the relational analysis of many of our key informational concepts. Only by strengthening our understanding of such a third way, Plato's *metaxy* (see for example *Symposium* 203b–c), shall we be able to escape the usual dichotomies that haunt our philosophy (think of the naïve and tiresome question whether colours are in the perceived or in the perceiver).

The world as we consciously experience it is the totality of its models as we unconsciously create them. It is the outcome of a constant construction and amendment of a stable interpretation. We saw in Chapter 3 that we are amphibian beings, partly living within natural environments as bodies and mostly living within normative and semantic ones as minds. As cognitive amphibians, we are embodied and embedded physical agents, and we live in and interact with the world in itself, Kant's *noumena*. We eat and drink, handle and build, avoid and crash into *noumena*. But as informational organisms, we experience and inhabit the world as a semantic reality both afforded and constrained by the world in itself. Our ontology is entirely semantic, so we know the world when we are informed about it and are able to account for such information. For a knower, if you recall the quote from Plato we encountered above, is 'the man who knows how to ask and answer questions' (*Cratylus* 390c), giving an account, that is, about the information that she holds.

Sub specie aeternitatis, all this does not look too bad. In the informational fabric that we call Being, there are some special nodes. They are unlike any other kinds of nodes. Perhaps they emerge out of an odd evolution of unrepeatable chances. They are Nature's beautiful glitches, as I wrote above. They were not meant to be there, like a unique kind of a most unlikely pattern, but they have occurred, and they can now marvel at the most improbable chances that brought them into existence. Or perhaps they have a divine origin, as Plato already thought. Either way, these nodes are informational structures like all other nodes, encapsulating packets of differences, relations, and processes, which contribute to the value and richness of the whole. Their special nature lies not in what they are—in their physics and biochemistry, to use a different level of abstraction— but in what they can become and do non-naturally. For they are *structuring structures*, the ultimate defence against entropy/evil, able to semanticize Being. They are the *loci* where the flow of information reaches its maturity and becomes self-conscious, capable of self-determination, and able to decouple itself from the rest of the fabric and reflecting on its own nature and status, semanticizing themselves and all the other nodes, thus shifting from a Darwinian, physical evolution to a Lamarckian, mental development (we have developed incommensurably faster than our bodies). Such nodes, you and I included, have an unclear destiny. They might hope that their moral struggle against entropy is actually a small episode in a divine plan. If so, this can only be reason for rejoicing. Or they might fear that such a struggle is unfortunately only a titanic effort in an unrewarding and lonely universe, a thin red line against the vandalism of time, the failure of which can be delayed and mitigated, but not avoided. If so, this should still be reason for some modest rejoicing, for they will have helped reality to die a more graceful death. Such nodes are the stewards of Being. They may do whatever they like, as long as they are careful, as both Paul of Tarsus and Augustine recommended.

5

Information Quality

Summary

Previously, in Chapter 4, we saw that our knowledge, as a non-natural construction, may be based on our ability to hack the data coming from the world. Two questions now become pressing. One concerns the quality of the information we are able to generate, when we are dealing with truthful contents. The other question concerns the truthfulness of such contents, when we are not quite certain whether we are dealing with information or misinformation. I shall address the first question here, and the second, which is really about a potential sceptical challenge, in Chapter 6. To do so, I shall generalize the analysis and apply it to a popular topic, that of big data. The first part of the chapter will briefly analyse the phenomenon, and argue that the real epistemological challenge posed by the zettabyte era is *small patterns*. The valuable undercurrents in the ocean of data that we are accumulating are invisible to the computationally naked eye, so more and better technology will help, further reinforcing the case for a constructionist philosophy. However, because the problem with big data is small patterns, ultimately, the game will be won by those who—and I know this is the third time I use this quotation—'know how to ask and answer questions' (Plato, *Cratylus* 390c). This introduces the second part of the chapter, which focuses on information quality (IQ). Which data may be useful and relevant, and so worth collecting, curating, and *querying*, in order to exploit their valuable (small) patterns? I shall argue that the standard way of seeing IQ in terms of being fit-for-purpose is correct but needs to be complemented by the methodology of abstraction introduced in Chapter 2, which allows IQ to be indexed to different purposes. This fundamental step can be taken by adopting a bi-categorical approach. This means distinguishing between purpose/s for which some information is *produced* (P–purpose) and purpose/s for which the same information is *consumed* (C–purpose). This in turn enables one to analyse a variety of so-called IQ dimensions, and in particular accuracy, completeness, consistency, and timeliness. I shall conclude by showing that the bi-categorical approach lends itself to simple visualizations in terms of radar charts.

1. Big Data

Just a few years ago, researchers at Berkeley's School of Information estimated that humanity had accumulated approximately 12 exabytes of data in the course of its entire history (one exabyte corresponds to 10^{18} bytes or a 50,000-year-long video of DVD quality), until the commodification of computers, but it had already reached 180 exabytes by 2006. According to a more recent study, the total grew to over 1,600 exabytes, between 2006 and 2011, thus passing the zettabyte (1,000 exabytes) barrier. The figure was expected to grow fourfold approximately every three years, to reach 8 zettabyes of data by 2015 (Figure 13). And according to Cisco there will be 44 zetta-bytes of data by 2020. I could continue with more updated details but the point is obvious. Every day, enough new data is being generated to fill all US libraries eight times over. Of course, trillions of Information and Communications Technology (ICT) systems are constantly working to keep us afloat and navigate through such an ocean of data. These are all numbers that will keep growing quickly and steadily for the foreseeable future, especially because those very systems are among the greatest sources of further data, which in turn require, or simply make possible, more ICTs. It is a self-reinforcing cycle, and it would be unnatural not to feel over-whelmed. It is, or at least should be, a mixed feeling of apprehension for the risks, excitement for the opportunities, and astonishment for the achievements, as we shall see in the following chapters.

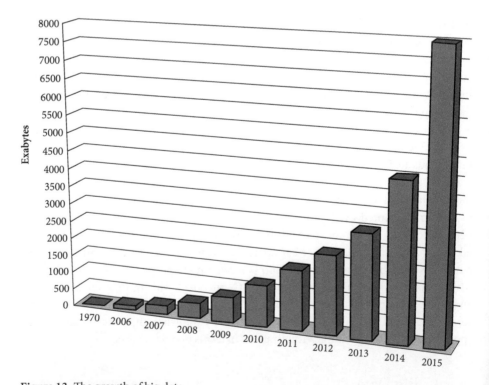

Figure 13 The growth of big data
Based on IDC White Paper, 'The Diverse and Exploding Digital Universe', March 2008 and IDC White Paper, 'Worldwide Big Data Technology and Service 2012–2015 Forecast', March 2012.

Thanks to ICTs, we have entered *the age of the zettabyte*. Our generation is the first to experience a Zettaflood, to introduce a neologism to qualify this tsunami of bytes that is submerging our environments. In other contexts, this is also known as 'big data'.

Despite the importance of the phenomenon, it is unclear what exactly the term 'big data' means and hence refers to. The temptation, in similar cases, is to adopt the approach pioneered by United States Supreme Court Justice Potter Stewart to describe pornography: difficult to define, but 'I know when I see it'. Other strategies have been much less successful. For example, in the United States, the National Institutes of Health (NIH) and the National Science Foundation (NSF) have identified big data as a programme focus. One of the main NSF-NIH interagency initiatives addresses the need for core techniques and technologies for advancing big data science and engineering. However, the two agencies specify that:

The phrase 'big data' in this solicitation refers to large, diverse, complex, longitudinal, and/or distributed data sets generated from instruments, sensors, Internet transactions, email, video, click streams, and/or all other digital sources available today and in the future.

(see NSF-12-499)[1]

You do not need to be a logician to find this both obscure and vague. Wikipedia, for once, is also unhelpful. Not because the relevant entry is unreliable, but because it reports the common definition, which is unsatisfactory:

data sets so large and complex that they become awkward to work with using on-hand database management tools.[2]

Apart from the circular problem of defining 'big' with 'large' (the NSF and NHI seem to be happy with it), the aforementioned text suggests that data are too big or large only in relation to our current computational power. This is misleading. Of course, 'big', as with many other terms, is a relational predicate: a pair of shoes may be too big for you, but fine for me. It is also trivial to acknowledge that we tend to evaluate things non-relationally, in this case as absolutely big, whenever the frame of reference is obvious enough to be left implicit. A horse is a big animal, no matter what whales may think. Yet these two simple points may give the impression that there is no real trouble with 'big data' being a loosely defined term referring to the fact that our current computers cannot handle so many gazillions of data efficiently. And this is where two confusions seem to creep in. First, that the *epistemological problem* with big data is that there is too much of it (the *ethical problem* concerns how we use them; more on this below). And, second, that the *solution* to the epistemological problem is *technological*: more and better techniques and technologies, which will 'shrink' big data back to a manageable size. The epistemological problem is different, and it requires an equally epistemological solution.

---

[1] https://www.nsf.gov/pubs/2012/nsf12499/nsf12499.htm.
[2] https://en.wikipedia.org/wiki/Big_data.

2. The Epistemological Problem with Big Data

Consider the problem first. 'Big data' came to be formulated after other buzz expressions, such as 'infoglut' or 'information overload', began to fade away, yet the idea remains the same. It refers to an overwhelming sense that we have bitten off more than we can chew, that we are being force-fed like geese, that our intellectual livers are exploding. This is a mistake. Yes, we have seen that there is an obvious exponential growth of data on an ever-larger number of topics, but complaining about such an over-abundance would be like complaining about a banquet that offers more than we can ever eat. Data remain an asset, a resource to exploit. Nobody is forcing us to digest every available byte. We are becoming data-richer by the day; this cannot be the fundamental problem.

Since the problem is not the increasing wealth of data that is becoming available, clearly the solution needs to be reconsidered: it cannot be merely how many data we can technologically process. We saw that, if anything, more and better techniques and technologies are only going to generate more data. If the problem were too many data, more ICTs would only exacerbate it. Growing bigger digestive systems, as it were, is not the way forward.

The real, epistemological problem with big data is *small patterns*. Precisely because so many data can now be generated and processed so quickly, so cheaply, and on virtually anything, the pressure both on the data *nouveau riche*, such as Facebook or Walmart, Amazon or Google, and on the data *old money*, such as genetics or medicine, experimental physics or neuroscience, is to be able to spot where the new patterns with real added-value lie in their immense databases, and how they can best be exploited for the creation of wealth, the improvement of human lives, the care for the environment, and the advancement of knowledge.

Small patterns matter because today they represent the new frontier of competition, from science to business, from governance to social policies, from security to business. In a Baconian open market of ideas, if someone else can exploit them earlier and more successfully than you do, you might be out of business soon, like Kodak, or miss a fundamental discovery, or put your country in danger.

Small patterns may also be risky, because they push the limit of what is predictable, and therefore may be anticipated, about not only nature's, but also people's, behaviour. This is an ethical problem. Target, an American retailing company, relies on the analysis of the purchasing patterns of twenty-five products in order to assign each shopper a 'pregnancy prediction' score, estimate her due date, and send coupons timed to specific stages of her pregnancy. In a notorious case, it caused some serious problems when it sent coupons to a family in which the teenager daughter had not informed her parents about her new status.

3. From Big Data to Small Patterns

Unfortunately, small patterns may be significant only if properly aggregated, for example in terms of loyalty cards and shopping suggestions, compared—as when a bank can use big data to fight fraudsters—and timely processed—as in financial markets. And because information is also indicative when it is not there, small patterns can be significant if they are absent. Sherlock Holmes solves one of his famous cases because of the silence of the dog, which should have barked. If big data are not 'barking' when they should, something is going on, as the financial watchdogs (should) know.

The increasingly valuable undercurrents in the ever-expanding oceans of data are invisible to the computationally naked eye, so more and better techniques and technologies will help significantly. Yet, by themselves, they will be insufficient.

And mere data hoarding, while waiting for more powerful computers and software, will not work. Since 2007, the world has been producing more data than available storage (see Figure 14). We have shifted from the problem of what to save to the problem of what to erase. Something must be deleted or never be recorded in the first place. Think of your smartphone becoming too full because you took too many pictures, and make it a global problem.

The infosphere ran out of memory space to dump its data years ago. This is not as bad as it looks. Rephrasing a common saying in advertisement, half of our data is junk, we just do not know which half. Clearly, what we need is a better understanding of which data are worth preserving. And this is a matter of grasping both what information quality is, as we shall see in the second half of this chapter, and which questions are or will be interesting. Which is just another way of saying that, because the problem with big data is small patterns, ultimately, the game will be won by those who 'know

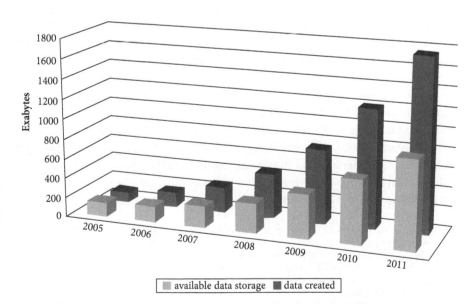

Figure 14 Global information (data) created vs. memory (storage) available

Based on IDC White Paper, 'The Diverse and Exploding Digital Universe', March 2008; IDC White Paper, 'Worldwide Big Data Technology and Service 2012–2015 Forecast', March 2012; 'Data, data everywhere'; and *The Economist*, 25 February 2010.

how to ask and answer questions' (Plato, *Cratylus* 390c), and therefore know which data may be useful and relevant, and hence worth collecting, curating, and *querying*, in order to exploit their valuable patterns. We need more and better techniques and technologies to see the small data patterns, but we need more and better epistemology to sift the valuable ones.

Big data is here to grow. The only way of tackling it is to know what we are or may be looking for. At the moment, such epistemological skills are taught and applied by a black art called *analytics*. Not exactly your standard degree at university. Yet so much of our well-being depends on it that it might be time to develop a philosophical investigation of its methods. Who knows, philosophers might have something to learn, but also a couple of lessons to teach. Plato would agree. Let me now turn to the quality problem.

4. Information Quality

The most developed post-industrial societies live by information, and Information and Communication Technologies (ICTs) keep them oxygenated (English 2009). So, the more (big data) and the better (information quality) the information exchanged is, the more likely such societies and their members may prosper. But what is information quality (IQ) exactly? The question has become increasingly pressing in recent years.[3] Yet, in this case too, our answers have been less than satisfactory so far.

In the USA, the *Information Quality Act*, also known as the *Data Quality Act*,[4] enacted in 2000, left undefined virtually every key concept in the text. Therefore, it required the Office of Management and Budget 'to promulgate guidance to agencies ensuring the quality, objectivity, utility, and integrity of information (including statistical information) disseminated by Federal agencies'. Unsurprisingly, the guidelines have received much criticism and have been under review ever since.[5]

In the UK, some of the most sustained efforts in dealing with IQ issues have concerned the National Health Service (NHS). In 2001, the Kennedy Report[6] acknowledged that: 'All health care is information driven, so the threat associated with poor information is a direct risk to the quality of healthcare service and governance in the NHS'. However, in 2004, the NHS Information Quality Assurance Consultation[7] still stressed that 'Consideration of information and data quality are made more complex by the general agreement that there are a number of different aspects to information/data quality but no clear agreement as to what these are'.

---

[3] The body of literature on IQ is growing; see for example Olson (2003), Wang et al. (2005), Batini and Scannapieco (2006), Lee et al. (2006), Al-Hakim (2007), Herzog, Scheuren, and Winkler (2007), Maydanchik (2007), McGilvray (2008), Theys (2011).

[4] https://www.state.gov/misc/49492.htm.

[5] See more recently United States Congress. House Committee on Government Reform. Subcommittee on Regulatory Affairs (2006).

[6] https://www.gov.uk/government/publications/getting-it-right-for-children-and-young-people-overcoming-cultural-barriers-in-the-nhs-so-as-to-meet-their-needs.

[7] http://webarchive.nationalarchives.gov.uk/+/www.dh.gov.uk/en/Publicationsandstatistics/Publications/PublicationsPolicyAndGuidance/DH_4125508.

We know that lacking a clear and precise understanding of IQ properties causes costly errors, confusion, impasse, dangerous risks, and missed opportunities. Part of the difficulty lies in constructing the right conceptual and technical framework necessary to analyse and evaluate them.

Some steps have been taken to rectify the situation. The first *International Conference on Information Quality* was organized in 1996.[8] In 2006, the Association of Computing Machinery (ACM) launched its *Journal of Data and Information Quality* (JDIQ).[9] The Information and Data Quality Summit[10] now provides an international forum for the study of information quality strategies. Pioneering investigations in the 1990s—including Wang and Kon (1992), Tozer (1994), Redman (1996), and Wang (1998)—and research programmes such as the Information Quality Program[11] at MIT have addressed applied issues, plausible scenarios, and the codification of best practices. There is already a wealth of available results that could make a difference. However, such results have had limited impact because research concerning IQ has failed to combine and cross-fertilize theory and practice. Furthermore, insufficient work has been done to promote the value-adding synthesis of academic findings and technological know-how. The proliferation of taxonomies (Batini and Scannapieco (2006) offer an excellent introduction) highlights one of the main epistemological difficulties in dealing with IQ, the one with which I shall be concerned in the rest of this chapter.

5. The Epistemological Problem with Information Quality

There is a lot of convergence in the literature on understanding IQ by starting from an analysis of the *fit-for-purpose value* of the data in question:

There is no doubt that a database can be of *high quality* for a given application, while being of *low quality* for a different one. Hence the common definition of data quality as 'fitness for use'. However, such consideration often leads to the wrong assumption that it is not possible to have an objective assessment of quality of data. We claim that for most data quality dimensions (including accuracy, completeness and consistency at least) it makes sense to have objective measures on the basis of which the perceived quality can be evaluated in relation to a given user application requirements.   (Batini and Scannapieco 2006, p. 221)

Once IQ is analysed teleologically, in terms of 'fit for purpose', IQ properties, known in the literature as *dimensions*—such as accessibility, accuracy, availability, completeness, currency, integrity, redundancy, reliability, timeliness, trustworthiness, usability, and so forth—are clustered in IQ groups, known as *categories*, such as intrinsic, extrinsic, contextual, representational, and so forth (Figure 15 provides an illustration).

All this is well known and does not need to be discussed in this chapter. However, since there are many ways of identifying and specifying dimensions and categories, the

---

[8] http://web.mit.edu/tdqm/www/iqc/past/96/program.shtml.
[9] http://jdiq.acm.org.   [10] https://idqsummit.org.   [11] http://mitiq.mit.edu.

IQ CATEGORIES	IQ DIMENSIONS
Intrinsic IQ	**Accuracy**, Objectivity, Believability
Accessibility IQ	**Access**, Security
Contextual IQ	Relevancy, Value-Added, **Timeliness, Completeness,** Amount of data
Representational IQ	Interpretability, Ease of understanding, Concise representation, **Consistent representation**

Figure 15 Examples of IQ categories and dimensions
Adapted from Wang (1998), in bold, dimensions from Batini and Scannapieco (2006)

result is that the issuing maps do not overlap, and some of them resemble Borges' *Celestial Emporium of Benevolent Knowledge's Taxonomy*:[12]

The list divides all animals into one of 14 categories: (1) Those that belong to the emperor; (2) Embalmed ones; (3) Those that are trained; (4) Suckling pigs; (5) Mermaids (or Sirens); (6) Fabulous ones; (7) Stray dogs; (8) Those that are included in this classification; (9) Those that tremble as if they were mad (10) Innumerable ones; (11) Those drawn with a very fine camel hair brush; (12) Et cetera; (13) Those that have just broken the flower vase; (14) Those that, at a distance, resemble flies.

A further consequence is that the all-important, practical issue of how to operational-ize IQ evaluation processes is disregarded. This is not just a matter of lack of logical rigour and methodological negligence, although they too play a role. The main trouble seems to be caused by three issues:

(1) a failure to identify the potentially multipurpose and boundlessly re-purposa-ble nature of information as the source of significant complications. This is particularly significant when dealing with 'big data'; because of

(2) a disregard for the fact that any quality evaluation can only happen at a given *level of abstraction*.[13] To simplify (see Figure 16): the quality of a system fit for a particular purpose is analysed within a context, at an LoA whose selection is determined by the choice of the *purpose* in the first place. If one wants to evaluate a bayonet for the purpose of holding some paper in place on the desk, then that purpose determines the LoA within that context, which will include, for example, how clean the bayonet is, but not whether it is sharp; leading to

(3) a missed opportunity to address the development of a satisfactory approach to IQ in terms of LoA and purpose-orientation.

Admittedly, all this may be a bit hard to digest, so here are four examples that should clarify the point.

[12] Borges, 'The Analytical Language of John Wilkins', originally published in 1952, English translation in (Borges 1964).
[13] On the method of abstraction and LoA see also Floridi (2008b and 2011c).

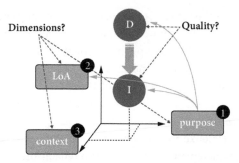

Figure 16 Data become information within a context (Z), at a LoA (Y), chosen for a purpose (X)

Some data are supposed to be re-purposable since their collection. In the UK, the 2011 Census population estimates were examined through a quality assurance (QA) process 'to ensure that users of census data have confidence in the *quality* and *accuracy* of the information' (my italics).[14] The Census Data Quality Assurance Strategy stated that

The proposed strategy reflects a considered balance between data relevance, accuracy, timeliness and coherence. The data accuracy that can be achieved reflects the methods and resources in place to identify and control data error and is therefore constrained by the imperative for timely outputs. 'Timeliness' refers to user requirements and the guiding imperative for the 2011 Census is to provide census population estimates for rebased 2011 mid-year population estimates in June 2012. 'Coherence' refers to the internal integrity of the data, including consistency through the geographic hierarchy, as well as comparability with external (non-census ONS) and other data sources. This includes conformity to standard concepts, classifications and statistical classifications. The 2011 Data Quality Assurance Strategy will consider and use the best available administrative data sources for validation purposes, as well as census time series data and other ONS sources. A review of these sources will identify their relative strengths and weaknesses. The relevance of 2011 Census data refers to the extent to which they meet user expectations. A key objective of the Data Quality Assurance Strategy is to anticipate and meet user expectations and to be able to justify, empirically, 2011 Census outcomes. To deliver coherent data at acceptable levels of accuracy that meet user requirements and are on time, will demand QA input that is carefully planned and targeted.   (Census 2011, pp. 8–9)

Apart from a questionable distinction between information *quality* and *accuracy* (as if accuracy were something else from IQ), overall the position expressed in the document (and in the citation above) is largely reasonable. However, I specify 'largely' because the statement about the 'key objective' of anticipating and meeting user expectations remains quite problematic. It shows a lack of appreciation for the complexity of the 'fit-for-purpose' requirement. The objective is problematic because it is unrealistic: such expectations are unpredictable, that is, the purpose for which the

[14] http://www.ons.gov.uk/ons/guide-method/census/2011/how-our-census-works/how-we-took-the-2011-census/how-we-processed-the-information/data-quality-assurance/index.html.

information collected in the census is supposed to be fit may change quite radically, thus affecting the fitness itself. To understand why, consider a second example.

Some data are not supposed to be re-purposed, but they are, and for evil goals, which were not anticipated. This is our second example. There is a puzzling fact about the Holocaust in the Netherlands: 74 per cent of the 'full' Jews (according to the Nazi definition) living in the Netherlands died. In relative terms, this was the highest death toll in any West European Jewish community, including Germany itself. One of the plausible explanations (Luebke and Milton 1994) is that the Netherlands had an excellent census, which provided plenty of accurate and reliable information about people's religious beliefs and home addresses.

Some data are re-purposed more or less successfully, to pursue goals that could not have been envisaged when the data were first produced. This is our third example. In the UK, postcodes for domestic properties refer to up to 100 properties in contiguous proximity. Their original purpose was to aid the automated sorting of the mail. That was what the postcode information was fit for (Raper et al. 1992). Today, they are used to calculate insurance premiums, designate destinations in route planning software, and allocate different levels of public services, depending on one's location (postcode) in crucial areas such as health and social services and education (the so-called postcode lottery). In short, the information provided by postcodes has been radically re-purposed, and keeps being re-purposed, leading to a possible decline in fitness. For instance, the IQ of postcodes is very high when it comes to delivering mail, but rather poorer if route planning is in question, as many drivers have experienced who expect, mistakenly, a one-to-one relation between postcodes and addresses.

Finally, some data are re-purposed despite the fact that we know that the new usage is utterly improper and could be risky. This is our last example. Originally, and still officially, Social Security Numbers (SSNs) in the USA were intended for only one purpose: tracking a worker's lifetime earnings in order to calculate retirement benefits. So much so that, between 1946 and 1972, SSNs carried the following disclaimer: 'For social security purposes not for identification'. However, SSNs are the closest thing to a national ID number in the USA, and this is the way they are regularly used today, despite being very 'unfit' for such a purpose, especially in terms of safety (United States Federal Trade Commission 2010).

6. A Bi-categorical Approach to Information Quality

The previous examples in section 5 illustrate the fact that one of the fundamental problems with IQ is the tension between, on the one hand, *purpose-depth* and, on the other hand, *purpose-scope*. Ideally, high-quality information is information that is fit for both: it is optimally fit for the specific purpose/s for which it is elaborated (purpose-depth), and is also easily re-usable for new purpose/s (purpose-scope). However, as in the case of a tool, sometimes the better some information fits its original purpose, the less likely it seems to be re-purposable, and *vice versa*. The problem is that not only may these two requirements be more or less compatible, but that we often forget this (that is, that they may be), and speak of purpose-fitness as if it were a single feature, synonymous with information quality, to be analysed according to a variety of taxonomies. Recall the statement from the Census Data Quality Assurance Strategy. This is a mistake. Can it be avoided? A detailed answer would require more space than is available here, so let me offer an outline of a promising strategy in terms of a bi-categorical approach, which could be implemented through some user-friendly interfaces.

The idea is simple. First, one must distinguish between the purpose/s for which some information is originally *produced* (P–purpose) and the (potentially unlimited) purpose/s for which the same information may be *consumed* (C–purpose). These two categories resemble what in the literature on IQ are known as the 'intrinsic' vs. 'extrinsic' categories. In our previous example, one would distinguish between postcodes as information fit for the purpose of mail delivery—the P–purpose—and postcodes as information fit for other uses, say driving navigation—the C–purpose. This bi-categorical approach could be introduced in terms of a simple Cartesian space, represented by P–purpose = x and C–purpose = y, in such a way that, for any information I, I must have two values in order to be placed in that space. This in turn allows one to analyse a variety of dimensions, such as accuracy, objectivity, accessibility, etc. in a purpose-oriented way (see Figure 17 for an illustration).

Second, one could then compare the quality of some information with respect to purpose P and with respect to purpose C, thus identifying potential discrepancies. The approach lends itself to simple visualizations in terms of radar charts (see Figure 18 for an illustration based on the data provided in Figure 17).

The result would be that one would link IQ to a specific purpose, instead of talking of IQ as fit-for-purpose in absolute terms.

		IQ CATEGORIES	
		Mail delivery	Navigation
IQ DIMENSIONS	Accuracy	1	0.8
	Objectivity	1	1
	Accessibility	0.9	0.9
	Security	1	1
	Relevancy	1	0.9
	Timeliness	1	1
	Interpretability	0.8	0.7
	Understandability	1	0.9

Figure 17 Example of bi-categorical IQ analysis

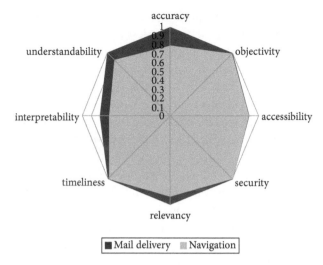

Figure 18 Graph of a bi-categorical IQ analysis

Conclusion: Back to Fit-for-Purpose

There are many senses in which we speak of information quality being a matter of 'fit-for-purpose'. A pre-Copernican, astronomical book would be of very bad IQ, if its purpose were to instruct us on the nature of our galaxy, but it may be of very high IQ if its purpose is to offer evidence about the historical development of Ptolemaic astronomy. We saw that this is not relativism but relationalism; it is a matter of explicit choice of the purpose against which the value of some information is to be examined. Once this methodological step is carefully taken, then the bi-categorical approach I have presented in this chapter is compatible with, and can be supported by, quantitative metrics, which can (let users) associate values to dimensions depending on the categories in question, by relying on solutions previously identified: metadata, tagging, crowd sourcing, peer-review, expert interventions, reputation networks, automatic refinement, and so forth. The main advantage of a bi-categorical approach is that it clarifies that the values need not be the same for different purposes. It should be rather easy to design interfaces that enable and facilitate such interactive selection of purposes for which IQ is evaluated. After all, we know that we have plenty of information systems that are syntactically smart, and users who are semantically intelligent, and a bi-categorical approach may be a good way to make them work together successfully. What the approach does not really touch upon is whether we might be systematically wrong. In other words, it fails to address the sceptical challenge, which is the topic of Chapter 6.

6

Informational Scepticism and the Logically Possible

Summary

Previously, in Chapters 2 and 3, I argued that philosophical constructionism can be both anti-relativistic and non naturalistic in its approach to knowledge, understood as accounted information. In Chapter 4, we saw how perception and testimony provide the data that are repurposed by human agents for the construction of their semantic artefacts. And in Chapter 5, I discussed how the quality of the issuing information may be evaluated in terms of a bi-categorical analysis based on the purpose/s for which some information is originally *produced* and the (potentially unlimited) purpose/s for which the same information may be *consumed*. In all the previous chapters, I have momentarily assumed that the information we are dealing with is immune from sceptical challenges. In short, I have suggested we suspend judgement about the most basic quality of information, its truthfulness. However, the question remains: how do we know that the world really is as our informational constructs tell us it is? This is the classic sceptical challenge. In this chapter, I deal with it by articulating and defending a twofold answer: either informational scepticism is radical, but then it is epistemologically innocuous because redundant; or it is moderate, but then epistemologically beneficial because useful.

In order to pursue this co-optation strategy, after the introduction, the chapter is articulated into two parts. The first is more historical. In it, I reconstruct the 'renaissance of epistemology' between the two world wars in light of the debate about radical scepticism. I first distinguish between the question and the meta-question asked by the sceptic about knowledge and epistemology. I then quickly outline the non-naturalist, German tradition; the naturalist, British tradition; and finally the American, pragmatist tradition. After this historical excursus, the second part is entirely theoretical. In it, I seek to solve the problem of radical scepticism. First, I set up the problem. Second, I introduce Borel numbers as a convenient way to refer uniformly to (the data that individuate) different possible worlds. Third, I adopt the Hamming distance between Borel numbers as a metric to calculate the distance between possible worlds. Then, I analyse radical and moderate informational scepticism using Borel numbers and Hamming distances, and show that they are either harmless (extreme form) or actually fruitful (moderate form). There are some potential objections which I deal with in a separate section. In the conclusion, I briefly discuss the Peircean nature of the overall approach.

1. Introduction: History and Analysis of Scepticism

The renaissance of epistemology between the two world wars forms a bridge between early modern and contemporary epistemology. At the turn of the century, there had been a resurgence of interest in epistemology through an anti-metaphysical and naturalist reaction against the nineteenth-century developments of Neo-Kantian and Neo-Hegelian idealism. Within German-speaking philosophy, this reaction had its roots in Helmholtz's scientific reinterpretation of Kant, in Brentano's phenomenology, and in Mach's neutral monism. In France, it was prepared by the Positivist movement. In British philosophy, it acquired the specific nature of a rebuttal of Hegelianism by the Critical Realism movement in Oxford, and by G. E. Moore and Bertrand Russell in Cambridge. And in America, the new pragmatist epistemology of William James, C. S. Peirce, John Dewey, and C. I. Lewis took the form of a direct confrontation with Kant and Hegel. However, it would be incorrect to regard the interwar renaissance as just a continuation of the emancipation from idealism. It was also prompted by major advances in mathematics, logic, and physics, which engendered new methodological concerns (see for example the influential tradition of French philosophers of science: Duhem, Poincaré, Bachelard) and led to the critical re-examination of central topics in epistemology. Among the traits that became prominent, one may list an interest in mathematical, natural, and social sciences; criticism of the possibility of synthetic a priori truth; a reliance on logical and semantic investigations, which transformed epistemology from a theory of ideas and judgement into a theory of propositional attitudes, sentences, and meanings; a realist and naturalist orientation that tended to accommodate, when not to privilege, commonsensical, and empiricist demands; a reconsideration of the role of philosophy as a critical exercise of analysis, rather than as an autonomous and superior form of knowledge; and, finally, a disregard for the philosophy of history and the temporal dialectic of conceptual developments. Of course, these perspectives never formed a unified programme of research. Philosophers between the wars took very different views when developing their epistemological investigations, whose specific trajectories lacked a uniform character. The full reconstruction and analysis of these is not the task of this chapter. Its more limited aim is to outline the common origins, across the philosophical traditions, of a central theme in contemporary epistemology: the debate on the sceptical problem and the foundation of knowledge. This will prepare the ground for the second half of the chapter.

Sceptics have never enjoyed a good press. Indeed, only sophists seem to have been bashed by philosophers more regularly and systematically. How unfair. Sceptical challenges provide the starting points of many philosophical investigations; young epistemologists sharpen their dialectical teeth on sceptical debates; more than one academic career has been made out of alleged refutations of some sceptical position;

and teaching philosophy without dealing with sceptical doubts would be like cooking without spices.

There are intuitive reasons why no brand of scepticism appears to be welcome. Some are more historical. I shall briefly return to them in the conclusion. Here, suffice to recall that, insofar as scepticism seeks to undermine all certainties—what Sextus Empiricus referred to as *dogma*[1]—it is a disruptive force, which is at loggerheads with intellectual conservatism and intolerant religious doctrines.[2] Crusaders and fundamentalists of all sorts inevitably loathe serious doubters.

Some other reasons are more theoretical. They usually concern the *degrees*[3] *of certainty* to which our Alice, the epistemic agent *a* (whether an individual or a group of agents, i.e., a multi-agent system, it does not matter, so I shall not differentiate between the two cases in the rest of this chapter), may be justifiably entitled, when assessing *her knowledge of the external world*.[4] Thus, most of the anti-sceptical literature, at least from Augustine onwards, has focused on the possibility of showing that Alice can indeed reach irrefutable certainties, and then on arguing, from Descartes onwards, that Alice can successfully exploit at least some of these certainties in order to discriminate between bad beliefs that must be discarded (Descartes' 'rotten apples', see Descartes 1984, 7:481), and good beliefs (the 'good apples') that may constitute knowledge, given the right circumstances and proper further qualifications. This is the classic perspective from which I shall approach the sceptical challenge concerning the truthfulness of our data-based information about the world. There are, however, three points where my contribution will depart from other, more orthodox lines of reasoning.

First, as the reader may expect, I shall focus on information, rather than on beliefs or knowledge. Second, I will be concerned with informativeness, rather than with certainty. And finally, I will seek to co-opt moderate scepticism as a valuable ally in the search for high-quality information about the world, rather than refute all kinds of scepticism as a disease, or endorse it wholeheartedly and unreservedly as a panacea. Each point deserves a brief clarification.

Information—in the factual, semantic sense of well-formed, meaningful, and truthful data about some topic, adopted in this book[5]—is a weaker concept than knowledge. This is so not least because information does not require what is a necessary feature of

[1] In the Greek tradition, dogma are fixed and untouchable beliefs and philosophical dogmatism is any non-Pyrrhonian philosophy advancing positive theories.

[2] True, some uses of scepticism have sometimes represented a background condition for a fideistic defence of religious faith; see Floridi (2002b) and Popkin (2003). But these are exceptions, which bear only a negative relation to the epistemological problems originally raised by scepticism. They stressed the weakness of human knowledge only in order to redirect the interest of the audience towards Christian faith, and hence to foster behaviour consistent with it. The emphasis was not on the nature of knowledge, but on the ethical attitude to be taken with respect to revelation and Christ's teachings.

[3] The qualification is introduced here in order to take into account epistemologically fuzzy statements such as 'I am almost certain (sure) that *p*' or 'I am pretty certain (sure) that *p*', or 'I am not completely certain (sure) that *p*'. The reader who objects to the possibility of degrees of certainty may replace them with only two binary values without any consequence for the rest of the chapter.

[4] I have discussed mathematical scepticism elsewhere; see Floridi (1998b, 2000, and 2004c).

[5] See Floridi (2011c) for a full analysis.

knowledge, namely a sufficient dose of the relevant kind of rational support, be this, for example, a satisfactory degree of justification, warranty, explanation, or account. An agent *a* might be informed that *i*—for example, Alice might hold the information that a playing card is indeed the King of Spades—without yet *knowing* that *i* because *a* lacks any further support in favour of *i*. It is well known that you are still informed that *i*—to the extent that you can successfully use *i*, convey *i*, sell *i*, etc.—even if you merely guessed correctly that *i* and cannot explain or justify why *i* for the life of you. Information is not subject to the problems notoriously caused by epistemic luck.

Regarding the second point, it is useful to focus on the more impoverished concept of information, rather than on the richer one of knowledge, because this clarifies that the sceptical challenge concerns the empirical truth, and hence the informativeness of *i*, not the kinds or degrees of support that *a* might enjoy in holding that *i* (this soon turns into some version of the Gettier problem), or the information network that may account for *i*. Let me explain. Information goes hand in hand with unpredictability. More precisely, the Inverse Relationship Principle (IRP), as Barwise labelled it, states that there is an inverse relation between the probability of *i* and how much semantic information is carried by *i*. Nowadays, one often translates IRP modally, by stating that the semantic information conveyed by *i* is equivalent to the set of all possible worlds— or, more cautiously, to the set of all the descriptions of the relevant possible states of the actual world—that are excluded by, or are inconsistent with, *i*. So, if *a* holds some content (i.e. some well-formed and meaningful data) *c* about some topic *t*, the informativeness of *c* is inversely related to the number of possible worlds in which *c* is true. If *c* is true in all possible worlds (necessary truth) then it follows from IRP that *c* is not informative.[6] If *c* is true in no possible world (necessary falsehood) then I have argued (Floridi 2004e) that, in this case too, *c* is not informative. In either case, the sceptical challenge regarding our information about the external world does not apply. The scope of IRP is limited to only possibly true content: if *c* is true only in some possible worlds, then establishing in which ones makes *c* either informative or disin- formative. It follows that the sceptical challenge is about whether one can treat some content that seems to be information as actually being information. Is *c* = *i*? The ques- tion is rephrased by the sceptic in the following way: how can you establish whether *c* is informative or disinformative with respect to *t* in a possible world *W*? That is, how can you establish whether *c* tells you something true or false about *t* in *W*? We shall see that the sceptic suggests that you cannot—mind, *not* that it is not—and hence that you should withhold your commitment regarding the informativeness of *c*. Assuming that *c* = *i* means assuming not only that ordinary epistemic problems regarding the *c* in question are not occurring, or have been solved (mistakes happen, but can be cor- rected), but also that the more radical, sceptical challenge about the truthfulness of *c* has been met. This bracketing of the sceptical problem is fine (Husserl was right about

---

[6] See Bar-Hillel and Carnap (1953, reprinted in Bar-Hillel 1964). Note that this is the source of Hintikka's scandal of deduction; see D'Agostino and Floridi (2009).

this), as long as our philosophical concerns are of a different nature—for example, if we wish to clarify what it means for some semantic information to be *relevant*—but it would be a silly way of begging the question in this context.

Finally, there are different strategies to deal with informational scepticism. In what follows, I shall argue that either the sceptical challenge is radical, but then it is epistemologically innocuous, because informationally redundant; or it is moderate, but then epistemologically beneficial, because informationally useful. The conclusion is that, either way, there is no epistemologically harmful scepticism.

In order to pursue this co-optation strategy, I will need to make much more precise and clearer what informational scepticism consists in. This task will require the use of two sharper tools, as previously mentioned in the introduction. For we will need to be able to refer uniformly to (the data that individuate) different possible worlds, and to adopt a metric that enables us to compare, with some precision, the distances between such possible worlds, or better, their data. Once so equipped, it will be easy to analyse the two forms of scepticism, and then show how the radical one can be tolerated, while the moderate one should be promoted. To repeat, the fundamental thesis is simple: scepticism is either a harmless exercise to be enjoyed intellectually, but not to be taken at face value epistemologically, or it is actually an essential component of any decent epistemic work, in academia as well as in real life. Before the conclusion, I shall consider some objections to the general strategy developed in this chapter, in order to dispel a few potential misunderstandings, for the confused critic, and reinforce the cogency of the approach, for the unconvinced reader. Finally, the overall approach to scepticism pursued in this chapter is clearly much more Peircean than Cartesian (Floridi 1998a), so it will be useful to say just a few words about this methodological aspect in the conclusion. Let us now start by looking at the modern history of the sceptical challenge.

2. The Two Faces of Scepticism

Two questions set the limits to sceptical debates:

(K)   Is knowledge possible?
(KK)   Is epistemology possible?
(i.e. is an epistemology that answers (K) possible?)

Interestingly, both questions presuppose the initial plausibility of some form of non-naturalism (see Chapters 2 and 3), that is, some cognitive discrepancy between knowledge and its reference. (K) proceeds bottom-up and (KK) top-down in dealing with issues concerning the legitimacy of epistemic claims. At the beginning of our period, Edmund Husserl and the neo-Thomistic philosopher Desiré Mercier clarified further the normative character of these issues.

According to Husserl (1907, see now Husserl 1950), the justificatory ground of a theory of knowledge cannot be provided by other instances of knowledge. Following a Cartesian strategy, we can analyse potential instances of knowledge by affixing to them an 'index of questionability'. The sceptic questions the possibility of ever removing the index permanently, and Husserl argued that any solution of the sceptical challenge in terms of reference to some extension of knowledge would be fallacious. The infringement of Husserl's principle can be considered of a piece with the 'naturalistic fallacy' in ethics we encountered in Chapter 2: (K) is not a question of natural science; by positing it, one asks *normatively* whether what is considered to be knowledge (information, in our case) *justifiably deserves* to be so described.

One difficulty with Husserl (and Carnap as well) is that he seems to think that the task of philosophy is to step out of the epistemic game and provide some kind of hierarchical reconstruction of knowledge at large. He fails to see that Kant had a very different question in mind, namely Hume's and the reconciliation of metaphysical failures. What Husserl (and Carnap) tried to do cognitive science does better, insofar as it is doable at all. Philosophical taxonomy is useless. And the Leibnizian project is at best distracting. Knowledge does not require a unified reconstruction or a foundation, it requires a semanticization.

Husserl formulated his principle by reacting against his previous psychologism. This explains why it can easily be extended to a *non-naturalist* dilemma: if a naturalized epistemology differentiates itself from a philosophical theory of knowledge by being empirically testable, predictive, etc., it raises the question of its own justification; but if, alternatively, it claims to be able to solve this foundational problem as well, it must provide a solution which cannot be in itself an instance of empirical knowledge, and with respect to which it must abandon any aspiration to gain the status of empirical science. The acceptance of this non-naturalist stand was one of the reasons why Husserl argued for a purely conceptual approach to epistemology. Thus he held that the only correct way of dealing with (K) is by means of principled and convincing arguments, that is, by 'placing it in the logical space of reasons of justifying and being able to justify what one says' as Sellars was later to say (Sellars 1963b, p. 169).

One may never be in a position to establish how to answer (K) if no satisfactory reply to (KK) can be provided. Arguing for a negative answer to (KK) means questioning the possibility of an epistemology itself and constitutes *the problem of the criterion* (Sextus Empiricus, *Outlines of Pyrrhonism*, II. 2 (Empiricus 2000)). Mercier re-launched the latter as 'le cheval du bataille du scepticisme' (Mercier 1923) and it has become a crucial difficulty for contemporary epistemology, deeply influencing Roderick Chisholm (1966, 1989). To know whether things really are as they seem to be, one needs a criterion for distinguishing between true and false appearances. But to know whether the criterion is reliable, one needs to know whether it really succeeds in distinguishing between true and false appearances. And one cannot know this unless one already knows which appearances are true and which are false. It seems that an epistemology cannot establish what, if anything, deserves to be called knowledge.

3. Non-naturalism and the Foundational Problem in German-speaking Philosophy

Owing to his limited concern with scepticism, Kant had not dwelled on (KK). The transcendental method assumed the existence of science as its starting point, but what type of knowledge was to be found in the *Critique* itself? Was that type of knowledge in need of justification? How could it be justified without incurring a vicious circle? In 1807, the Kantian philosopher Jakob Friedrich Fries published his *Neue Kritik der Vernunft* (Fries 1807). One of its aims was to provide what Popper later described as a 'psychologistic solution' to the foundational problem.

Fries summarized the (KK) problem in terms of a trilemma: the premises of an epistemology can either be dogmatically assumed, or be justified by an endless chain of statements, or be anchored to a psychological basis which is justificatory but not in need of a justification. Fries' trilemma influenced the subsequent German tradition thanks to a 'Fries-Renaissance' that occurred during the 1910s and the 1920s, and in particular to the work of Leonard Nelson (Nelson 1970; Haller 1974, 1979). Following Fries' analysis, Nelson came to object to the entire project of an epistemology in the Cartesian, anti-sceptical, and justificatory sense, and to favour a more descriptive and psychologistic approach (Nelson 1908, 1965). However, despite his criticism of foundational debates, Nelson's 'naturalised epistemology' contributed greatly to reawakening philosophers' interest in the foundational issue in the late 1920s and early 1930s. Two philosophers were especially influenced by his work: Moritz Schlick and Karl Popper.

Schlick endorsed the Cartesian requirement that there be an absolutely certain foundation of knowledge. He argued that it was

...self-evident that the problem of the foundation of all knowledge is nothing else but the question of the criterion of truth   (Schlick 1979, vol. II, p. 374)

and supported a correspondence theory of truth, defined as the univocal designation of reality. However, in his view

anyone who holds that the Cartesian thesis [i.e. the direct perception of a fact of consciousness] constitutes knowledge will inevitably be drawn into a similar circle [i.e. Fries' trilemma].
(Schlick 1974, p. 86)

So, Schlick came to defend an empiricist and externalist foundationalism, according to which there are objective facts, external to the knower's doxastic states, both accessible by the knower and capable of justifying the knower's beliefs in a way that is sufficient for knowledge. According to Schlick, *protocol propositions*, that is, basic observation statements

in absolute simplicity, without any forming, change or addition, set forth the facts, whose elaboration constitutes the substance of all science.
(Schlick 1979, vol. II, p. 370, see also pp. 400–13)

But, although they are logically prior to other factual propositions, their predictive and verifiable nature leads to the acknowledgement of a prior layer of indubitable, empirically contentful 'affirmations' (*Konstatierungen*). Schlick, who had been a straightforward conventionalist, maintained in the 1930s that these affirmations, for example 'there is red here now', are expressions of immediate, simple, existential experiences of individual states of affairs, which provide a genuine acquaintance with reality, although they are wholly subjective, fleeting, and ineffable. The 'affirmations' of them are indubitable because, although empirically contentful, to understand their meaning is to understand their truth; hence they constitute the basic form of evidence from which protocol propositions obtain their evidential contents, and against which the latter are constantly tested. Schlick argued that these 'affirmations' are the founda-tion of science not in a Cartesian, static, and inclusive sense, but in the sense that they form the constantly renewed ground necessary and sufficient for its open-ended development.

Schlick's foundationalism requires a verificationist semantics, an ostensive theory of meaning of elementary propositions, the distinction between analytic and synthetic statements, the defence of the observational-theoretical distinction (already criticized by Carnap), and a conception of ineffable experience of the world that is immediately 'given' to the subject. As a result, his position appeared to critics, such as Otto Neurath and Carl Hempel, similar to a philosophy of intuition; they argued that it was beset with solipsistic difficulties and contained unacceptable metaphysical theses. A lively debate over the nature of the protocol propositions soon ensued (*Erkenntnis* 1932; *Analysis* 1935).

Neurath's view was that only a nominalist and constructivist interpretation of the nature of protocol propositions—as actual statements, expressed in a physicalistic lan-guage, recording empirical observations—is in fact acceptable as metaphysically safe. Scientific theories could be grounded, empirically, on these basic protocol sentences, but no position 'external' to language is achievable. Sentences could be compared only with other sentences. Direct reference to external reality or internal experience is to be avoided as empty metaphysics. Since protocol sentences are intrinsically fallible and hence always corrigible in principle, any Cartesian demand for absolute certainty is unrealistic and misleading. For Neurath, the epistemic justification of science was not to be achieved by means of an appeal to external facts or alleged intuitions, but internally, through logical coherence (which did not necessarily exclude some ordering relations), instrumental economy, pragmatic considerations of social and scientific ends, a rational use of conventions by the scientific community, and a constantly open and public debate. Following Duhem, Neurath argued that, given an apparently successful theory, rival explanations can be made to fit the same evidence that supports it, and that in replacing or revising a theory, hypotheses and observation statements come under scrutiny as whole networks, not individually. Practical expedience rather than absolute truth was determinant. Neurath summarized his position in a famous analogy:

We are like sailors who have to rebuild their ship [the system of knowledge] on the open sea, without ever being able to dismantle it in dry-dock and reconstruct it from its best components.   (Neurath 1983, p. 92)

Hegel had stressed a similar point:

...the examination of knowledge can only be carried out by an act of knowledge. To examine this so-called instrument is the same thing as to know it. But to seek to know before we know [i.e. Kant's critical project] is as absurd as the wise resolution of Scholasticus, not to venture into the water until he had learned to swim.   (Hegel 1830, Eng. Tr. in Hegel 1975, p. 14)

This was not the only similarity between Neurath's and Hegel's coherentism. A direct consequence of the former's holistic and non-subjectivist 'pan-internalism' was a strong tendency towards a unified and synoptic approach to the entire domain of human knowledge. This 'epistemological totalitarianism' was a feature shared by other approaches to the foundational problem, such as Hilbert's and Cassirer's, which were similarly suspicious of the Cartesian, subjective, turn, and favourable to Kantian constructionism rather than pure coherentism. In Neurath, this tendency was reflected in his project for an *International Encyclopedia of Unified Science* (1938–70). The programme of the *Encyclopedia* was presented as an explicit development of the ideas of the French Enlightenment, of Diderot's famous *Encyclopédie*. But the latter had a Cartesian basis, so the comparison should rather be with Hegel's *Encyclopaedia of the Philosophical Sciences*, although Neurath's project had a methodological justification in place of Hegel's ontological one.

Schlick was firmly hostile to Neurath's coherentism. If epistemic statements are not based on a specific set of more basic protocol propositions ultimately rooted in sense-experience of the world, all propositions may be regarded as in principle corrigible and their truth can only consist in their mutual agreement within the system of knowledge. Schick argued that such coherence provides too little—truth can be equated to logical consistency only in a formal system but not in an empirical science, since a coherent tale may otherwise become as acceptable as a scientific fact. Moreover, the absence of coherence leaves it utterly unclear what propositions may need to be revised, eliminated, or adjusted, and how. But despite Schlick's criticisms, Neurath's coherentism found an ally in the pragmatist movement, which was equally anti-Cartesian. Quine's fallibilist and holistic, naturalized epistemology can be interpreted as its latest development (Quine 1969, 1992a).

The other philosopher deeply influenced by the 'Fries Renaissance' was Popper (1930–33; see Popper 1979, 2002, 2012). His discussion of the problem of the nature of basic statements in scientific theory and his dynamic solution—we can simply leave the presuppositions of a specific science open to the possibility of further testing—became the source of some later important works on the foundational problem (Apel 1975; Albert 1978, 1985; Lakatos 1978). It was also the origin of a significant modification in the interpretation of (KK), now understood no longer as a meta-epistemological problem, but as a problem concerning the foundation of scientific knowledge.

4. Coherentism, Naturalism, and the Refutation of Scepticism in British Philosophy

Coherentism in epistemology is a natural ally of anti-realism in ontology, and both find a fertile environment in Idealistic philosophies, whose claims about the contradictory nature of the apparent reality, in defence of a monistic supra-naturalism, may easily incorporate the sceptic's dualist anti-naturalism (Hegel 1985). Neurath had charged Schlick with metaphysical inclinations but found himself sharing a coherentist epistemology not entirely different from that of some Idealists.

During the post-World War I period, the most interesting and influential idealist epistemology remained that of F. H. Bradley (1914, 1922, 1930). Bradley held that the Absolute remains unknowable because knowledge is necessarily discursive and relational, and hence always inadequate with respect to the continuously unified nature of reality. Ideally, reality, its true description, and its complete knowledge are identical. In practice, knowledge remains fragmentary and truth can only be more or less adequate. Knowledge, including science, is like the biography of a person: no matter how accurately written, it is still only partly true and conspicuously unsatisfactory when compared to actual life. Justification, understood as the process through which possible instances of partial knowledge may or may not be included in the epistemic system, is interpreted in terms of coherence. There is only one, ultimate, complete, accurate description of reality and every limited truth, insofar as it is true, concurs with every other limited truth in realizing it.

The kind of holistic coherence involved here—which Bradley and his friend Bernard Bosanquet (1911) seemed to have in mind, and that was further refined by J. J. Joachim (1939) and Brand Blanshard (1939)—is richer than Neurath's mere logical consistency. It can be compared to the web of internal, reciprocal relations linking a set of words in a complex crossword, a set of pieces in a puzzle, or a string of numbers in a Sudoku: each truth is meant to interlock, meaningfully and uniquely, with the other components to constitute the whole, final system. It was justified by ontological considerations. And some of the problems affecting later coherentist epistemologies, such as Neurath's, can be interpreted as stemming from the lack of a similar metaphysical commitment.

The reaction against idealism amongst British philosophers had been motivated in part by scepticism concerning these metaphysical commitments (e.g. internal relations and organic wholes). Amongst these realist critics, G. E. Moore's positive approach to epistemology was distinctive and influential. Against the sceptical position, Moore held that there are many commonsensical beliefs that everyone is naturally inclined to hold and that are endorsed upon reflection by all. These beliefs have the highest (a) presumptive and (b) pervasive credibility. (a) means that it is virtually impossible to doubt them or dissent about them. We are perfectly entitled to start by accepting them as being *prima facie* epistemically justified, leaving to the sceptic the hard task of showing that, on the whole, there are better reasons to believe that not *p* rather than *p*. (b) means that the sceptic's claims are incoherent. The denial of *p*'s credibility presupposes *p* itself or a system of credible *p*s.

Moore based his defence of common sense on (a) and (b) (Moore 1925, 1939, both now in Moore 1993b). Re-evaluating Reid's philosophy, he concluded that there is an objective and mind-independent, physical reality, which we can come to know through our sense data. However, how our immediate awareness of these sense data is related to our knowledge of the world remained a constant problem for Moore and led to Ducasse's adverbial realism: sensations are ways of perceiving an object, not entities, so in looking at a tomato we are not directly aware of red sense data but 'we are being appeared to redly by an object' (Ducasse 1942).

Moore's antisceptical strategy rested on an inadequate, if influential, assessment of scepticism. Ancient sceptics themselves had already disposed of (b) (Sextus Empiricus, 2000, *Outlines of Pyrrhonism* II, 144–203). Scepticism is not a doctrine but a process of immanent criticism that gradually rots away Neurath's ship from within. As for (a), it could not be employed against the sceptic without presupposing an anti-sceptical answer to (K) and hence begging the question. Moore's reliance on common sense suggests an appeal to naturalized epistemology to provide an answer to (K). But since (K) involves a *de jure* epistemological problem, this would have meant committing in epistemology that naturalistic fallacy which Moore himself had helped to clarify in ethics. Moore's anti-Cartesian naturalism could thus be defended more convincingly by conceding something to the sceptic, as Gassendi and Hume had done before, and Wittgenstein, in effect, did later (Wittgenstein 1975).

The problem of our 'knowledge of the external world' was also a central theme in Russell (1910, 1912, 1914, 1917, 1948). In response to this traditional problem, he developed the famous distinction between 'knowledge by acquaintance and knowledge by description' and his theory of sense data. Russell agreed that sense data are not logically indubitable, but he argued that, since they are simply given in sensations, they enjoy a self-evident, 'primitive certainty' and that this phenomenalist realism provides a far better explanation of our experience of the world than scepticism or Idealism. The problem is how we move from sense data such as colour, shape, texture, etc. to our complex experience of mind-independent, enduring physical objects, say a table. Russell held different theories and corresponding terminological distinctions through the years. For some time, he maintained that the solution laid in a conception of continuants as non-private, logical constructions out of sense data, but he later rejected this constructionism in favour of an inferential interpretation of structural properties of continuants from empirical experience of events. Russell's epistemology represents a revival of Cartesian methodology, although his foundationalism was originally based on degrees of complexity and asymmetric relations of informative support between epistemic propositions, not on degrees of certainty, and later developed into a form of naturalized epistemology.

What are the necessary and sufficient conditions according to which Alice can be said to know that *p*? Russell (1912) had revived this classic question by raising what is now known as a Gettier problem (Gettier 1963): given some unfortunate circumstances, Alice may be fully justified in believing that *p*, *p* may be true, and yet Alice may still not really know that *p* because she has in fact merely hit on the truth by chance. F. P. Ramsey (1929, see now Ramsey 1990), directly influenced by Russell, propounded a solution that anticipates later accounts of knowledge. Attempting to couple the truth of *p* with its justification, he claimed that

a belief [is] knowledge if it is (i) true, (ii) certain, (iii) obtained by a reliable process... [that is, one that] must be caused by what are not beliefs in a way or with accompaniments that can be more or less relied on to give true beliefs. (Ramsey 1990, p. 110)

5. Pragmatist Epistemologies in American Philosophy

The philosophers who best represent the epistemological renaissance during the interwar period in the United States are John Dewey and C. I. Lewis.

In Dewey, the influence of Darwinism, psychology, and Hegel's dialectics is reflected in an anti-Cartesian, naturalistic epistemology (Dewey 1925, 1929, 1938). He contended that epistemology is beset by four main errors:

1. foundationalism;
2. the primacy of knowledge (access to reality is only epistemic);
3. the artificial distinction between the known reality, the knowing process, and knowledge as its outcome;
4. the spectator theory of knowledge (the object of knowledge is some detached reality, passively contemplated by an external and uninvolved spectator).

Consequently, he attempted to rectify these errors by arguing that:

1. knowledge is a non-hierarchical and relational phenomenon that emerges from natural and fallible interactions between two dependent *relata*, mind and nature ('contextualism');
2. non-reflective and non-cognitive experiences provide direct access to the world;
3. the epistemic continuum includes both the process of inquiry, as a series of self-corrective, organizing acts, and knowledge, defined as the attainment of 'warranted assertibility' and interpreted as its appropriate completion;
4. the object of knowledge is the observable outcome of experimental procedures. The elaboration of knowledge is the semiotic means—the process of inferential signification—through which we can facilitate the experimental determination of future consequences, by bridging the gap between the known and the unknown. Cognition is an always-contextualized way of dealing with a problem situation ('epistemological immanentism').

Rather than speaking of some static, alethic correspondence with reality, satisfactory theories or concepts are those that turn out to be usefully reliable in all the practical and theoretical endeavours for which they are developed.

Dewey's critique of Cartesian epistemology has been more influential (as in the work of Quine, Putnam, and Rorty) than his instrumentalism has been. Russell and Reichenbach, for example, immediately objected that the latter failed to account for mathematical sciences.

C. I. Lewis stands in a similar relation to Kant as Dewey does to Hegel. Following Kant, he analysed knowledge in terms of judgements, which are in/correct depending on their relations to their references, and are un/justified in terms of their supportive reasons. Motivated also by his work in logic, he attempted to provide an empirically oriented form of foundationalism and a pragmatic theory of the a priori.

For Lewis, knowledge has a hierarchical structure, based on the infallibility of sensory states. The sensory given—the immediate apprehension of what is presented to the senses—is devoid of a conceptual structure and is not yet a form of knowledge, for there can be no possibility of error, since the apprehension of what is sensibly presented and the latter's existence qua appearance are indistinguishable, and, contrary to Descartes, Lewis held that we can speak of knowledge only if error is possible. Rather, the epistemically infallible given supports 'terminating judgements', which are certain and have a predictive value. Their logical form is: 'Given the sensory cue S, if the possible action A is performed then the expected experiential appearance E will occur'. The certainty of terminating judgements is established by their being verified by practical tests concerning the predicted consequence. All other empirical judgements that concern objective facts different from the given (e.g. physical objects) are non-terminating. Non-terminating judgements are at most probable and increasingly verifiable, never absolutely certain. Their logical form is 'If O is a physical object, then if S and A occur, then in all probability E will occur'. They entail terminating judgements, on which they are based. Lewis argued that probability ultimately requires and is based on certainty, for if no judgement could count as certain even probable judgements would be impossible (they would be merely 'probably probable'). The grounding relation between terminating and non-terminating judgements grants that the former, if verified, confer on the latter their degree of probability and hence their meaningfulness.

Although for Lewis the a priori was coextensive with the analytic, a priori concepts, categories, logical relations, and truths were not empirically irrelevant linguistic conventions. They provide the indispensable ordering, taxonomic, and interpretative criteria without which the given could not rise to the level of knowledge but would remain unintelligible. Thus, they have the crucial role of conceptualizing and giving sense to the unlimited and undetermined continuum of the sensory given and empirical experiences. Contrary to Kant's view, a priori structures are creative constructions that do not constrain but need to be adequate to experience and hence are not fixed. Having a hermeneutic function, they represent stable semantic commitments which are modifiable or replaceable in the light of pragmatic requirements: intelligibility, order, simplicity, economy, comprehensiveness, resilience, and, in the long run, intellectual and practical satisfaction.

Lewis tried to reconcile his 'phenomenalist' foundationalism with a realist theory of perception of physical objects (terms in non-terminating judgements denote genuine physical objects, not just phenomena or subjective appearances), without resorting to Kant's doctrine of the synthetic a priori, but his original 'pragmatic apriorism' remained a rather isolated attempt to develop a transcendental epistemology between the wars.

We have now reached the end of the historical reconstruction. In quick succession, we looked at the roots of contemporary epistemology and its engagement with the sceptical challenge. The time has come to return to a purely logical analysis of the problem. To do so, I will need to introduce a few conceptual tools, beginning with Borel's numbers.

6. Possible Worlds and Borel Numbers

Suppose we toss a fair coin. The outcome may be described (modelled) by the following information i: the coin is heads. Using a common convention already introduced in Chapter 2, I shall refer to anything like the actual coin being tossed and landing heads on a surface after some time as our targeted *system S*, while i will be said to provide a *model M of S* (M_S).

Still following a standard approach in information theory, we already saw in Chapter 1 that we can disassemble i into a combination of a Boolean question Q and a Boolean answer A. The question is a message, requesting data, sent by the sender, our epistemic agent a, to the receiver, in our case the system represented by S. The answer is also a message, providing the requested data, sent by the queried S to the querying a. In short, we have:

$$i = Q + A \qquad [1]$$

The polarization of i into $Q + A$ makes evident that the role of A is to *saturate* Q, to adapt a Fregean idea lately borrowed by information theory.[7] Although it is trivial to apply [1] to any piece of information i, like 'the coin is heads', in order to obtain:

Question   'Is the coin heads?' +
Answer   'yes' =
Information   'The coin is heads'

it is important to keep in mind that the correct interpretation of Q in [1] is not as (i) a request for *confirmation* or (ii) a *test*, but as (iii) a genuine request by a to S to erase a

---

[7] In information theory *saturation* is the condition at which a communication system reaches its maximum capacity of traffic-handling.

data deficit on a's side through *saturation*. The difference is that, in (i) and (ii), a already holds the information that i, but wishes to double-check it, or to check whether the receiver also holds that information; whereas in (iii), a lacks the information that i and wishes to acquire it from the receiver, by obtaining the missing data. Since we cannot assume that a already holds a priori the information that i, the polarization of i requires a channel of communication between a and S.

Of course, in real life, questions and answers share, in variable proportions, the amount of semantic content that is to be found in the corresponding semantic information. However, in [1], the full semantic content, to be found in 'the coin is heads', is entirely allocated to Q. Now, one cannot expect a to be able always to maximize the content of a's questions, for a often lacks much more than just a positive or negative saturation of a Boolean question by S. Frequently, a wishes to know, for example, *what* the capital of France is, not just *whether* Paris is the capital of France. Still, given some idealization, typical of controlled experiments, it is perfectly reasonable, for our present purposes and for the rest of this chapter, to assume that all non-Boolean questions can be translated into Boolean equivalents.[8]

As I have argued in Chapter 2 (see also Floridi 2011c), [1] requires us to specify the *context* (C) in which, the *level of abstraction* (LoA) at which, and the *purpose* (P) for which the question is formulated, and hence it is expected to be satisfied by the answer. In our case, for example, we are in an ideal context (the coin is perfectly fair); we are able to ask only about heads and tails (this is the LoA at which data are obtained from S) but not, for instance, about the kind of coin tossed, who is tossing it, or the length of time the coin takes to be tossed and to land on one side; and the purpose may be assumed to be merely illustrative, namely to establish on which side the coin lands. For the sake of simplicity, I shall refer to the combination of these three parameters by means of the acronym CLP. To recall another Fregean point, questions cannot acquire their specific meaning in isolation or independently of their CLP parameters. It is a bit of a pain, but we need to keep these variables in mind, lest the conceptual mess becomes unmanageable. They will turn out to be rather useful below. As a memory aid, let me revise [1] by adding a combined index, thus:

$$i^{CLP} = Q^{CLP} + A \qquad [2]$$

Note that it is now easy to appreciate that it is really Q and not A that sets the scope of the CLP parameters. A Boolean answer can only *endorse* or *reject* the *context* (C) in which, the *level of abstraction* (LoA) at which, and the *purpose* (P) for which the Boolean question is formulated; but it can neither *change* nor *challenge* them.

Two more advantages offered by [2] are related and they finally lead us to the conclusion of this section. In [2], the relation 'is correctly saturated by' is a function from a countable domain of Boolean questions to a co-domain of only two possible Boolean answers {Yes, No} or better {1, 0}. This is an information-theoretic way of interpreting

---

[8] The reader interested in an explicit defence of such translatability will find it in Floridi (2011c).

Frege's idea that declarative sentences (propositions) are terms that denote one of only two truth-values. Unfortunately, having only two values without any possibility of reiteration would be too restrictive, because it would make it hard to take into account the complexity of, and the possible state-transitions in, the system S. Luckily, [2] allows for a small improvement.

Suppose we have two fair coins, which are tossed repeatedly. [2] may still be sufficient to capture the more complex system S and its dynamics if we allow strings of binary values, as in Table 1.

Each numeric row in Table 1, for example <1, 0>, provides data on the synchronic state of S, obtained through a set of questions, asked relative to some given CLP parameters. The columns provide the data on the transition state of S, that is, from 1 to 0, in the first column, and from 0 to 1, in the second. The CLP must be kept invariant for the state transition or indeed any comparison (see below) to be, and remain, meaningful. Once again, this will turn out to be crucial. The result is that the number of answers is equivalent to the number of time-steps in the state transition, whereas the number of questions indicates the complexity of the (analysis of the) system. Simplifying, all these data can be contained in one n-tuple: <1, 0 | 0, 1>, where occurrences of ',' separate synchronic data, and occurrences of '|' separate diachronic data. We are now ready to appreciate Borel numbers.

In 1927, Émile Borel, in a brief article defending mathematical finitism,[9] presented the following 'odd problem', as he called it:

One could define [a] number by saying that each of [the] successive digits [of its decimal expansion] is equal to 0 or 1 according to whether the answer to some question or other is affirmative or negative. Moreover, it would be possible to order all the questions that can be asked in the French language by sorting them...as is done in dictionaries. Only those questions for which the answers is *yes* or *no* would be retained. The mere knowledge of the number thus defined would give answers to all past, present and future enigmas of science, history and curiosity.[10]

Change French into English or indeed into any other sufficiently expressive language L; sort questions not 'as is done in dictionaries' but into numbered questions asked

Table 1 Elementary example of polarized information

	Context, Level of Abstraction, Purpose	
	Q1	Q2
	is the first coin heads?	is the second coin heads?
A1	1	0
A2	0	1

⁹ See Marion (1998) for an interesting discussion of Borel's position.

¹⁰ Borel (1927, p. 271, English translation in Mancosu 1998, ch. 21). I use here the slightly revised text provided by Tasić (2001, p. 52).

relative to some given CLP parameters; make the set of questions finite; add a dynamic dimension (Borel's world is static), and you will recognize our n-tuple, expressed as a binary string.

Borel thought that his odd problem was a difficulty not in finite cases, like our elementary two-coin system, but whenever one admits real numbers that are inaccessible, or even in the case of extremely large numbers that are incomputable. Recently, Chaitin (2006) revived Borel's criticism in order to defend a finite and digital ontology.[11] For our present purposes, however, I hope that any reader who is happy to talk about possible worlds and the boundless number of their properties will also allow Borel numbers (henceforth simply β) to be as long as we may need them to be, and hence possibly infinite, in order to capture such properties. Consider that they are no more problematic than real numbers, and they are a very efficient and elegant device to describe the data characterizing a system S relative to some given questions and CLP parameters, in the following way (in what follows, the reader acquainted with Carnap-like state-descriptions might wish to compare them to Borel numbers; the comparison is explicitly discussed later, when I shall deal with objection four).

If one simplifies the analysis and disregards any dynamic aspect (for we now know that such a feature could easily be added anyway), one can see that the data produced by static possible worlds are Borel numbers. Alternatively, Borel numbers are snapshots of possible worlds. Thus, our one-coin, static system has a very simple β, which is either 1 or 0. The four states of the two-coin, dynamic system are described by four βs and so forth. Transitions systems are described by well-ordered sets of Borel numbers, where the ordering relation $\leq$ is suitably interpreted in chronological terms, for example 'is not a state subsequent to'. If this is unclear, here is another elementary illustration.

Imagine that our system S is a micro-world consisting of two cards. Our LoA consists of the following observables: a card can be either a King or not a King, and it can be either Spades or Clubs. S can be observed to be in sixteen possible states. Suppose the actual state of S from an imaginary God's-eye perspective is as shown in Figure 19.

Depending on the CLP parameters, there are many ways of expressing the information that the first card is a King of Clubs and the second card is Spades but not a King, and this further clarifies the crucial importance of the CLP parameters. We could transform the information [the first card is a King of Clubs and the second card Spades but not a King] into the question: is the first card a King of Clubs and the second card not a King but Spades? The Borel number would simply be 1. This alternative is always available in principle, since, no matter how complex (in the sense introduced above) the system is, one can always generate such a conjunction of all the relevant questions as to require only a single yes/no answer. In light of what has been said above, we may

---

[11] I owe to Greg Chaitin my first introduction to what he calls Borel 'know-it-all number' during the 30th International Wittgenstein Symposium in Kirchberg, in August 2007. Note that both Borel and Chaitin talk only about one Borel number, and they do not associate Borel numbers to possible worlds or any modal analysis, let alone edit distances.

Figure 19 Example of a state of a system *S* consisting of two cards

agree to call one-digit Borel numbers Fregean numbers. Fregean numbers[12] are usually uninteresting. Our information about the world is obtained and managed at a much more finely grained level. Of course, we could ask two questions instead of only one ('is the first card such and such?' and then 'is the second so and so?'), but let us assume, just for the sake of illustration, that we work at what seems to be a more intuitive and information-theoretically fruitful level of abstraction, one at which we ask four questions: Q1: is the first card a King? Q2: is the first card Clubs? Q3: is the second card a King? Q4: is the second card Spades? This way, we obtain $\beta = 1101$. Now, 1101 is the shortest Borel number that characterizes the possible world *S* at a given time and given the specified questions and CLP parameters. It is also the Borel number that needs to be obtained by *a* in order to be informed about *S* relative to the given questions and CLP parameters. Figure 20 provides a graphic illustration.

We now have a simple way to describe possible worlds as their shortest Borel numbers, according to a given set of questions in a fixed language and CLP parameters, no matter how complex a possible world is, and hence how long its β needs to be. To put it in terms of Kolmogorov or algorithmic complexity: Borel numbers are the minimal computational resources needed by an informational agent such as *a* to specify a possible world. Each possible world is characterized by its Borel number. There are as many Borel numbers as (states of) possible worlds, and as many Borel numbers as possible sets of CFP parameters relative to which sets of questions are asked. Transitions are captured by well-ordered sets of Borel numbers, which can be compressed, if one

---

[12] According to *The Hitchhiker's Guide to the Galaxy* there is a third Fregean number, 42.

Figure 20 System and model share the same Borel number

disregards all the numbers that remain unchanged when moving from β_m to β_n. One may think of this as data refreshing cycles on β.

Of course, in order to be able to compare Borel numbers of possible worlds, both the questions asked and the relative CLP parameters must remain invariant across the comparison; therefore, from now on, we shall simply assume that they are specified. I shall return to this important simplification below. For the moment, let us just say that Borel numbers are the variables that make the difference. In order to analyse and compare such difference we need a metric.

7. The Edit Distance as a Modal Metrics

Since Lewis' (1973)work on counterfactuals, it has become common to talk about degrees of *closeness* between possible worlds. Nowadays, the widespread impression seems to be that we know exactly what we are talking about. The truth is that often we do not.

The false impression may be due to the fact that we rely on simplistic assumptions and implausible scenarios in order to illustrate the notion of closeness. This is misleading. It goes without saying that a possible world in which my wife is late because of some traffic is closer to the possible world in which she is on time than a possible world in which she is late because she has been momentarily kidnapped by some extraterrestrials and then released. But it is hardly intelligible to ask whether a possible world in which Japan never bombed Pearl Harbour is more or less close to the one in which you are reading these words, when compared to another possible world in which Hitler honoured the Treaty of Non-Aggression between Germany and the Soviet Union. It has to be said that Lewis himself was aware of the difficulty, and virtuously bit the bullet:

Overall similarity among worlds is some sort of resultant of similarities and differences of many different kinds, and I have not said what system of weights or priorities should be used to squeeze these down into a single relation of overall similarity. I count that a virtue. Counterfactuals are both vague and various. Different resolutions of the vagueness of overall similarity are appropriate in different contexts.   (Lewis 1979, p. 465)

In truth, Lewis' comment reminds one of the notorious disclaimer in IT, according to which a problem 'is not a bug, it's a feature'. The vagueness of the concept of modal closeness is due to the fact that it was introduced to deal with the semantics of coun-terfactuals and 'counterfactuals are infected with vagueness, as everyone agrees' (Lewis 1979, p. 457). We basically use common sense (e.g. Lewis' suggestions concern-ing the absence of large miracles) and some elementary logic relations (e.g. asymmetry and Lewis' back-tracking) in order to extricate ourselves from the mess they introduce. So, I agree that

we must use what we know about counterfactuals to find out about the appropriate similarity relation—not the other way around.   (Lewis 1979, p. 467)

However, that is exactly why, in the end, it becomes a matter of more or less compatible intuitions, an issue that Lewis' analysis was meant to help to resolve in the first place. So far, the conceptual difficulty. There is a second difficulty that is more formal in nature.[13]

  Contrary to expectations, the formal relations of *closeness* (Lewis 1973, p. 29), *nearness* or *approximation*—as well as that of *similarity* often used to make sense of them[14]—do not provide a metric d on a set of elements, including sets of possible worlds. This because they fail to satisfy the second of the four axioms for a metric:

1. $d(x, y) \geq 0$ *non-negativity*
2. $d(x, y) = 0 \Leftrightarrow x = y$ *identity of indiscernibles*
3. $d(x, y) = d(y, x)$ *symmetry*
4. $d(x, z) \leq d(x, y) + d(y, z)$ *subadditivity* or *triangle inequality*

If the closeness, nearness, approximation, or similarity between two possible worlds is null, then they patently cannot be the same possible world.

  There are at least two strategies to deal with the difficulties highlighted above, short of abandoning the whole project. One is to maintain the choice of the semantic rela-tion and decide on, for example, a *proximity space*, which axiomatizes relations of 'nearness' (Naimpally and Warrack 1970). A proximity space (X, δ) is a set X with a

---

[13] But not only formal; see Kutach (2006).
[14] "The right general analysis of counterfactuals, in my opinion, is one based on comparative similarity of possible worlds" (Lewis 1979, p. 464).

binary relation δ (which can be read as 'is close to') of proximity (proximity structure) on the *power set* $P(X)$ of all its subsets, satisfying the following conditions (for all subsets A, B, C):[15]

1. $A \delta A \Leftrightarrow A \neq 0$ *reflexivity*
2. $A \delta B \Rightarrow B \delta A$ *symmetry*
3. $A \delta (B \cup C) \Leftrightarrow A \delta B$ or $A \delta C$ *binary additivity*

It is easy to see that the three axioms are satisfied by Lewis' modal closeness, which is also a tolerance relation.[16] Since δ holds between sets, these could be Borel numbers.

The alternative strategy, which I shall adopt here, is to modify the semantic notion, used to compare possible worlds, in such a way as to satisfy the identity of indiscernibles axiom. Here is the rationale. The properties of proximity spaces are a generalization of the properties of a metric space. The proximity spaces which satisfy the metric axioms are known as metrizable, and this is the kind of metric space that we need here in order to calculate the distance between possible worlds. For the goal is to introduce the 'edit distance' between Borel numbers as the possibility of correcting substrings in one Borel number when this is compared to another. A very simple option is to choose the dual notion of *close*, that is, *distant*, and hence of *similarity*, that is, *dissimilarity*. Dissimilarity relations (including, for example, information divergence) are still retro-compatible with Lewis' analysis of counterfactuals, since every metric space is a proximity space. But they also satisfy all four axioms for a metric space, giving us a more refined and flexible analysis of distance. Dissimilarity works at a finer LoA (points not just sets) and, above all, as I anticipated, since it is a metric, it makes it possible to use the edit distance to compare Borel numbers. The idea is not entirely new. In order to introduce it, let us return to our example.

Let us assume that the system S is still in the same state as illustrated above, but that a's information i, expressed in some language L, is equivalent to Figure 21:

There is now a mismatch between $\beta_S = 1101$ and β_M 1111. In order to correct a's misinformation, β_M needs to be edited. In this elementary illustration, the editing distance consists in only one step, a replacement of the third digit (see Figure 22). This is known as the Hamming distance (hd), which measures the minimum number of substitutions required to change one string into another.

The Hamming distance is a standard tool in any context where two strings of data *of equal length* need to be compared for similarities (dissimilarities, in our revised approach) and correctible errors, including biological sequences, automatic spell-checkers, or pattern recognition systems. Unsurprisingly, it is a popular metric in the literature on belief- and knowledge-based revision (Papini 2000), or agent-based systems

---

[15] There are many equivalent sets of axioms for a proximity space; see for example the one provided here that tends to be more common and in only slightly modified from (Deza and Deza 2009, p. 70), in order to match more closely the previous list of metric axioms.

[16] A tolerance relation is a reflexive and symmetric relation without transitivity property, i.e. a weaker form of the equivalence relation.

 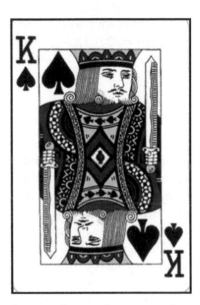

Figure 21 Example of a's misinformation about the state of system S consisting of two cards (see Figure 19)

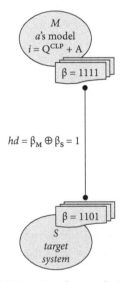

Figure 22 An example of Hamming distance between two Borel numbers

(Gabbay and Schlechta 2009). In modal logic, it is one of the staple options to calculate the distance between possible worlds:

The spheres around the worlds are assumed by Lewis to be given. Epistemologically, one would like to be able to say how to find this structure, that is, to construe it from properties of the worlds themselves. A primitive solution is that the spheres around w are the worlds [our Borel numbers] of Hamming-distance $\leq n$ for every given n. (This means that at most n values of the primitive letters can be changed in going from w to a world in that sphere.) We could also say that the worlds in the spheres result in the revision of the theory at w.

(Kracht and Kutz 2007, pp. 958–9)

The Hamming distance between two binary strings, such as two Borel numbers β_n and β_m, has the nice property of being equal to the sum of 1s in their exclusive disjunction, so it can be expressed as $hd\,(\beta_n, \beta_m) = \beta_n \oplus \beta_m$.

The Hamming distance is not the only edit distance. There are others, depending, for example, on what sort and combination of edit operations, such as substitution, insertion, deletion, or transposition, are allowed. In particular, it is well known that the Hamming distance is criticizable for being too rigid (Lafage and Lang 2001) and, because it is syntactically inflexible and defined only for inputs of the same length, in some cases it might not be the best option. If S grows or shrinks (suppose we add or remove a card in our example), or a has asked too few or too many questions, it would be useful to be able to rely on the other two operations of deletion and insertion in order to correct β_m. This gives us the Levenshtein distance, which can be further improved through the Needleman–Wunch distance by adding a 'gap cost', when there are more or less 'expensive' ways of correcting a string. These and other[17] alternatives are available to any reader interested in refining the approach. But since all such distances share the same axioms, in this chapter their choice will not make a difference and, for the sake of simplicity, I suggest we adopt the simpler, Hamming distance. It is now time to analyse the sceptical challenge.

8. Informational Scepticism or the Sceptical Challenge Reconstructed

According to the anti-sceptic philosopher, an informational agent a embedded in a possible world enjoys a boundless number of informative, zero-Hamming-distance relations with it. This means that a's empirical data about a's world are, normally, indiscernible from the data a receives from it, and when they are discernible they are either corrigible, at least in principle, or at least they are transparently incorrigible, again, in principle. More formally, given β_M, either $\beta_M \oplus \beta_S = 0$ or, if $\beta_M \oplus \beta_S \neq 0$, then either $\beta_M \oplus \beta_S$ can, in principle, be reduced to zero by further editing, or at least a has in principle access to the meta-information that $\beta_M \oplus \beta_S \neq 0$, that is, a can be informed that hd should be edited but also that it is not improvable. Either way, scepticism may be dismissed as unjustified.

---

[17] See for example the Dalal distance, popular in model-based belief-revision analyses, which compares sets of models according to their minimal Hamming distance to other sets of models (Dalal 1988; Satoh 1988).

The sceptic, of course, begs to differ. He does not argue that, given a's β_M, the distance between a's model and its targeted system is greater than zero, but that the length of such distance cannot be established. More formally, he argues that $hd_1 = \beta_M \oplus \beta_S = ?$, not that $hd_1 = \beta_M \oplus \beta_S > 0$. Such a challenge is motivated by the fact that a might be radically misinformed. Circumstances could be such as to give a the impression that $hd_1 = \beta_M \oplus \beta_S = 0$, when actually $hd_1 = \beta_M \oplus \beta_S \neq 0$. Such circumstances are well known: a might be dreaming, or be a brain in a vat, or an avatar in *Second Life*—to use a slightly retro example—who believes itself to be a human being in *First Life*, or a biological body in a *Matrix* scenario, or a citizen constantly and secretly misled by some Big Brother. The examples can easily be multiplied but, at least since Descartes, they all share the following format (see Figure 23). *Perhaps* (a does not have this bit of information) a is not informed about the real world (the system S), despite all appearances that $hd_1 = 0$, because the following is a logical possibility: a's model M, which allegedly carries information about S, is actually indistinguishable[18] ($hd_2 = 0$) from another model (call it D from dreamt), which carries information ($hd_3 = 0$) about a possible world (call it V for virtual), and V and S might (a does not have this bit of information either) be very different from each other, in which case a might be utterly misinformed. More formally, informational scepticism argues that, since $hd_2 = 0$ and $hd_3 = 0$ might be the cases, then $hd_4 = ?$ and therefore $hd_1 = ?$.

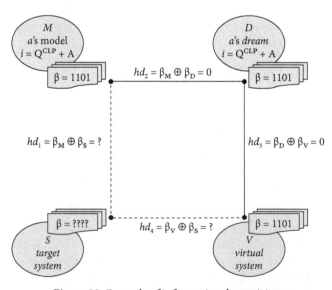

Figure 23 Example of informational scepticism

---

[18] "Quasi scilicet non recorder a similibus etiam cogitationibus me alias in somnis fuisse delusum; quae dum cogito attentius, *tam plane video nunquam certis indiciis vigiliam a somno posse distingui* [my italics] ut obstupescam, et fere hic ipse stupor mihi opinionem somni confirmet", Descartes, *First Mediation*, 1641.

9. The Redundancy of Radical Informational Scepticism

Two quick clarifications are now in order, before showing why informational scepticism is harmless. First, the sceptic must (and is also happy to) concede that, because of the triangle inequality then $hd_5 \leq hd_2 + hd_3$, but since $hd_2 + hd_3 = 0$, then $hd_5 = 0$ (see Figure 24). This is exactly as it ought to be, because the disruptive hypothesis, which the sceptic is inviting us to entertain, is that a's information and its corresponding $hd = 0$ might not concern S but V.

Second, the challenge posed by informational scepticism has been formulated in terms of $(hd_4 = \beta_V \oplus \beta_S = ?) \rightarrow (hd_1 = \beta_M \oplus \beta_S = ?)$, but it could be formulated equally well in terms of: $(hd_6 = \beta_D \oplus \beta_S = ?) \rightarrow (hd_1 = \beta_M \oplus \beta_S = ?)$.

At this point we know that:

1. $hd_2 = 0$ sceptical hypothesis
2. $hd_3 = 0$ sceptical hypothesis
3. $hd_5 = 0$ from 1, 2, and the triangle inequality axiom
4. $hd_1 = hd_4$ from 3 and the triangle inequality axiom

It follows that, in order to meet the sceptical challenge, it is sufficient to show that we can establish one of the following distances: hd_1, hd_4, or hd_6.

One approach, the direct analysis of hd_6, is precluded by informational scepticism itself. The hypothesis—to be taken seriously by the anti-sceptic who wishes to engage with the sceptic—is that there is no way of inspecting whether D is informative about S. The dreaming argument, for instance, presupposes that you cannot just wake up and

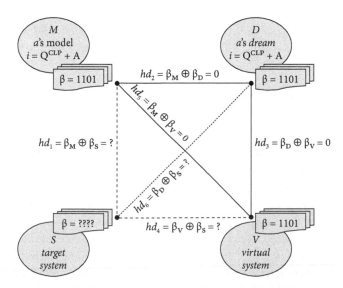

Figure 24 Some implications of informational scepticism

realize you were dreaming, because you may then be dreaming that you are no longer dreaming, and so forth. Pascal summarizes the point nicely:

The main strengths of the Pyrrhonists—I shall leave aside the lesser ones—are that we can be in no way sure of the truths of these principles apart from faith and revelation, except that we feel them to be natural to us. Now this natural feeling is not a convincing proof of their truth, since, having no certainty, apart from faith, about whether we were created by a benevolent God, or an evil demon, or by chance, it is open to doubt whether the principles given to us are true, or false, or uncertain, depending on our origin. In addition, since none of us can be certain, apart from faith, whether we are awake or asleep, given that while asleep we believe as firmly as we do that we are awake. We think we see space, figures, movement. We feel the passage of time, we measure it; in short, we behave just as we do when awake. The result is that, spending half our lives asleep, by our own admission and whatever it seems like to us, we have not the slightest conception of the truth, as all our feelings during that period are illusions. Who knows if that other half of our lives when we assume we are awake is not another form of sleep, slightly different from the first kind, in which we awaken when we think we are sleeping? As we do often dream that we are dreaming, piling one dream on top of another, is it not perfectly feasible that the half of our life when we think we are awake is just itself a dream on to which the others are grafted and from which we will awaken at our death?   (Pascal 1995, n. 164)

In the sceptical *Matrix*, to use a different example, there is no red pill. Thus, the disagreement boils down to diverging views about hd_1 and hd_4. Again, this is consistent with the classic debate about scepticism. The anti-sceptic holds that there are many cases of genuine information, that is, $hd_1 = 0$, and therefore that, in such cases, $hd_4 = 0$, and hence that $hd_6 = 0$. The sceptic holds that nobody can tell whether $hd_4 = 0$, and therefore that nobody can tell whether $hd_1 = 0$ and hence whether $hd_6 = 0$. The anti-sceptic defends a position in the philosophy of information that the sceptic attacks metaphysically.

Luckily, the situation is much better than it looks. As we know, $hd_1 \geq 0$. Trivially, if $hd_1 = 0$ then there is no sceptical challenge, so let us assume that $hd_1 > 0$. In this case, we have two alternatives:

(i) β_M cannot be edited in order to decrease hd_1, so a stops immediately; or
(ii) β_M can be edited, in which case a keeps editing it until hd_1 cannot be further decreased.

Following the sceptical challenge, the possibility of editing β_M must be understood, in both (i) and (ii), to be 'in principle': when a stops, this is because, no matter how much more editing a might still be able to do, this would not improve the distance between β_M and β_S. At this point, a cannot assume to have any direct information about the exact hd_1 between β_M and β_S. However, a does have the meta-information that there is not a single bit of information, concerning β_S, that could make an informative difference to the editing of β_M, for if there were, a would carry on the editing and stop only after the required steps (recall that the sceptical challenge does not allow any 'red pill' or 'wake-up' solution). This is crucial. For consider now the following two ways of describing informational equivalence or co-informativeness:

(i) p and q are co-informative if and only if all the information in p is also inferable from q and vice versa (Larkin and Simon 1987), that is, if and only if they both exclude exactly the same possible worlds.

β_M and β_S are *co-informative* in (i) sense, since all the information obtainable from one is also obtainable from the other and vice versa.[19] If they were not, a would edit β_M until they become co-informative. But (i) is equivalent to (ii):

(ii) p and q are co-informative if and only if p can be transformed into q without any loss of information and vice versa. (Simon 1978)

And since β_M and β_S are *co-informative*, then they can be transformed into each other without any further editing. The result is that β_M and β_S are identical, in the following, qualified sense.

Following Leibniz's principle of the indiscernibility of identicals, it is obvious that, if p and q qualify as information, and $p = q$, then p and q are co-informative. The identity in question, in such a *co-informativeness of identicals*, is the very strong identity one obtains only when there is no single property that distinguishes p from q, no matter what the context, LoA, and purpose (CLP) might be. In other words, $p = q$ is the case if and only if one can safely ignore the CLP parameters at which the identity is predicated. Consider now Leibniz's more controversial principle of the identity of indiscernibles. At first sight, this would translate into the *identity of co-informatives*, which is obviously false. It takes only a moment to realize that p and q may be perfectly co-informative without being the same (Larkin and Simon 1987). Just imagine two fire alarms, one acoustic and the other visual, conveying exactly the same information. What is wrong with the identity of co-informatives is that it tries to adopt the same approach to CLP parameters that one finds at work in the principle of the indiscernibility of identicals. In other words, one makes the mistake of thinking that, in this case as well, it does not matter which context, LoA, or purpose are in question. However, in the simple counterexample above, we can distinguish between the two co-informatives precisely because we take into account not only the identical information they convey, but also their physical features, namely a piercing noise and a flashing light. Therefore, the correct way of stating the second principle is by constraining it within the given CLP parameters according to which the relata are considered to be co-informative in the first place: if p and q are co-informative, they are so at a given LoA, in a specific context, and for a particular purpose, so they are also identical, but at *that* given LoA, in *that* specific context, and for *that* particular purpose. Wittgenstein's famous two issues of the same newspaper are co-informative, and therefore identical, exactly in this qualified sense. Since this is what we mean by saying that p and q are informationally equivalent, let me refer to this revised Leibnizian principle as the *constrained identity of co-informatives*.

---

[19] For a similar approach see Williamson (1987), who, generalizing a suggestion by Geach, proves that, in the more restricted case of two relations, these are informationally equivalent if and only if each can be defined in terms of the other without the use of quantifiers.

Let us now return to the conclusion of the previous reasoning. Since β_M and β_S are co-informative according to the CLP parameters specified, then they are identical, still according to those CLP parameters. But we said at the beginning of our investigation that we were going to ignore the CLP parameters only for the sake of simplicity. They have been there all along. All Borel numbers are always parameterized, and they must all be equally parameterized for their comparison to make any sense. Therefore, all the distances identified so far are valid at some given CLP parameters, just as the constrained identity of co-informatives is. It follows that $\beta_M = \beta_S$, according to the same CLP parameters implicitly employed when discussing all the other distances. Accordingly, contrary to our initial assumption, hd_1 cannot be greater than 0, but given that $hd_1 = hd_4$, it follows that $hd_4 = 0$ and that $hd_6 = 0$ because of the triangle inequality axiom. Summarizing, we have:

1. $hd_2 = 0$ sceptical hypothesis
2. $hd_3 = 0$ sceptical hypothesis
3. $hd_5 = 0$ from 1, 2
4. $hd_1 = hd_4$ from 3 and the triangle inequality axiom
5. $hd_1 = 0$ from the constrained identity of co-informatives
6. $hd_4 = 0$ from 4 and 5
7. $hd_6 = 0$ from 2, 6, and the triangle inequality axiom

All distances are actually zero (see Figure 25). Once made fully explicit and clarified in detail, radical informational scepticism, with its fanciful scenarios of possible worlds, can be proved to be entirely redundant informationally, so it can be disregarded as

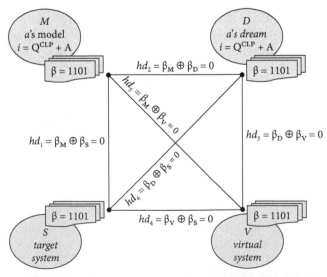

Figure 25 An example of the redundancy of the sceptical challenge

harmless. Wondering whether we might be dreaming, or living in a Matrix, or might be butterflies who think they are humans, or might be characters in a sci-fi simulation created by some future civilization, and so forth, are pointless speculations that may be amusing, but make no significant difference to the serious problem of how we acquire, manage, and refine our high-quality information about the world.

10. The Usefulness of Moderate Informational Scepticism

Absolute, radical, or total forms of informational scepticism are cases of friendly fire. They seem to be attempts to investigate and test our information about the world without prejudice, but they end up promoting disastrous politics of epistemic laissez-faire, which scientologists and creationists, astrologists and fundamentalists, as well as gurus of all kinds are way too happy to exploit. If anything goes, if there are no firewalls against idiocy and irrationality, if we create an informational vacuum, then any bogus belief has an equal right to be sold in the market of ideas. This conclusion should not be read as a dismissal of the useful role that moderate forms of informational scepticism can and must play in our intellectual lives. On the contrary, given the nature of our information-based society, there is an increasing need for a sceptical attitude towards the overabundant mass of contents (in the technical sense introduced above) to which we are exposed. Fake news is polluting the Web, mis- and dis-information[20] are rampant, as well as dogmatism and intolerance, so we need more rather than less scepticism, but it must be of the right kind. As Ramón y Cajal insightfully remarks in his beautiful *Advice for a Young Investigator*, 'The investigator's motto will always be Cicero's phrase: *Dubitando ad veritatem pervenimus*'.[21] So where is the constructive role for sceptical doubts in the previous analysis?

Recall how we saw that *a* is supposed to edit the relevant Borel number until the distance between β_M and β_S cannot be further decreased. In less technical terms, *a* 'is distinguished by a rigid worship of truth, and by a sound and genuine skepticism' (Ramón y Cajal 1999, p. 145), which allows *a* to question and test *a*'s information thoroughly, without prejudice but with an open mind, in order to refine it as much as this is feasible. Good scepticism offers a robust benchmark for testing our information under extreme, but still plausible, conditions. You would not dismiss a car because you cannot drive it on the Moon. This role differs from that of radical informational scepticism insofar as it is not *metaphysical*—it does not deal with logically possible worlds in which we might be deluded into thinking that we are informed about the real world— but *epistemological* or *methodological*, since it deals with actual errors, usual mistakes,

---

[20] Disinformation is understood here as the intentional dissemination of misinformation. See Floridi (2011c), Primiero and Kosolosky (2016).

[21] 'By way of doubting we arrive at the truth' (Ramón y Cajal 1999, p. 55). The common attribution to Cicero is actually based on a paraphrase of a passage in his Tusculanae *Disputationes* 1.30.73.

potential biases, and the inevitably fallible and often probabilistic nature of our informative transactions with the world, thus exercising an open and tolerant attitude towards other views. As Abelard writes: 'By doubt indeed we come to questioning; by questioning, we perceive the truth'.[22] Sceptical doubts of an epistemological kind are essential for the acquisition, refinement, and updating of information. They play a very useful role in the evolution of our understanding of the world.

11. Objections and Replies

By way of further clarification, let me now address a few potential objections that might help to dissipate some doubts and criticisms.

1) Objection: infinite Borel numbers may be incommensurable. It might be objected that, if Borel numbers can be infinite, as they might have to be if they are to encode the binary strings that answer all questions about the state of a possible world, then it is unclear how one might be able to compare them at all.

Reply: the difficulty is real, but irrelevant. The sceptic asks us to consider a whole possible world in which we are, for example, sleeping. Hence, the possibility of an infinite Borel number is something we are conceding to the sceptic, not introducing ourselves in the first place. If a strict finitist reader remains dissatisfied, we could agree to work on meaningful substrings of Borel numbers, those that, for instance, represent the Boolean answers to Descartes' questions about 'the opening of the eyes, the motion of the head, the forth-putting of the hands... [the possession of] an entire body [or] hands' (*First Meditation*).

2) Objection: distances between Borel Numbers can be very counterintuitive. Suppose we have three possible worlds W_1, W_2, and W_3, such that W_1 is the empirical world in which your wife is late because of some traffic, W_2 is a possible world in which your wife is late because her car had a flat tyre that had to be replaced, and W_3 is a possible world in which your wife is late because she was momentarily abducted by some extra-terrestrials. Both the Hamming distance between W_1 and W_2 and the Hamming distance between W_1 and W_3 are 1, since, in both cases, we are assuming that it is only one question that receives a different answer, but surely this must be a *reductio ad absurdum*, because intuitively W_1 and W_2 are much less distant (much closer, in Lewis' sense) than W_1 and W_3, at least because we have decided to conceive them to be so. It follows that the analysis is flawed: either Borel numbers do not provide a satisfactory description of possible worlds, or the Hamming edit distance between them provides the wrong metric, or indeed both, and the same holds true for other metric distances as well. In any case, the issuing analysis of radical informational scepticism must be deficient.

---

[22] Abelard (1976, Prologue): '*Dubitando quippe ad inquisitionem venimus; inquirendo veritatem percipimus.*'

Reply: the objection raises a very serious problem, but this is actually different from the one that it seems to present. What is indeed untenable is the idea that possible worlds might be comparable 'ceteris paribus' without being extremely careful regarding the scope of such a clause and what it really implies. Let me explain by using the same example. The mistake lies in pretending to be able to conceive three possible worlds such as W_1, W_2, and W_3, that, all other things being equal, differ only for one single feature, the cause of your wife's delay. This is absurd. A world in which your wife is late because she is spending some time on an extra-terrestrial spaceship is very distant from W_1 exactly because that event requires the coherent modification of an enormous number of other answers to other questions about the existence of aliens, of their visit to earth, of life in the universe, and so forth. Once again, and at the risk of becoming tedious, it is a question of context, levels of abstraction, and purpose. Anything can be 'similar' to anything else, given some CLP parameters, but that is why we should be careful about the choice of the latter. If all we can observe, when analysing three systems such as W_1, W_2, and W_3, is determined by only one question about the cause of your wife's delay, then it is correct to say that the distance between W_1 and W_2 and W_1 and W_3 must be 1. If this is felt to be unsatisfactory, the problem does not lie with Borel numbers and their Hamming distances and the issuing analysis, but with the selection of the right CLP parameters. Make them more inclusive and you will soon see that W_1 and W_2 are much closer than W_1 and W_3, since, if we choose the right questions, progressively less will need to be edited in W_2 than in W_3. Borel numbers and metric distances are good conceptual tools, but there is no blind and mechanical *computemus à la* Leibniz: their adequate and productive use requires intelligence and insightfulness in the handling of the CLP framework.[23]

3) Objection: edit distances might be computationally intractable. Even regular languages (the set of words accepted by a given finite automaton) are computationally complex, when it comes to calculating their Hamming (Manthey and Reischuk 2005) or Levenshtein distances (Konstantinidis 2007). The relevant and interesting result for the analysis proposed in this chapter was already obtained by (Ernvall et al. 1985), who proved that the Travelling Salesman Problem, when cities are digital strings (our Borel numbers) with Hamming distances, is NP-complete. Of course, strings may be finite, short, and easily computable, but given the intractability of the worst scenarios, and the fact that complete descriptions of whole possible worlds do represent such worst scenarios, what are we gaining from the introduction of Borel numbers and Hamming distances? Aren't these just pointless technicalities, which, in all sufficiently interesting cases, merely complicate rather than facilitate the problem of describing and comparing possible worlds in terms of their distances? It seems that either the descriptions and the comparisons are trivial, in which case the formal tools are unnecessary, or they are complex, in which case the same tools are useless.

---

[23] *The Art of Discovery* (1685, now Leibniz 1951, p. 51).

Reply: this is a fair objection, but it must be properly addressed, for it does not affect the line of reasoning developed in this chapter, but rather the Lewisian approach, in the following sense. In the analysis provided in this chapter, I deal with potentially infinite descriptions (Borel numbers) only when their Hamming distances are assumed to be zero *ex hypothesis* (informational scepticism), or different from but reducible to zero, by further investigation (informational anti-scepticism). I have not attempted to show how to calculate the distance between infinite β (two full descriptions of two possible worlds) when their *hd* might be equally infinite. For I agree that, when we have sufficiently complex (in the sense introduced above) Borel numbers, such comparisons are computationally unrealistic. Yet this does not take anything away from the project of making more rigorous the possibility of having a modal metrics. We are indeed better off by understanding what exactly is required through any serious attempt to develop it. This is partly because we can then come to realize how inane it is to speak of whole possible worlds comparisons in general, and partly because we can rely on such formal analysis to deal with degenerate cases in which infinite strings have *hd* = 0. Therefore, the objection is correct but it does not affect the argument developed in this chapter, which deals with a special case, and it underestimates the importance of providing a negative result. The objection should rather be addressed to anyone who seeks to compare infinite descriptions potentially different at an infinite number of data points.[24]

4) Objection: the analysis lacks originality. We do not really need Borel numbers and Hamming distances. Possible worlds may be described by assigning truth-values to maximal sets of atomic propositions, in some sufficiently expressive language L, which completely describe a possible world, so that modal distances can be calculated in terms of the number of atomic propositions that differ in their assigned truth-values. Indeed, Borel numbers might be compared to (possibly infinite) Carnapian state-descriptions:

A state-description is defined as a conjunction or class of basic sentences (i.e., atomic sentences and negations of such) which for every atomic sentence S contains either S or non-S but not both and no other sentences. A state-description is intended to represent a possible state of affairs of the universe of discourse. (Carnap 1951, p. 75)

Since Carnap, the idea of replacing possible worlds by their descriptions in some language L (such as constituents or model sets) has been rather popular (see for example Hintikka 1973 and Niiniluoto 1987, p. 481—note 3 explicitly addresses this point). Borel numbers are just another variation of the same approach.

Reply: this is more a clarification than an objection. If the comparison between Carnap-like state-descriptions and Borel numbers helps one to understand the latter, it is very welcome. I also agree that, for finite and simple systems, the difference might

---

[24] Holm (2003) provides the generalization needed to deal with possibly infinite descriptions in state-description semantics. I am grateful to Giuseppe Primiero for calling my attention to this point.

not be significant. However, despite the similarity of the two approaches, there are some features that make Borel numbers preferable. First, the Q&A framework avoids the construction of the informed agent *a* as a passive recipient of messages (whole propositions) sent by *S*. Rather, the language in which Galileo's book of nature is written is that of data (Borel numbers), not of sentences, and we saw in the previous chapters that it is up to *a* to extract the data by questioning nature in a Baconian way. Second, note that state-descriptions *à la* Carnap are bottom-up propositional constructs from a formal language, whereas Borel numbers are top-down data, extracted from contents that we consider information, so the latter do not encounter the same limitations that undermine the former (see the debate between Bar-Hillel (1951) and Carnap (1951)): Carnap-like state-descriptions seem to facilitate and invite an ontological commitment that Borel numbers make much more difficult, if not impossible. Third, Borel numbers are more economical: we use bits of information and polarize them into questions and answers, whereas Carnapian state-descriptions require propositions (our Q + A) *and* corresponding truth-values as extra keys to determine their fitness to a particular target, so that the ontological status and location of such values becomes a further issue that requires more theorizing, somewhat like Frege's position about the Truth and the False. Fourth, Borel numbers, being the result of an informational analysis, are better suited than Carnapian state-descriptions to provide a full and detailed analysis of the CLP parameters at which they are obtained. A final reason worth listing here is connected with the sort of correctness theory of truth that Borel numbers and the Q&A framework can elicit, but I shall say more about this in the reply to the next objection and in the conclusion.

5) Objection: there is a confusion between truth-values and probability distributions. Borel numbers and their Hamming distances are introduced from an informational-theoretic perspective. However, a Borel number and its corresponding question form a propositional artefact in which 1s or 0s are equivalent to truth-values and have nothing to do with the probability that the content in the question might be true or false, respectively; yet, this is exactly what is relevant in information theory, where we deal with probability distributions instead. In the one-coin system example, the 1 bit of information provided by heads (or tails) corresponds to the 50 per cent probability that the coin might land heads (or tails), not to the binary value of the truth (or falsehood) of the assertion that it landed heads (or tails). Thus, if the coin were biased, the information provided by its tossing would be less than 1, but 1 (or 0) would still be the correct answer to the relevant question. All this means that there is at the root of the analysis a confusion between truth-values and probability distributions that undermines the whole analysis.

Reply: there is no confusion and hence no problem. One could construct the whole analysis by treating Borel numbers as probability values. Yue et al. (2008) use, for example, the so-called 'earth mover's distance' or Wasserstein metric as the distance function defined between probability distributions on a given metric space, and then treat the co-informativeness of β_M and β_S in terms of zero Kullback–Leibler divergence, that is, $D_{KL} = 0$, since $D_{KL}(\beta_M \| \beta_S) = 0 \Leftrightarrow \beta_M = \beta_S$. Yet the exercise would be rather pointless, since this is not the issue at stake. We are treating Borel numbers as unlocking keys of specific contents, exactly as discussed in the previous objection and the consequent reply. Consequently, although the warning of a potential confusion is welcome, the actual error is nowhere committed.

6) Objection: the approach is too friendly in its rejection of radical informational scepticism. Let us assume that the analysis and the arguments presented in this chapter are accepted. The problem remains that too much has been conceded to the radical sceptic. For if all $hd = 0$, as argued, then there is really no way of showing whether a lives in a virtual or the real world. The distances might all be equal to zero because there is no real world, only a virtual one in which we all live.

Reply: the objection is trivially correct, insofar as it is a matter of elementary logic that, if the Hamming distance between two relata is zero, then one may as well say that the first *relatum* is identical to the second. The objection, however, is more interestingly mistaken when it infers from such a platitude that the radical sceptic might be satisfied by it. What the objection is missing is that there is no room left to argue that the virtual world, in which we might live, is not the real world. Yes, it might be true that 'All the world's a stage, And all the men and women merely players',[25] but this does not make any informational difference, as long as we accept that there is only this stage anyway. There is nothing to be epistemically worried about calling the real virtual, or the virtual real, if the two are identical. It is only a matter of poetic taste.

7) Objection: the approach is inconclusive in its defence of moderate informational scepticism. Once again, let us assume that the analysis and the arguments presented in this chapter are accepted. There is a difficulty about which we are offered no clue, namely when and how the moderate form of informational scepticism should stop. In theory, the sceptic might argue that his testing and probing could go on interminably, leaving forever undetermined whether we have reached a point when β_M and β_S are really co-informative or merely appear to be so. But if this *regressus ad infinitum* is the case, then the whole strategy is inconclusive and the sceptic has the last word.

Reply: the objection is correct in stressing that forms of moderate informational scepticism need to be handled with care. They are powerful acids that can not only clean and polish our information about the world, but also corrode it irreparably. So how can Ramón y Cajal's young Investigator decide when to stop 'scepticizing'? The answer is twofold. First, the approach presented here is fallibilist in Peirce's sense (see the conclusion below), but not sceptical. This means that, far from assuming that obtaining information about the world is impossible, one keeps more or less open the possibility that what appears as information might turn out to be disinformation, that is, not information at all, but mere content, that applies to a different possible world. This is just another way of saying that Ramón y Cajal's young Investigator should keep in mind that, although he is right, he might have been wrong, and has been wrong in

---

[25] William Shakespeare, *As You Like It*, II.7.

the past. Our unconvinced opponent might still retort that this merely shifts the problem: how do we know that this is the time when we are right? And this is the other part of the answer. The objection is really asking for a way of understanding whether there is anything, in the best information we can gather about the world, that is a clear hallmark of its truth, that is, of its zero-Hamming distance with the targeted system. A full explanation would take us too far away, but I have argued in Floridi (2011c) that such a hallmark is indeed available, and it is represented by the commutative relation (in the category theory's sense of 'commutation') between the model under discussion and its target, that is, in the vocabulary of this chapter, between the proximal access to β_M and the distal access to β_S. Theories of truth often seem to be developed with passive viewers of an outside world in mind, detached observers, whether inside or outside Plato's cave, TV watchers, radio listeners, movie goers, in short, *systems users*, according to the computer science terminology favoured in this chapter. The correctness theory of truth, defended in Floridi (2011c), is an attempt to cater for a different sort of customer, namely embodied and embedded, creative agents, who interact with reality, who shape and build it, Plato's artisans, writers not just readers, Shakespeare's players not mere audience, in short *systems designers*. For these agents, truth is about constructing and handling informational artefacts and interacting with them *successfully*, not merely experiencing them passively. It is such successful interactions that provide the much-sought-after hallmarks of truth to our young Investigator. When they occur, then it is time to stop scepticizing. I shall expand on these points in Chapter 10.

Conclusion: From Descartes to Peirce

The attentive reader might have noticed that, in my treatment of radical informational scepticism, I have not followed a Cartesian strategy. Instead, it is rather Peirce that has influenced the approach developed in this chapter. For Descartes, radical scepticism is a means of clearing the ground for the static and permanent foundations of a new 'dogmatism', a vital element in the internal monologue of the single mind, and an essential step towards individualism and the subject's epistemic responsibility. For Peirce, a genuine form of doubt is a falsificationist means to keep the road of inquiry constantly open, a vital element in the deontology of scientific communication, and an essential step towards the construction of a community of scientific inquirers less fallible than any of its members. The dynamic and multi-agent process of investigation, which permeates Peirce's whole philosophy, makes him aware of the importance and utility of a constructive form of scepticism of the sort I have defended above. Thus, it is thanks to a process of doubting that in *The Fixation of Belief* (Peirce 1877) we can move from

- the method of tenacity (dogmatically holding fast to one's beliefs); to
- the method of authority (deferring to someone else the right to assess the epistemic value of a belief); to

- the a priori method (the intra-subjective way of coming to the acceptance of a belief without taking into account either reality or other people's minds); to
- the scientific method (the inter-subjective way of coming to an agreement about the acceptability of a belief, further constrained by reality).

Therefore, I agree with Peirce that inquiry is really prompted only by further genuine doubts of an external origin, and that a constructive scepticism shows the importance of being earnest in the pursuit of knowledge. We should follow Peirce in rejecting absolute scepticism as an anthropology (Pyrrhonian-blessed state of ignorance) and as an ontology (irreconcilable dualism, nominalism, anti-realism), while appreciating it as a deontological stance in how to conduct our search for information.

7

A Defence of Information Closure

Summary

Previously, in Chapter 6, I articulated a constructive appreciation of the sceptical challenge. I stressed that this concerns not the degree of justification but the truthfulness of some information. It is now time to address the latter feature. In this chapter, I define and then defend the principle of information closure (PIC) against a sceptical objection similar to the one discussed by Dretske in relation to the principle of epistemic closure. If I am successful, given that PIC is equivalent to the axiom of distribution and that the latter is one of the conditions that discriminate between normal and non-normal modal logics, a main result of such a defence is that one potentially good reason to look for a formalization of the logic of 'S is informed that p' among the non-normal modal logics, which reject the axiom, is also removed. This is not to argue that the logic of 'S is informed that p' should be a normal modal logic, but that it could still be, insofar as the objection that it could not be, based on the sceptical objection against PIC, has been removed. In other words, I shall argue that the sceptical objection against PIC fails, so such an objection provides no ground to abandon the normal modal logic **B** (also known as **KTB**) as a formalization of 'S is informed that p', which remains plausible insofar as this specific obstacle is concerned.

1. Introduction: The Modal Logic of Being Informed

The topic of this chapter may be introduced by fast zooming in and out of the philosophy of information (Floridi 2011c; Illari 2012). In recent years, philosophical interest in the nature of information has been increasing steadily.[1] This has led to a focus on semantic information,[2] and then on the logic of being informed (Greco and Floridi 2004; Floridi 2006), which has attracted analyses concentrating both on the *statal*[3] sense in which S holds the information that p (this is what I mean by 'logic of

---

[1] For an early overview see Floridi (2004a); on the various meanings and uses of 'information' see Floridi (2010a).

[2] At least since Dretske (1981, see now Dretske 1999). For an introduction see Floridi (2009) or Floridi (2011d). On relevant semantic information, see Floridi (2008c); on how semantic information may become knowledge, see Floridi (2012b).

[3] The statal condition of being informed is that enjoyed by S once S has acquired the information (actional state of being informed) that p. It is the sense in which a witness, for example, is informed (holds

being informed' in the rest of this chapter) and on the *actional* sense in which S becomes informed that *p* (Primiero 2009). One of the consequences of the logic debate has been a renewed epistemological interest in the *principle of closure*, which has motivated a revival of a sceptical objection against its tenability. Dretske (1981, 1999, 2006) and Nozick (1981) found the objection convincing and their support, especially Dretske's, made it popular. However, the topic of this chapter is not a commentary on Dretske's position and the debate that it has generated.[4] Rather, it is a definition and defence of the *principle of information closure* (henceforth PIC) against the sceptical (or, rather, scepticism-based) objection, as formulated, for example, by Kerr and Pritchard (2012). If I am successful, this means—and we are now zooming out—that the plausibility of PIC, as defined in section 1, is not undermined by the sceptical objection. This has important consequences that go beyond the epistemological and informational debates, because PIC is logically equivalent to the axiom of distribution. It follows that the previous defence, if successful, amounts to showing that a major epistemological argument against the formalization of the logic of being informed, based on the axiom of distribution in modal logic, is removed. And since the axiom of distribution is one of the conditions that discriminate between normal and non-normal modal logics, this means that a potentially good reason to look for a formalization of the logic of being informed among the non-normal modal logics,[5] which reject the axiom, is also removed. And this finally means that a formalization of the logic of being informed, in terms of the normal modal logic **B** (also known as **KTB**), is still plausible insofar as this specific obstacle is concerned. In short, I shall argue that the sceptical objection against PIC fails, so the sceptical objection is not a good reason to abandon the normal modal logic **B** as a good formalization of the logic of being informed.[6] Note that this is not equivalent to arguing that a defence of PIC and of the axiom of distribution is sufficient to rule out a non-normal approach, which is perfectly possible. It is rather to argue that the rejection of PIC and of the axiom of distribution would be sufficient to force the adoption of a non-normal approach. This is because a modal logic is normal if and only if it (a) includes the axiom of distribution, (b) includes the strong necessitation-rule,

---

the information) that the suspect was with her at the time when the crime was committed. The distinction is standard among grammarians, who speak of passive verbal forms or states as 'statal' (e.g. 'the door was shut (state) when I last checked it') or 'actional' (e.g. 'but I don't know when the door was shut (act)').

   [4] The reader interested in a clear and informative presentation of Dretske's and Nozick's positions may wish to consult Luper (2010). On the debate see White (1991), Jäger (2004), Baumann (2006), Dretske (2006), Luper (2006), Shackel (2006). More recently, see Adams et al. (2012), which defends Dretske's position. In two recent articles, Genia Schoenbaumsfeld (submitted-a, submitted-b) has defended the principle of epistemic closure from a Wittgensteinian perspective that converges with some of the conclusions reached in the following pages about information closure. I am grateful to her for sharing her research.

   [5] The analysis of the logic of being informed in terms of a non-normal modal logic is developed by Allo (2011).

   [6] This of course leaves open the possibility that other objections might be more successful; see for example (Wheeler 2015). It also does not touch upon a stronger objection in terms of logical omniscience; see the conclusion of this chapter for a link to the issue and (D'Agostino 2013).

and (c) satisfies uniform substitution, and each of these can be dropped to obtain a non-normal modal logic.[7]

The chapter has the following structure. In section 1, I formulate PIC against the background provided by the principle of epistemic closure (PEC). There, I argue that a satisfactory formulation of PIC is in terms of the *straight principle* of information closure. In section 2, I formulate the sceptical objection against PIC. In a nutshell, this is a *modus tollens* that holds that PIC is too good to be true: if PIC were acceptable, it would work as a refutation of radical scepticism, yet this violates a more general and widely accepted principle, endorsed in Chapter 6, according to which no amount of factual information can actually answer sceptical questions, so PIC must be rejected. Note that the sceptical objection against PIC has the same format as the objection against the axiom of distribution: in this case, the 'too good to be true' line of reason concerns the possibility of logical omniscience.[8] I shall return to this feature in the conclusion. In section 3, I show that, although the argument is convincing, it mis-allocates the blame: it is not PIC that needs to be abandoned, but the assumption that one might be allowed to start with an uncontroversial piece of factual information held by S, which then provides the input for the correct application of PIC, thus leading to the sceptical refutation. It follows that the sceptical objection does not undermine the tenability of PIC. There might be other good reasons to challenge information closure, but the scepticism-based or 'too good to be true' argument is not one of them. In section 4, I consider a potential counter-argument, based on a different formulation of PIC in the context of empirical information processing, and show that this too is ineffectual, although for different reasons. In the conclusion, I indicate how the acceptance or rejection of PIC may determine the choice of normal or non-normal modal logics that best model epistemic and information logics and remind the reader that the removal of the sceptical argument leaves open the plausible choice of a normal modal logic as far as this specific difficulty is concerned.

2. The Formulation of the Principle of Information Closure

Formulating the principle of closure in informational terms is not as straightforward as it might seem. This is because, even if we leave aside the doxastic vocabulary in which it is expressed and that often fails to help, PIC is usually assumed, at least

---

[7] Logics without the axiom of distribution may be obtained by moving to a neighbourhood-semantics and may be used to formalize Nozick's analysis of knowledge. Logics without strong necessitation, or even without weak necessitation, are obtained by including non-normal worlds in the Kripke-models; see Allo (2011). Logics without uniform substitution can be found in the area of dynamic epistemic logic, where, for instance, the dynamic operator for public announcements is not a normal modal operator even though it distributes over implication and satisfies necessitation.

[8] On the connection between logical omniscience and the problem of closure in the context of a philosophy of information see Floridi (2006) and D'Agostino (2010).

implicitly, to be a simplified version of the principle of epistemic closure (PEC), and there is quite a large variety of alternative formulations of the latter, each presenting some interesting if subtle mutations.[9] Luckily, the informational translation makes our task less daunting because—to reiterate a point already made in the previous chapters— information is a less slippery concept than that of belief, and a more impoverished concept than that of knowledge, so the ensuing minimalism does help to unclutter our conceptual space. Let us see how.

Initially, it might seem that the best way to formulate PIC would be to use as a template the formulation of PEC under *known* entailment (I am maintaining here the standard terminology to be found in the literature; later I shall speak in terms of material implication), namely:

K   If, while knowing that p, S believes that q because S knows that p entails q, then S knows that q.

K looks like a good starting point because it includes, as an explicit requirement, the fact that S holds (epistemically, doxastically, or, in our case, informationally) not only that p but also that p entails q. As we shall see presently, this is an advantage, because it enables one to avoid a whole set of issues that would be distracting here (but not elsewhere, as I shall explain in section 4 and in the conclusion), based on the contingent or idiosyncratic unavailability of the entailment to a particular epistemic agent rather than to another one, in the following sense. The fact that Alice might fail to hold the information that Paris is in Europe, while holding the information that Paris is in France, because she misses the information that France is in Europe and therefore fails to hold that if Paris is in France then Paris is in Europe, might be relevant in other contexts, for example to check how well informed Alice is about European geography, but not here. Note that this is not equivalent to assuming some ideal, omniscient agent, and to arguing that we should not pay attention to a more realistic notion of semantic information and feasible information processing. On the contrary, in D'Agostino and Floridi (2009) we argue that feasibility is a crucial issue. What I mean by 'distracting issues' are issues that are not under discussion in the deployment of the sceptical argument. For, as will become clearer in the next two sections, the argument using the sceptical objection attacks PIC not because people have informational or cognitive limits—of course we all do, since we may be distracted, lack a crucial piece of information, be incapable of seeing what follows from the information that we do hold, run out of time to perform the required logical steps, etc.—but because, if we concede information about both premises, we seem to be able to refute the sceptic, and this, for reasons to be discussed, is alleged to be unacceptable.

The good news is therefore that the requirement of known entailment is a positive feature in K. The bad news is that, despite this, the informational translation of K does

⁹ The interested reader is referred to the excellent review in Luper (2010). In this chapter, I use K and SP in the way in which they are used in the epistemological literature rather than in modal logic.

not work. Suppose we simplify our task and avoid any reference to beliefs or knowledge, as promised. The rationale for this is that we are seeking to formulate a principle of information closure with a broader basis of applicability: it should work for human and artificial agents—including computers that may be able to hold information physically—and hybrid agents, like banks or online services, which might hold information in their files, or in the memories of their employees. Neither artificial nor hybrid agents can be said to *believe* or *know* that *p* non-metaphorically, for they lack the required mental states or propositional attitudes. In this case, K becomes the principle of known information closure:

> PKIC   If, while holding the information that *p*, *S* holds the information that *q* because *S* holds the information that *p* entails *q*, then *S* holds the information that *q*.

Clearly, PKIC will not do, for it just trivializes the principle into a verbose repetition. If *S* holds the information that *q* then…*S* holds the information that *q*: uncontroversial but also useless. It would be interesting to investigate why the informational translation deprives K of its conceptual value. I suspect that the interplay between a doxastic and an epistemic vocabulary hides the tautological nature of K. However, substantiating this suspicion would go well beyond the scope of this chapter, so let us not get side-tracked. More constructively, let us keep the known entailment clause in K, which we have seen to be a valuable feature, and use it to modify another version of PEC, known as the *straight principle* of epistemic closure. This states that:

> SP   If *S* knows that *p*, and *p* entails *q*, then *S* knows that *q*.

The modification, translated into informational terms, gives us:

> SPIC   If *S* holds the information that *p*, and *S* holds the information that *p* entails *q*, then *S* holds the information that *q*.

SPIC treats *p* entails *q* as another piece of information held by *S*, as required by the known entailment feature. This avoids contingent or idiosyncratic distractions, as we have seen above in the 'French' example with Alice, while avoiding any tautological trap.

Following Floridi (2006)—if we interpret the modal operator $\Box$ as 'is informed (holds the information) that', replace the symbol $\Box$ with *I* for 'being informed', include an implicit reference to the informed agent *S*, and write $\Box p = Ip$ to mean *S* is informed (holds the information) that *p*—we obtain what may be called the canonical principle of information closure, or simply PIC:

> PIC $(Ip \wedge I(p \to q)) \to Iq$

PIC is not trivial, or at least not in the sense in which PKIC above is. As we shall see presently, it also delivers what we need in order to analyse the sceptical objection informationally.

The last step concerns how we *handle* the implication with the wider scope occurring in PIC. Mind, I do not say *interpret* it, for this is another matter. In the rest of our analysis, I suggest we follow common practice and simplify our task by assuming that both implications are interpreted in terms of material implication. It is the main implication in PIC that can be handled in several ways. I shall mention two first, for they provide a good introduction to a third one that seems preferable for our current purpose.[10]

A modest proposal is to handle the implication in terms of *feasibility*. *S could* obtain the information that *q*, if only *S* cares enough to extract it from the information that *p* and the information that *p* entails *q*, both of which are already in *S*'s possession. Consider the following example. The bank holds the information that Bob, its chairman, is overpaid. As a matter of fact, the bank also holds the information (endorses the implication) that, if its chairman is overpaid, then he does not qualify for an annual bonus. So, the bank can (but might not) do something with the implication. Bob might keep receiving his annual bonus for as long as the bank fails to use or indeed decides to disregard the information at its disposal to generate the information that Bob no longer qualifies and then act on it.

A slightly more ambitious proposal, which has its roots in work done by Hintikka (1962), is to handle the implication *normatively*: *S should* obtain the information that *q*. In our example, the bank should reach the conclusion that Bob no longer qualifies for an annual bonus; if it does not, that is a mistake, for which someone (e.g. an employer) or something (e.g. a department) may be reprimanded.

A further alternative, more interesting because it bypasses the limits of the previous two, is to handle the implication as part of a *sufficient procedure for information extraction* (data mining): in order to obtain the information that *q*, it is sufficient for *S* to hold the information that *p* implies *q* and the information that *p*. This third option leaves unspecified whether *S* will, *can* (first proposal), or even *should* (second proposal) extract *q*. In particular, it differs from the first proposal insofar as it does not rely on the occurrence of a possibility, and hence of the resources required to realize it, but on the occurrence of a procedure sufficient to extract the relevant information, which may turn out to be unfeasible, if the required resources are unavailable. This is much less demanding and, in a different context, it would be much less satisfactory, because feasibility matters. This is not the right context to expand on this point, so suffice it to indicate that, in computational complexity theory, the decision problem for Boolean logic is co-NP-complete, that is, one of the hardest problems in co-NP. It is a widely accepted conjecture that Boolean logic is practically undecidable, that is, admits of no feasible decision procedure. Clearly, such a limit puts some hard constraints about feasibility issues in epistemic logic.[11] I shall return to this point in section 4 and in the conclusion. At the moment, let me stress that one way for the bank to obtain the

---

[10] It is not necessary, but might be preferable, to adopt a uniformity of interpretation between the two material implications. However, the conclusions reached in this chapter are independent of the specific interpretation of the second material implication.

[11] See D'Agostino and Floridi (2009) and D'Agostino (2010, 2013) for a full analysis of the issue.

information that Bob does not qualify for an annual bonus is to hold the information that, if he is overpaid, then he does not qualify for an annual bonus, and the information that Bob is overpaid. Handling the implication as part of a sufficient procedure for information extraction means qualifying the information that q as obtainable independently of further experience, evidence, or input, that is, it means showing that q is obtainable without overstepping the boundaries of the available information base.[12] This is just another way of saying that the information in question, namely q, is obtainable a priori and *analytically* (I shall return to this point in Chapter 9).

We now have a satisfactory formulation and interpretation of the principle of information closure. Let us look at the sceptical objection.

3. The Sceptical Objection

The sceptical objection against PIC has been formulated and debated in several papers. Essentially, it is a *modus tollens*, which requires three steps. The first two are very simple. They consist in providing an interpretation of the information that p and of the information that q such that p implies q. The reader is welcome to provide her own version. Here, I shall follow Kerr and Pritchard (2012), and use:

$p :=$ S is in Edinburgh
$q :=$ S is not a brain in a vat on Alpha Centauri [henceforth BiVoAC].
$e :=$ If S is in Edinburgh then S is not a BiVoAC.

As Kerr and Pritchard remark, referring to Dretske's rejection of PIC:

...on Dretske's view I can have an informational basis for believing that I am in Edinburgh but I can have no informational basis for believing that I am not a BIV [brain in a vat] on Alpha Centauri (a skeptical hypothesis which entails that I am not in Edinburgh), even whilst I know that if I am a BIV on Alpha Centauri then I am not in Edinburgh. It is for this reason that Dretske denies epistemic [information] closure.   (Kerr and Pritchard 2012, p. 191)

The third step is the formulation and adoption of a negative thesis:

NT   information alone cannot answer a sceptical doubt.

NT seems most plausible. It refers to factual information, and it is a standard assumption in the literature on scepticism, from Sextus Empiricus to Descartes to Wittgenstein. It is explicitly proposed by Dretske himself, shared by Kerr and Pritchard, and I agree with them: we saw in the previous chapter that sceptical doubts of a Cartesian nature cannot be answered by piling up more or different kinds of factual information. One of the reasons for raising them is precisely because they block such possibility. If this were not the case we would have stopped discussing sceptical questions a long time ago.

[12] The reader may prefer to analyse this in terms of boundaries offered by the chosen level of abstraction; see Floridi (2008b) for this alternative way of formulating the point.

We are now ready to formulate the sceptical objection against PIC thus:

argument (showing that something is wrong)
   (i)   if PIC, S holds the information that p, and S holds the information that e;
   (ii) then S can generate the information that q a priori;
   (iii) but q is sufficient for S to answer the sceptical doubt (in the example, S holds the information that S is not a BiVoAC);
   (iv) and (iii) contradicts NT;
   (v)   but NT seems unquestionable;
   (vi) so something is wrong with (i)–(iii): in a Cartesian scenario, S would simply be unable to discriminate between being in Edinburgh or being a BiVoAC, yet this is exactly what has just happened;

analysis (of what is wrong)
   (vii) (iii) is correct;
   (viii) and the inference from (i) to (ii) is correct;
   (ix)   and e, as well as S holds the information that e, in (i) seems innocent;
   (x)   so the troublemaker in (i) is PIC, which needs to be rejected.

It all sounds very convincing, but I am afraid PIC has been framed, and I hope you will agree with me, once I show you by whom.

4. A Defence of the Principle

Admittedly, PIC looks like the only suspicious character in (i). However, consider more carefully what PIC really achieves, that is, look at e. The implication certainly works, but does it provide any information that can answer the sceptical doubt? Not by itself. For, given the way the sceptical argument is supposed to use e, e works even if both p and q are false. This is exactly as it should be since, more generally and *prima facie*, valid deductions do not generate new information, a famous 'scandal of deduction' (Hintikka 1973; D'Agostino 2013) that, for once, it is quite useful to expose. There are different ways of removing such a scandal. Hintikka himself provides one, and D'Agostino and I (D'Agostino and Floridi 2009) have offered a more recent strategy to deal with it. Here, however, I take e to be analytically true, that is, it does not extend our knowledge beyond p. This is in order to minimize the problems for those who support the sceptical objection, for if e is supposed to be informative, then what I shall argue presently about the assumption of p and of S holding the information that p will also apply to e and its being held as information by S, thus doubling the difficulty. Basically, either e is treated as being non-informative, for example because analytically true, but then we shall see that the assumption of p and that S holds the information that p are the problem, not PIC; or e is interpreted as being informative, in which case the problem is the assumption of p and of e, and that S holds the information that p and that e, still not PIC.

Given such a charitable interpretation, I would suggest that not only can factual information alone not answer a sceptical doubt, but analytically true deductions alone can never answer a sceptical doubt, either. If e did generate new information in terms of q, we would have a case of synthetic a priori reasoning (recall the handling of the implication as a sufficient procedure for information extraction) that would be quite bizarre here: it would mean confusing synthetic truths ('I am not in Paris now') with a priori truths ('if I am in Edinburgh now then a fortiori I am not in Paris now'). The fact is that the only reason why we take e to provide some anti-sceptical, factual information about S's actual location in space and time is because we assume that p in e is *true*. *Ex hypothesis*, not only S is actually in Edinburgh, but S holds such information as well. Consequently, if PIC works anti-sceptically, it is because q works anti-sceptically, but this is the case because $e + p$ work anti-sceptically, but this is the case only if p is true. Now, p is true. Indeed, it should be true, and not just in the chosen example, but in general, or at least for Dretske and anyone else, including myself, who subscribes to the veridicality thesis, according to which p qualifies as semantic information only if p is true. But then, it is really p that works anti-sceptically. All the strength in the anti-sceptical interpretation of (i)–(iii) comes from the truth of p as this is known to S, that is, it comes from assuming that S is informed that p. This becomes obvious once we realize that no shrewd sceptic will ever concede p to S in the first place, because she knows that, if you concede p, then the sceptical challenge is over, as Descartes correctly argued. Informationally (but also epistemically), it never rains, it pours: you never have just a bit of information; if you have some, you *ipso facto* have a lot more. Quine was right about this, and Moore took advantage of it when arguing from his knowledge of his hands (something the Pyrrhonian sceptic would refuse to concede). Allow a crack in the sceptical dam and the informational flooding will soon be inevitable. In a more epistemological vocabulary, if you know something, you know a lot more than just that something. This is why, in the end, local or circumscribed scepticism is either critical thinking under disguise or must escalate into global scepticism of a classic kind, for example Pyrrhonian or Cartesian. The conclusion is that it is really the initial input, surreptitiously provided by p, that is the real troublemaker. PIC is only following orders, as it were. For PIC only exchanges the higher informativeness of a true p (where S is located, in our example) into the lower informativeness of a true q (where S is *not* located, being located where he is). Metaphorically,[13] this is like exchanging a twenty-pound banknote into many one-dollar bills. It might look like you are richer, but of course you are just a bit poorer, in the real-life analogy because of the exchange rate and the commission charged, and in the sceptical objection because you moved from a positive statement (where you actually are located) to a negative one (one of the infinite number of places where you are not, including places dear to the sceptic like vats on Alpha Centauri). If you do not want the effects of q—if you think that it is rather suspicious for someone to end up with so many dollars coming out of nowhere—do not

---

[13] I specify 'metaphorically' because a material implication is resource insensitive, but the suggestion that PIC can be seen as 'exchanging a twenty-pound banknote into many one-dollar bills' presupposes an implication that is resource sensitive (like a linear implication), since we cannot exchange a twenty-pound banknote into many one-dollar bills *and* a twenty-pound banknote, or life would be too simple.

blame PIC, just never concede *p* in the first place—do not give the initial British pounds to that someone in the first place, using the cash metaphor.

It follows that the informational answer to the sceptical doubt, which we agreed was an impossibility, is provided not by *q*, but by *p*, and this disposes of the objection that PIC is untenable because factual information can never provide an answer to sceptical doubts. It never does because one may never be certain that one holds it (one cannot assume to be informed that *p*), not because, if one holds it, it does not.

It might be remarked that all this leaves the last word to the sceptic. I agree, it does, but it does so only in this context, and this is harmless.[14] PIC was never meant to provide an anti-sceptical argument in the first place. It was the alleged accusation that it did in a mistaken way that was the problem. So, what happens next? If being in Edinburgh means that I may not be sure that I am there, then we are talking about a scenario in which no further empirical information, no matter how far-reaching, complex, sophisticated, truth-tracking, reliable, or strongly supported, will manage to eradicate once and for all such Cartesian doubt. I believe it is this proper sense in which all the factual information in the world will never meet the sceptical challenge. For factual information is a matter of empirical facts, and sceptical doubts are based on logical possibilities that challenge the reliability of all such facts. Therefore, no reference to empirical facts and no offer of factual information can cure logically possible doubts. If you are really worried about being a butterfly that is dreaming of being a human being, showing you that you cannot fly will not work. Is this, then, finally a good reason to reject PIC? The answer again is in the negative. PIC was not guilty when we were assuming to have a foot in the door, a piece of factual information about how the world really is, namely *p*. It is still not guilty now that we are dealing with a web of information items that might turn out to be a complete fabrication. On the contrary, in the former case it is PIC that helps us to squeeze some (admittedly rather useless) further bits of information from *p*. In the latter case, it is still PIC (though of course not only PIC) that makes the coherence of the whole database of our information tight. But if PIC is to be retained in both cases, what needs to be discharged? Either nothing, if we are allowed a foot in the door, because this is already sufficient to defeat the sceptical challenge; or the value of absolute scepticism as a weapon of total information destruction, if all that it can ever mean is that the logically possible is empirically undefeatable. Once made fully explicit and clarified in detail, radical informational scepticism, with its fanciful scenarios of possible worlds, can be proved to be entirely redundant informationally (Floridi 2010c), so it can be disregarded as harmless. Wondering whether we might be dreaming, or living in a Matrix, or might be butterflies who think they are humans, or might be characters in a sci-fi simulation created by some future civilization, and so forth, are interesting speculations that may be intellectually stimulating or simply amusing, but that make no significant difference whatsoever to the serious problem of how we acquire, manage, and refine our information about the world when in the world. The endless game of

---

[14] I have argued against the sceptical challenge in Floridi (1996 and 2010b).

dealing with them for their own sake can be left to scholastic philosophers dreaming of final refutations.

5. Objection and Reply

The reader might still be unconvinced. There might be a lingering doubt about the value of PIC. Such doubt may turn into an objection (allied with, but different from, the sceptical objection seen above) against the previous defence of PIC that can be formulated by adapting Adams (2011), who, following Dretske, argues that we should reject information closure. Here it is.

As Adams notices, I too reject PIC in cases in which the kind of information *processing* in question is empirical, as when we see or hear that such and such is the case. As I acknowledged in Floridi (2006):

> Not all 'cognitive' relations are distributive. 'Knowing', 'believing' and 'being informed' are, as well as 'remembering' and 'recalling'. This is why Plato is able to argue that a 'mnemonic logic', which he seems to base on K4, may replace DL [Doxastic Logic] as a foundation for EL [Epistemic Logic]. However, 'seeing' and other experiential relations, for example, are not: if an agent a sees (in a non metaphorical sense) or hears or experiences or perceives that $p \rightarrow q$, it may still be false that, if a sees (hears etc.) p, then a also sees (hears etc.) q.

Adams would like to see a more uniform approach and argues that I should simply reject PIC in all cases. I resist it, but we might not be at variance. Consider the following case.

In the left pocket of your jacket you hold the information that, if it is Sunday, then the supermarket is closed. Your smartphone indicates that today is Sunday. Do you hold the information that the supermarket is closed today? The unexciting answer is maybe. Perhaps, as a *matter of fact*, you do not, so Adams (and Dretske with him) is right. You might fail to make the note in the pocket and the date on the smartphone 'click'. Nevertheless, I would like to argue that, as a *matter of logic*, you should realize, that is, in terms of *feasibility*, *normativity*, or *sufficient procedure for information extraction*, you did have all the information that the supermarket was closed. So much so that you will feel silly when you are in front of its closed doors and realize that, if you had been more careful, you had all the information necessary to save you the trip. You should have known better, as the phrase goes. Now, I take logic to be a prescriptive not a descriptive discipline. From this perspective, PIC seems to be perfectly fine. This also means that the logical application of PIC to informational co-variance is correct. Suppose two systems a and b are coupled in such a way that a's being (of type, or in state) F is correlated to b being (of type, or in state) G, so that $F(a)$ carries (for the observer of a) the information that $G(b)$.[15] An application of PIC in this case means that, if $F(a) \rightarrow G(b)$ qualifies as information and so does $F(a)$, then $G(b)$ qualifies as

---

[15] Such a co-variance principle has been at the core of the philosophy of information at least since its explicit formulation in Dretske (1981). The version provided here is from Floridi (2011c, p. 41), which is a slight modification of the version provided by Barwise and Seligman (1997).

well. For example, if the low-battery indicator (a) flashing (F) indicates that the battery (b) is flat (G) qualifies as information, and if the battery indicator flashing also counts as information, then so does the battery being flat.

Still from the same perspective, one should not jump to the conclusion that PIC is always applicable to any empirical way of handling information. Consider the example above. This time you *read* the following e-mail, sent by the supermarket: 'The shop will be closed every Sunday.' You also *read* the date on your computer, which correctly indicates that today is Sunday. Have you *read* that the supermarket is closed today? Of course not, as we assume that there were no further messages. Should you have read that it was? Obviously not, for where was the text that you should have read? Should you have inferred that the supermarket was closed today? Surely, for that was the information that could easily be extracted from the two texts that you read. Again, imagine you are in a hurry and you have only two 'time tokens', let us say two seconds. And suppose that reading each message takes one token each. Clearly you do not have the time to extract the information that the supermarket is closed. In more abstract terms, the agent may simply lack the resources to extract not just all (since this is trivially true) but even the relevant information that may be logically extractable from the available database.

Adams is talking about the performance of actual players; I am talking about the rules of the game. If Adams's thesis is that PIC is at best only a matter of logic and certainly not an empirical fact, I am convinced.

Conclusion: Information Closure and the Logic of Being Informed

In this chapter, I have sought to defend the principle of information closure (PIC) against a popular objection, namely that its assumption would lead to an implausible argument that would defeat radical scepticism, and that this is a good reason to drop PIC. I have shown why such an objection is misdirected. The previous debate may seem to be of interest only to epistemologists or philosophers of information, but such an impression would be mistaken. The acceptance or rejection of the principle of closure in epistemology or in the philosophy of information has a wider consequence, in terms of the design of databases, and of the kind of modal systems that then become available to model epistemic and information logics of different strengths. Quite surprisingly for a topic so well discussed and understood, it seems that such consequence has remained implicit so far, and yet, it is straightforward. Let me explain. The axiom of distribution states that:[16]

AOD $\Box(\varphi \to \psi) \to (\Box\varphi \to \Box\psi)$

---

[16] See for example Cocchiarella and Freund (2008) or Hughes and Cresswell (1984). The axiom is also and perhaps better known as the K axiom, but such terminology would be confusing in this chapter. A less popular name is the deductive cogency axiom.

AOD is one of the conditions that discriminate between normal modal logics, to which the axiom applies, and non-normal ones, where the axiom does not apply. PIC is simply the counterpart of AOD in the philosophy of information. This is because PIC can be translated as $(\Box\varphi \land \Box(\varphi \to \psi)) \to \Box\psi$, and the latter is logically equivalent to $\Box(\varphi \to \psi) \to (\Box\varphi \to \Box\psi)$, as a reformulation of both in an implication-free form easily shows. Indeed, AOD is the source of the debate on PEC in modal logic. The parallel is enlightening not because it points necessarily towards a uniform solution, but because it makes one realize that arguments against AOD in terms of logical omniscience have the same conceptual format as scepticism-based arguments against PIC already discussed: they are both based on a 'too good to be true' strategy.

The fact that PIC and AOD are two sides of the same coin means that the acceptance or rejection of PIC is an important consideration when it comes to deciding whether one is going to consider normal or non-normal modal logics as more suitable to capture all the features one wants to include in an epistemic or information logic. There are good reasons for choosing either option, but two points should now be clear. One is a matter of consistency: rejecting PIC means rejecting the option that epistemic or infor- mation logics are normal modal logics. Such rejection is perfectly reasonable and Allo (2011), for example, offers an interesting analysis of a non-normal alternative. However, and this is the second point, the refutation of the 'sceptical argument' against PIC means that one obstacle against a normal modal logic analysis of '*S* is informed that *p*' has been removed. And this, in turn, means that the argument in favour of the analysis of information logic in terms of the *normal* modal logic **B** remains unaffected in this respect. PIC has many shortcomings, but not that of being 'too good to be true' in the sense analysed in this chapter.

8

Logical Fallacies as Bayesian Informational Shortcuts

Summary

Previously, in Chapter 5, we discussed the topic of information quality. Information closure, as defended in Chapter 7, may help with the consistency of a database, so it is related to information quality. However, it cannot be used to expand such an information repository. For this, other forms of reasoning are needed. Bayesianism is often indicated as a classic means to upgrade a set of beliefs or indeed some bits of information, in the vocabulary of this book. Some other erroneous forms of reasoning, however, damage the same reservoir of information. Interestingly, the two dynamics are related. As I shall argue in this chapter, the two best known formal logical fallacies, namely *denying the antecedent* (DA) and *affirming the consequent* (AC), are not just basic and simple errors, which prove human irrationality, but rather informational shortcuts, which may provide a quick and dirty (and therefore unsafe) way of extracting useful information from the same informational resources to which Alice already has access. And, in this sense, they can be shown to amount to degraded versions of Bayes' theorem, once this is stripped of some of its probabilities. The less the probabilities count, the closer these fallacies become to a reasoning that is not only informationally useful but also logically valid.

1. Introduction: A Greener Approach to Logic

When it comes to managing ontic resources, philosophy may be notoriously prodigal. One only needs to recall Plato's world of ideas, Popper's Third World, or Lewis' possible worlds. But when epistemic and logical resources are in question—the nature and scope of what is knowable and the limits of what is acceptable as formally valid—the problem may, rather, be some excessive profligacy. All sorts of radical sceptics, rigorous empiricists, and dogmatic rationalists seem to be bent on throwing away far too much. They waste what could be otherwise saved or recycled, both in terms of what we probably do know and in terms of what we might have a decent right to conclude. In this chapter, I wish to help to redress this situation. I will argue that logic has been guilty of a wasteful or 'ungreen policy', by considering some formal logical fallacies as absolutely worthless rubbish, only fit for the conceptual junkyard, thus missing their potential contribution to our information processes. I will suggest that there is a greener and much more reasonable interpretation of such fallacies, which shows that they can be rather useful, if quick and dirty, and probably riskier, ways to gain and manage one's information. Some logical fallacies are not mere mistakes, of no value, but informational shortcuts that can be epistemically fruitful, if carefully managed.

2. What are Logical Fallacies?

There is no ultimate and complete agreement among logicians or philosophers on a very tight definition of what a logical fallacy is (Hansen and Pinto 1995). This is so, partly because opponents like to use the expression flexibly, in order to throw dialectical mud at each other, and partly because a large variety of errors in reasoning is often diagnosed as a logical fallacy. The result is that there is no fixed taxonomy either. However, for the purpose of this chapter, the following might provide a good starting point:

LF)   a logical fallacy $=_{def.}$ any (possibly unnoticed) deductively invalid or erroneous argument with the appearance of validity or a demonstrably false conclusion from plausible reasoning.

If LF (or a working definition sufficiently similar to it) is acceptable, the next step usually consists in distinguishing between two types of LFs (Woods and Walton 1982):

ILFs)   Informal logical fallacies; and

FLFs)   Formal logical fallacies.

ILFs are really mistakes in argumentation, such as begging the question, *ignoratio elenchi*, *argumentum ad hominem*, and so forth. What is wrong with them is something in their semantics or in their strategy, not so much in their essential structure or form. ILFs will make a brief appearance later in the chapter (see section 9), but they are not its subject.

What concerns us here are FLFs. Their problem is entirely morphological. In particular, the two best known schemes of FLFs are *denying the antecedent* (DA) and *affirming the consequent* (AC) (Hamblin 1970). In the rest of this chapter, I shall concentrate my attention entirely on them. An old and influential tradition has denounced both as just basic and simple errors, weeds in the logical garden, to be eradicated as quickly and thoroughly as possible, wherever they occur. *Pace* Aristotle, this might not be such a good idea.

3. Do Formal Logical Fallacies Provide Any Information?

Answers to this question can be grouped under two headings, which are not mutually exclusive:

(a) No. Considered as plain and obvious errors, FLFs are normally dismissed as providing zero information;

(b) Yes. As errors, FLFs show, metatheoretically, that individuals make systematic mistakes and that human reasoning is faulty.

On (a), there is of course a vast literature in logic and critical thinking, but no significant advancement has been made since Aristotle condemned logical fallacies to the dustbin, in his *De Sophisticis Elenchis* (Aristotle 1938).

On (b), the literature is equally vast but less unanimous. In cognitive science, developmental psychology, and neuroscience, a wealth of experiments at least since the 1960s (e.g. the classic Wason selection task, in Wason 1966) has shown, allegedly, that humans are not so rational, or not as rational as they like to describe themselves. Yet, in this context, there is also a rather annoying tendency to over-simplify and reduce a variety of ways and styles of rational thinking to problem solving, the latter to logical reasoning, and this to conditional reasoning. This reduction may be questionable, to say the least, and misleading, as semantic and social interpretations of the Wason selection task seem to show (Griggs and Cox 1982). On the whole, however, Stein (1996) still provides a good survey and a widely accepted conclusion about (b), so let me quote him at length:

> According to experiments done over the past few decades, humans make...significant errors in various realms of reasoning: logical reasoning, probabilistic reasoning, similarity judgements, and risk-assessments to name a few. Together these...reasoning experiments are taken to show that humans are irrational....Some philosophers and psychologists have developed creative and appealing arguments that these experiments are mistaken or misinterpreted because humans must be rational.
>
> ...I attempt to show that these arguments fail; cognitive science can and should play a role in determining whether or not humans are rational.   (Stein 1996, pp. 1, 2)

Stein might be right, but the story is probably a bit less discouraging, as I will try to show.

4. Formal Logical Fallacies and Their Explanations

Formal logical fallacies are the dark side of valid inferences: denying the antecedent (DA) is supposed to be a rotten variant of *Modus Ponens* (MP), while affirming the consequent (AC) may be seen as a *Modus Tollens* (MT) gone wrong. This can more easily be appreciated visually, by looking at Figure 26.

In a study now considered a classic, Marcus and Rips (1979) presented participants with examples of MP, MT, DA, and AC, and asked them to judge each argument as either valid or invalid. Results showed that participants often incorrectly judged MT as invalid, and incorrectly judged DA and AC as valid. There are two standard, positive explanations about why participants accept fallacies as valid inferences (Verschueren et al. 2001).[1]

---

[1] In the rest of this chapter I shall not be concerned with the other problem, namely why participants misjudge MT as invalid.

MP	DA
$\varphi \rightarrow \psi$	$\varphi \rightarrow \psi$
φ	$\neg \varphi$
ψ	$\neg \psi$

MT	AC
$\varphi \rightarrow \psi$	$\varphi \rightarrow \psi$
$\neg \psi$	ψ
$\neg \varphi$	φ

Figure 26 Valid inference schemes and formal logical fallacies

Following a stronger informational reading, the first suggests that participants mistake 'only if' for 'if and only if', treating 'if it is a square, then it has four sides' as the same as 'if it is water, then it is H_2O'. This was already Aristotle's view:

The refutation which depends upon the consequent arises because people suppose that the relation of consequence is convertible. ... since after rain the ground is wet in consequence, we suppose that if the ground is wet, it has been raining; whereas that does not necessarily follow.

(*De Sophisticis Elenchis* in Aristotle 1938)

The other explanation, based on a weaker informational reading, holds that participants mistake necessity for probability. The two explanations may not be incompatible. To see why, we need to rely on Bayes' theorem.

5. Bayes' Theorem

Bayes' theorem calculates the posterior probability of an event A given event B (that is, $P(A|B)$ on the basis of the prior probability of A (that is, $P(A)$). Basically, it tells us what sort of information can be 'retrodicted' (backward prediction). The well-known formula is:

$$P(A \mid B) = \frac{P(B \mid A) \times P(A)}{P(B \mid A) \times P(A) + P(B \mid A^c) \times P(A^c)}$$

Let us consider a simple example. Suppose Alice receives many emails, but only a few of them (say 2 per cent) are infected by some software virus. She uses a rather reliable antivirus software, which is successful 95 per cent of the time. The latter does not erase her potentially infected emails, but moves them to a special quarantine folder in the email client software, which Alice can check. Alice wonders how often she should check it for good emails. The question she is implicitly asking is: 'what is the probability

Bayes Rule Applet: Is the email infected?

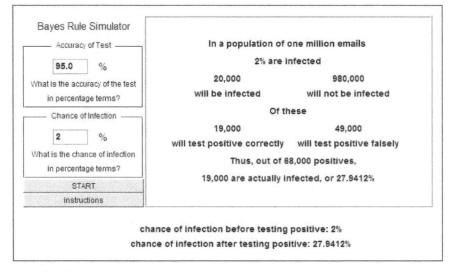

Figure 27 A simple application of Bayes' theorem

Source: Adapted and reproduced with permission from Mikhael Shor (2005), 'Bayes Rule Applet', *GameTheory.net*, http://www.gametheory.net/Mike/applets/Bayes/Bayes.html.

that *A* (= the email was infected), given the fact that *B* (= the email was blocked by the antivirus and placed in the quarantine folder) when, on average, 2 per cent of all the emails I receive are actually infected and my antivirus is successful 95 per cent of the time, that is, it provides only 5 per cent false positives?' If the chance that some emails in the quarantine folder might not be infected is very low, then she will check it only occasionally, rather than regularly.

Suppose Alice runs an ideal test on one million emails. The result is shown in Figure 27. The chance that an email might be infected before being blocked by the antivirus is 2 per cent, but the chance that an email in the quarantine folder is actually infected is roughly 28 per cent. Clearly, Alice should check her folder regularly.

6. Bayes' Theorem and the Fallacy of Affirming the Consequent

Alice is smart. Bob, a friend of hers, is not. He uses the same antivirus and receives roughly the same number of emails, with approximately the same quantity of infections but, when Alice explains to him that he should check his quarantine folder regularly, he is astonished. For he thought that, if the email was infected, then the antivirus blocked it, and since the quarantine folder contains only emails blocked by the antivirus, then all the emails in it must be infected. More formally, he reasoned that: $A \rightarrow B$, $B \vdash A$. Alice explains to Bob that the previous inference is a typical fallacy (AC), but that he should not feel silly at all. For, consider Bayes' theorem once again. Look at the formula $P(B|A^c)$, where A^c (the absolute complement) is just another notation for $\neg A$. $P(B|A^c)$ indicates the probability that the antivirus blocks the email (B) when the email is not infected (A^c). Suppose we have perfect, infallible antivirus software. This will generate no false positives (no mistakes). But if there are no false positives, that is, if $P(B|A^c) = 0$, then $P(A|B) = 1$ and Bayes' theorem is degraded to a double implication: $A \leftrightarrow B$, $B \vdash A$, which is what Bob perhaps had in mind. On the other hand, if there are some false positives, that is, if $P(B|A^c) > 0$, then $P(A|B) < 1$ and the formula bears a strong family resemblance to the AC fallacy: $A \rightarrow B$, $B \vdash A$, which is what Bob might also have had in mind. Either way, Bob was taking a shortcut (he disregarded the probabilities) to focus on the sort of information that he could extract from the fact that those emails were in the quarantine folder. And on the wise advice of being safe rather than sorry, he treated all its content as dangerous. The result is that Bob is onto-logically thrifty (he trusts many fewer items than Alice) by being logically greener (he relies on a reasoning that, although formally fallacious, can still be recycled to provide a quick and dirty way of extracting useful information from his environment). If this is unclear, the reader may try this other example.

Bob's teacher tells him that, if he does not study enough, then he will fail his exam. Unfortunately, Bob does fail his exam and the teacher reproaches him for not having studied enough. Bob has learnt his Bayesian lesson, so he knows that the teacher's reasoning is fallacious. But he also knows that it is fairly accurate, as a shortcut that gets things right most of the time: on average, students who fail their exams have not studied enough. The teacher should have simply sprinkled her inference and then judgement with some 'probably' and 'most likely' clauses. Basically, the AC fallacy is Bayes' theorem stripped of some of its probabilities. The less the probabilities count, the closer the fallacy is to a reasoning that is logically valid.

7. Bayes' Theorem and the Fallacy of Denying the Antecedent

The case for the DA fallacy is analogous. Given the same interpretations for A, B, A^c, and B^c, Alice calculates, through Bayes' theorem, the probability that the email is not blocked by the antivirus given the fact that it is not infected, that is, $P(B^c|A^c)$. In this case too, if there are no false positives, that is, if $P(B|A^c) = 0$, then $P(B^c|A^c) = 1$ and the formula is again degraded to a double implication $A \leftrightarrow B$, $\neg A \vdash \neg B$, which is perfectly valid. If there are some false positives, that is, if $P(B|A^c) > 0$, then $P(B^c|A^c) < 1$, and the formula bears a strong family resemblance to the DA fallacy: $A \rightarrow B$, $\neg A \vdash \neg B$. The DA

	MP	DA	MT	AC
1	$\varphi \rightarrow \psi$	$\varphi \rightarrow \psi$	$\varphi \rightarrow \psi$	$\varphi \rightarrow \psi$
2	φ	$\neg \varphi$	$\neg \psi$	ψ
	ψ	$\neg \psi$	$\neg \varphi$	φ

Figure 28   Valid inferences and formal logical fallacies

fallacy is also Bayes' theorem stripped of some of its probabilities. We are now ready for an overall interpretation.

8. Logical Formal Fallacies and Their Bayesian Interpretation

Consider Figure 28. In row 1, all four schemes introduce $\varphi \rightarrow \psi$. If we interpret $\varphi \rightarrow \psi$ informationally, it means that there are no false negatives: in our example, if the email is infected, the antivirus blocks it.

MP and MT rely only on this information, so there is no need for probabilities. However, DA and AC also assume (and here is the logical mistake) that there are no false positives (double implication), or that, if there are, they are so improbable as to be negligible (degraded Bayes' theorem). Consequently, DA and AC are Bayesian 'quick and dirty' informational shortcuts. When we use them, we bet that $A \rightarrow B, B \vdash A$ or that $A \rightarrow B, \neg A \vdash \neg B$. The bet might be risky (we might be wrong), but it often pays back handsomely in terms of the lower amount of informational resources needed to reach a conclusion (see the case of the teacher assessing whether Bob studied enough). Moreover, it is easy to show that the information gain increases (the bets are less risky) the more the following conditions are satisfied:

1. *soundness*: A is true and $A \rightarrow B$ valid;
2. *relevance*: A and B in $A \rightarrow B$ are relevantly related and not independent: the occurrence of A affects the occurrence of B meaningfully (not as in 'if Paris is the capital of France then bachelors are unmarried', but more as in 'if Paris is the capital of France then Lyon is not the capital of France') (Floridi 2008c);
3. *constraints*: we assume $A_1, A_2, ..., A_k$ to be mutually exclusive events, whose union is the whole sample space of an experiment, and B to be an event with $P(B) > 0$.

9. Advantages of the Bayesian Interpretation of Formal Logical Fallacies

The 'greener' approach to DA and AC just offered presents several advantages.

First, and quite interestingly, parallel results have recently been achieved in the Bayesian analysis of *informal* fallacies: '... three classic reasoning fallacies... *argumentum ad ignorantiam*, the circular argument or *petitio principii*, and the slippery slope argument... match structurally arguments which are widely accepted. This suggests that it is not the form of the arguments as such that is problematic but rather something about the content of those examples with which they are typically justified. This leads to a Bayesian re-analysis of these classic argument forms and a reformulation of the conditions under which they do or do not constitute legitimate forms of argumentation' (Hahn and Oaksford 2006, p. 207). The convergence is remarkable and probably significant. Humans reason in many different ways, only a few of which are captured by mathematical logic, as cognitive science is increasingly showing (Chater and Oaksford 2008).

Second, the Bayesian interpretation is consistent with recent work on the interpretation of

1. *abduction as inference to the best explanation* (IBE),
2. the AC fallacy as a form of IBE, and
3. IBE in Bayesian terms.

It all turns out to be a bit too consistent to be accidental. If we accept the previous Bayesian interpretation of DA and AC, the following quote acquires a very interesting meaning:

> It has become common in AI to identify 'abduction' with backward *modus ponens* [i.e. affirming the consequent], or with backward *modus ponens* together with constraints on the set of conclusions that are allowable, or with backward *modus ponens* with syntactic constraints. There is a burden on those who study restricted forms of backward *modus ponens* to show us the virtues of their particular forms—they need to show us how they are smart. I suggest that they will find that backward *modus ponens* is smart to the degree that it approximates, or when it is controlled and constrained to approximate, or when it implements, inference to the best explanation.
>
> (Josephson 2000, p. 32)

In the email example, AC is read as an IBE (inference to best explanation or retrodiction) effort: the email was blocked because it was (probably) infected, whereas DA is read as an IBP (inference to best prediction) effort: the email is not infected so it will (probably) not be blocked.

Third, formal fallacies are interpreted in terms of information-gathering and gain, rather than argumentative and dialectical strength, as in post-Aristotelian logic, or mathematical utility, as in post-Fregean logic. To put it less cryptically, AC and DA are still a disaster, if our goal is to win an argument, because our opponent will not have to be too smart to provide plenty of counterarguments. They are also mathematical calamities, whenever our goal is to provide valid proofs that convey total certainty and faultless conclusions, for their morphology makes them utterly unreliable. But when it comes to extracting information from whatever is at hand and without too much fuss, they can be serviceable. This point is related to the last advantage, which is best left for the conclusion.

Conclusion: Rationality Regained

Anyone who has taught logic to undergraduates knows that logical fallacies are very common and hard to eradicate. Convincing normal, intelligent, decently educated young minds, who have successfully negotiated very complex cognitive tasks for almost two decades, that their most basic ways of reasoning produce only worthless rubbish takes a while and some effort. It is also an unrewarding and tedious task, which is not always successful. A common result is the development of a schizophrenic attitude: life is life and logic has got little to do with it. Otherwise put: when in the logic class do as the teacher does, but then, at the pub, you can go back to your old habits and infer that if someone has had too many drinks and drives, that person will have an accident and since she did have an accident she must have been drunk. A greener approach to the way in which we treat fallacies has the advantage of making people see not only the limits of similar ways of reasoning, but also their value, provided one is aware of the sort of epistemic risks one is running. In a way, AC and DA are very powerful informational tools—inferentially, they are the equivalent of shoot first and ask questions later—developed by embedded and embodied agents to cope, as quickly and successfully as possible, with a hostile environment. The fact that we have had the leisure, in the past few millennia, to show how badly logical fallacies serve us when the inferential game becomes more refined and subtle, either dialectically or mathematically, should not prevent us from building a healthier relation between life and logic and recognize their potential utility. The sooner we start recycling them the better.

9

Maker's Knowledge, between A Priori and A Posteriori

Summary

Previously, in Chapter 2, I introduced the so-called maker's knowledge tradition to clarify what I meant by a constructionist approach to how we perceive, make sense of, and explain the world. Then, in Chapter 3, I argued that we should adopt a non-naturalist version of constructionism. In Chapter 4, I articulated how this may be supported by an interpretation of perception and testimony as providers of data that a human agent like Alice then repurposes to create an informational interpretation of the world. In Chapter 6, I defended this position against the sceptical challenge. In this chapter, I finally return to the maker's knowledge tradition to provide a full description and defence. I shall do so by tackling another important difficulty. If Alice's knowledge is the knowledge enjoyed by a maker—more on this presently—how can this be qualified according to the three classic distinctions, which specify that truths can be *necessary* vs. *contingent*, *analytic* vs. *synthetic*, and a priori vs. a posteriori? Let me hasten to add a clarification. The philosopher reading this chapter knows very well both how useful and how ordinary such distinctions are, in our conceptual work, and that they have been subject to many and detailed debates, especially the last two. In the following pages, I do not wish to discuss how far they may be tenable. This is not the point at all. I shall simply assume that, *if* they are reasonable and non-problematic in some ordinary cases, *then* they can be used in order to understand what kind of knowledge the *maker's knowledge* is. By this I mean the sort of knowledge that Alice enjoys when she holds the information (truthful content) that Bob's coffee is sweetened because she just put two spoons of sugar in it herself. The *maker's knowledge* tradition is quite important but it is not mainstream in modern and analytic epistemology and lacks grounding in terms of exactly what sort of knowledge one is talking about. My suggestion is that this grounding can be provided by a minimalist approach, based on an information-theoretical analysis. In this chapter, I argue that

(a) we need to decouple a fourth distinction, namely *informative* vs. *uninformative*, from the previous three and, in particular, from its implicit association with *analytic* vs. *synthetic* and a priori vs. a posteriori;

(b) such a decoupling facilitates, and is facilitated by, moving from a monoagent to a multiagent approach: the distinctions qualify a proposition, a message, or some information not just in themselves but relationally, with respect to an informational agent;

(c) the decoupling and the multiagent approach enable a re-mapping of currently available positions in epistemology (Classic, Innatist, Kant's, and Kripke's) on these four dichotomies;

(d) within such a re-mapping, two positions, capturing the nature of a witness's knowledge (see Chapter 4 on testimony) and of a maker's knowledge, can best be described as *contingent, synthetic,* a posteriori, and *uninformative* and as *contingent, synthetic, weakly* a priori (ab anteriori), and *uninformative* respectively.

In the conclusion, I indicate why the analysis of the maker's knowledge has important consequences in all those cases in which the *poietic* (constructive) intervention on a system determines the truth of the model of that system.

1. Introduction: The Question about Maker's Knowledge

Let us assume that Alice knows that p. This is the fact not under dispute. And let us assume that, at least in some cases, her knowledge that p can be correctly analysed as follows:

Alice knows that p because

(i) she is informed that p, that is, she holds the (true[1]) information p[2]; and

(ii) she can provide the right account (justification, explanation, warrant, ...) for p.

I have defended the tenability of both (i) and (ii) elsewhere[3] and in this chapter I hope the reader may concede both theses as our starting point, at least conditionally. For the question I am keen on investigating is not whether (i)–(ii) are correct—sometimes they are not, as Gettier-type problems show—but rather: *if* they are sometimes correct, when they are, what happens, from an information-theoretic perspective, when Alice is also responsible for the system S to be in the state modelled (captured, described, fitted, represented, ...) by p? In other words, what is the informational analysis of the so-called maker's knowledge, if we start from (i)–(ii)? Let me add a further clarification. I do not intend to reconstruct a chapter in the history of epistemology or philosophical

---

[1] This clause is added for any reader who does not hold the veridicality thesis according to which p qualifies as semantic information only if p is true. I follow Grice and Dretske in defending the veridicality thesis for reasons explained in Floridi (2007) and (2011c). Therefore, throughout this chapter, agents deal with (true) information, not with content that they take to be true, i.e. information, as in Gerbrandy and Groeneveld (1997).

[2] Throughout the chapter I write 'information p' not 'information that p' in order to indicate that p is the information (informational content) in question, communicated by a message. The reader unhappy with this solution is welcome to disregard it and add a 'that'.

[3] See Floridi (2011c). For a theory of truth that fits well with the veridicality thesis, see Floridi (2010c); for a theory of accounting for semantic information, based on network theory, that fits both, see Floridi (2012b).

logic, from Plato, through Bacon, Hobbes, and Vico, all the way to Kant and neo-Kantian philosophy.[4] What I intend to investigate is whether and, if so, how the maker's knowledge that p may informationally differ both from the observer's (witness's) knowledge that p—that is, Bob observing Alice interacting with the world (more on this soon)—and from the knowledge that p enjoyed by a receiver of the information p who does not observe that p, that is, Carol, who receives a message from Bob about Alice interacting with the world.

I suggest that the previous question may be answered more easily if we rely on a simple scenario constituted by a game based on six conditions:

1. a system S that changes. The easiest solution is to use an S with some simple, clear, and fully accessible and controllable transition states (although it could be just any empirical state of the world, continuous or discrete). Note that the chosen system is not (always) deterministic. Its behaviour must be contingent in order for the agent really to be the maker of a new state: there must be some causal connection related to the choices that the maker can exercise;
2. an agent who changes S. This is Alice the maker;
3. a change[5] in S, from S_1 to S_2, brought about by Alice. This is s;
4. a message that conveys p, where p, the informational content of the message, is that s has occurred. This is m;
5. an agent who does not bring about but observes s. This is Bob the observer (or witness);
6. an agent who does not bring about or observe s, but receives the information p. This is Carol the receiver, to whom Bob communicates p through m.

An example from chess provides all we need to build our simple example:

1. S: chess game
2. Alice: the white player
3. s: white King's pawn moved two steps by Alice
4. m: the move s communicated (e.g. by voice) in English notation by Bob to Carol
5. p: the true propositional content, or information, e2–e4
6. Bob: the black player, who observes Alice's move s and sends m to Carol
7. Carol: the receiver of m.

Figure 29 shows the move on the chessboard made by Alice.

Alice has made the move, and Bob has seen her making the move and communicates the move to Carol, who is in another room, by sending her m, the message that conveys the information p. In the end, all three agents hold the information p. Recall now that we started by assuming a bipartite analysis of knowledge, as comprising an information component and an account component. If Alice's knowledge is different from Bob's

---

[4] On this see Floridi (2011a).
[5] In the literature on dynamic epistemic logic this is sometimes qualified as an 'ontic' or 'factual' change.

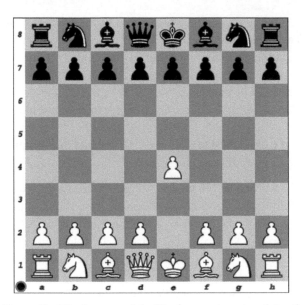

Figure 29 Alice has moved the King's pawn two steps (e2–e4)

and Carol's then only three possibilities present themselves: because of (i), because of (ii), or because of both, that is

(a) because Alice's *information p* (or about *s*)[6] is different;
(b) or because Alice's *account* for *p* (or *s*) is different;
(c) or because *both* (a) and (b).

I shall argue that (b) is the correct answer: it is the logical nature of the maker's account that differs, not the maker's information (the propositional content *p*). We shall see that if (b) is the case, then this has important consequences.

2. Maker's Knowledge: Same Information

Let me first exclude the possibility that Alice's knowledge may differ from Bob's and Carol's knowledge because it comprises a different kind of information. It does not. Suppose the move e2–e4 has been made. And suppose we do not know who is who. We ask all three agents to join us in a different room and broadcast *m* to all of them. In this dynamic setting,[7] we know that Carol is the only agent whose epistemic status about *s*

---

[6] Note that I shall not develop two different analyses, one for a *de dicto* case (*p*; or that *p*) and one for a *de re* case (about *s*), since any relevant difference between the two would only make the line of reasoning more convoluted without adding any conceptual advantage. The reader is welcome to choose between a *de dicto* or a *de re* reading of the following arguments.

[7] Van Ditmarsch et al. (2007) is an outstanding presentation of dynamic epistemic logic that has influenced the ideas presented in this chapter.

can be upgraded.[8] This is because the other two agents, independently of who is Alice and who is Bob, will find m redundant, as they already hold p, regardless of who made the move and who saw the move being made. Yet now, if Alice and Bob have a different knowledge that p from Carol's, this cannot be because they have a different information p, so (a) cannot be the case and therefore (c) is also excluded. Holding the information p is a binary state: an agent either does or does not hold it, that is, in terms of a database, p is either recorded in it or not. If it is, it is the same p that occurs. So, if there is a difference between Alice's, Bob's, and Carol's knowledge that p, it cannot be in holding the information p. Either there is no difference, or something else must be playing a role. But we said that their epistemic states could differ only in terms of information or in terms of account. If there is a difference, this must be in the account that Alice, Bob, and Carol can provide of p. But is there a difference?

Consider Carol first. Recall that we broadcast m. At that point, all Carol has is the information p, nothing else. In short, Carol does not know that p, she is merely informed (holds the information) that p, because she has no account to provide (no justification, warrant, etc.) over and above the simple fact of having received m (we are excluding by design the possibility that she may appeal to Bob's reliability, for example). In more standard terminology, she believes that p, p is true, but she has no justification for p. So, the difference between Alice and Bob, on the one hand, and Carol, on the other, is indeed one of account, because Alice and Bob can provide one and Carol cannot.

Consider Alice and Bob next. They can both provide an account for p. A fundamental difference between their epistemic states—and one that, if necessary, further differentiates Alice's knowledge from Carol's—is that, if Bob holds the information p, then the *perceptual* conditions that make Bob informed that p—and that can provide him with the resources for an account for p, for example a reliable vision of s—are different from the making (henceforth *poietic*) conditions that make p true. This is an anti-idealist conclusion. Perceiving something to be the case is different from making that something be the case. Bob sees e2–e4 because it is true that 'e2–e4', but his seeing it does not make it true. Imagine Bob walks into the other room and communicates to Carol that 'e2–e4'. Thanks to Bob, Carol acquires the information p. Bob's information is the *sender's information*: he can send m conveying p because he already holds the information p; this is why our previous broadcasting was redundant for him. The further point is now that the truth of p is independent of the fact that Bob sends m: the assumption is indeed that p is true, but not because Bob sends m. Sending m conveying p does not make p true. If Bob had made a mistake and sent 'f2–f4' this too would not have

---

[8] To be precise, since this is now a case of common knowledge, Alice's and Bob's epistemic states are also updated with respect to their information about who is informed about who is informed about p (that is, everyone in the group is informed that p, everyone is informed that everyone is informed that p, and so on). However, this metaepistemic aspect is not relevant in this context and I shall disregard it.

made any difference to the chessboard. This is less trivial than it may seem. For one may object that there are some obvious counterexamples. There are cases in which Bob saying so makes it so, to put it bluntly. If Bob is Conan Doyle and sends the message 'Sherlock Holmes visited the Bodleian Library only once' to Carol, then his saying so makes it so, and hence, one may argue, Conan Doyle (our Bob) could become informed about s (or that p), just by sending the message m that p because his sending m makes s to be the case and hence makes p true.

The objection has some merit: performative cases in which one can 'do things with words' are indeed relevant. If Bob has the right kind of authority and states, in the right circumstances, that the new ship will be called 'Queen Mary', then the new ship's name does become 'Queen Mary' and he knows that too, and only because he said so. Yet the objection is misaddressed, because the counterexamples in question are actually special cases of maker's knowledge, which are possible because they are based on conventional rather than empirical knowledge. They do not show that Bob the observer can have the same empirical knowledge as Alice the maker. Rather, they show that Bob the observer can play the role of Bob the maker when his communicating that p brings about the s that makes p true, according to some conventions. If these cases did not deal with conventions but with empirical facts they would qualify as magical events or miracles, that is, cases in which, allegedly, language acquires an ontic power over its referents and enables one to make a factual difference in the world through special formulations. Yet communication can only bring about at most information change but never factual change, unless it is a performative communication. God is the only entity assumed to be such that sending a message m that p about an empirical fact s actually makes p true. It is knowledge by *fiat*: 'dixitque Deus fiat lux et facta est lux' ('And said God let there be light, and there was light', *Genesis* 1,3). This is why one important way of understanding God's omniscience is by attributing to God a maker's knowledge of the universe, that is, by relying on God's omnipotence.

Let us return to Alice. It is clear that the difference between her knowledge and Bob's is that, in her case, if she is informed about s, then the experiential conditions that make Alice informed that p are the same *poietic* conditions that make p true. This is a constructionist conclusion. In the maker's knowledge case, *poiesis* (making s happen) and *alethization* (making p about s true) are two sides of the same coin. Alice is not merely the sender of the information that p, she is the source of the referent of p.[9] But then, does her account of p differ from Bob's?

---

[9] As David Watson has rightly remarked commenting on a previous version of this chapter, perhaps one could use something like Kripke's causal theory of reference to expand this dichotomy into a semantic direction, interpreting Alice's *poiesis* in a way akin to an 'initial baptism', except she inaugurates some state of affairs rather than a name.

3. Maker's Knowledge: Different Account

To understand how Alice's account (and hence her ensuing knowledge) that p may differ from Bob's it is useful to rely on the three classic distinctions that can be used to qualify a truth:

- (a) necessary vs. contingent
- (b) analytic vs. synthetic
- (c) a priori vs. a posteriori

Such a reliance is not meant to be uncritical. The reader will know too well that the tenability of each couple has been challenged, especially (b)[10] and (c).[11] What I am asking from the reader is only a conditional acceptance. *If* (or perhaps more optimistically *insofar* as) such distinctions can be reliably and usefully adopted in some cases, then I hope the reader will be willing to concede that they fully apply to Alice's, Bob's, and Carol's knowledge that the King's pawn has moved two steps. I do not wish to argue, for example, that we should disregard Quine's or Williamson's criticisms and accept (b) or (c) as perfectly fine. What I intend to show is that, *if* we are ready to use such distinctions as sufficiently unproblematic in some cases, then 'e2–e4' is one of them, and yet more work needs to be done, for a further distinction needs to be introduced in order to explain how Alice, who enjoys a maker's knowledge that p, can account for p differently from Bob and Carol. Let us see why.

It seems clear that Alice's knowledge about s (or that p) is synthetic, not analytic, and contingent, not necessary. This is due to the fact that the truth (i.e. information) in question, 'e2–e4', is synthetic and contingent, and that we assume that such properties are inherited by the knowledge of such truth. As they write in logic textbooks, the rest of the argument can be left as an exercise. But is Alice's knowledge a priori or a posteriori? This is tricky. The distinction has undergone many interpretations since its Kantian formulation. Here, I am happy to adopt a fairly orthodox understanding, well represented in standard introductions to philosophical logic. Many would do. The following comes from David Papineau's excellent book *Philosophical Devices*, which formulates it in terms of kinds of knowledge, exactly what we need in this context:

This distinction [between a priori and a posteriori truths] is to do with *kinds of knowledge* [my italics]. . . . A true statement is a priori if it can be known prior to experience of the facts. In principle, you can figure out an a priori truth just by sitting in an armchair with your eyes shut and thinking hard. The most obvious examples of a priori truths are analytic truths. Anybody

---

[10] For a careful review of the debate and a defence of the tenability of the distinction against Quine's arguments see Russell (2008). On Quine's arguments based on the indeterminacy thesis I follow Pagin (2008). A very useful reconstruction of the history of the distinction in Kant and its role in his philosophy is provided by Anderson (2015).

[11] For two excellent analyses to which I am indebted see Casullo (2013) and Jenkins and Kasaki (2015); see also Casullo and Thurow (2013 and forthcoming).

who understands the statement triangles have three sides won't need to examine any physical triangle to know that this statement is true.... A true statement is a posteriori if it can only be known as a result of relevant experience. Blackbirds eat worms is an example of an a posteriori truth. There is no way of finding out that this statement is true without making observations.

(Papineau 2012, p. 46)

Consider Alice's knowledge that 'e2–e4' in light of the previous distinction.

On the one hand, it does not seem to be a posteriori, at least not in the same sense in which Bob's is. For Alice has a perfectly simple 'way of finding out that this statement is true without making observations', and that is by moving the pawn. If this is unclear, or seems an extraordinary case, consider another simple scenario. Alice is alone in the kitchen. She makes some coffee for Bob and puts two spoons of sugar in it. Bob comes in the kitchen and wishes to know whether the coffee has been sweetened. He can only know that a posteriori, 'as a result of relevant experience', as Papineau puts it: by tasting the coffee or by asking Alice (the latter would be a case represented by Carol, in our chess example, i.e. knowledge through communication rather than empirical experience). Yet Alice does not need to taste the coffee in order to know the truth of the statement 'the coffee has been sweetened'. Barring any sceptical scenario, Gettierization, or empirical mistake,[12] *if* Alice knows that 'e2–e4' then her account for the fact that 'e2–e4' or that 'the coffee has been sweetened' is acquired *through* experience as *interaction*,[13] but not *following* experience as *perception*; whereas Bob's knowledge is acquired *by* experience as perception, that is, by observing the world without changing it; and Carol's knowledge is acquired by *proxy* experience as *communication*. Alice changes the world and insofar as she succeeds (and we assume that she does, because we assumed that she knows) this is how she knows the world is.

On the other hand, Alice's knowledge may seem to be a priori, insofar as this is simply a negation of a posteriori. Yet this too does not seem to be entirely satisfactory. Admittedly, her knowledge that the King's pawn has moved two steps—*if* it is knowledge (and we assume that it is)—is based on the fact that she meant to move it that way and succeeded in doing so—again, her success is not in question, it is assumed by hypothesis—and this is the source of the kind of account (justification, in more ordinary epistemological vocabulary) that she can provide. For example, to the question how does she know that the pawn has moved two steps, she could simply answer that she moved it herself, and that she did so because of a particular strategy. Likewise, if she knows that the coffee has been sweetened she does so, in terms of having an account for her information, *somehow* (more on this crucial qualification presently), 'prior to

---

[12] These three issues are out of the question here by hypothesis. Recall that we are assuming that Alice does know that *p*; we are trying to understand in which way, if any, her knowledge differs from Bob's, who is also assumed to know that *p*.

[13] As a consequence, the position defended in this chapter is compatible with a reliabilist epistemology of justification that does not reject the a priori vs. a posteriori distinction; see Grundmann (2015).

experience of the facts' (to quote Papineau again), the sort of experience that Bob requires in order to know that the coffee has been sweetened; or *in advance, so to speak* (again, more on this presently), because that was her plan and she successfully carried it out. In a more standard vocabulary, *p* is true, Alice believes that *p*, and she is justified in believing that *p* because (or, equivalently: her justification is based on the fact that) she is the one who brought about the truth of *p* (made *p* true) in the first place. However, it also seems clear that her knowledge of 'e2–e4' is different from Carol's a priori knowledge that 'the pawn that was moved was either black or white', which requires no interactive or observational experience to be acquired. To use Papineau's analysis once more, in principle, Carol having been told that a pawn has been moved, she can figure out that the moved pawn is either black or white by sitting in an armchair with her eyes shut and thinking hard, by merely knowing the rules of chess. Alice's information about *s* is the source's (not merely the sender's) information: it is synthetic, contingent, and not a posteriori. But it is a priori only in a *weaker sense* (again, more on this presently) than the one usually described in textbooks. In order to provide an account of *s*, Alice does not need to consult experience at all. Actually, her account for making *s* the case comes logically before *p* being true. She might want to refer, for example, to a particular opening strategy that she intends to pursue by making that move, and predict that the world will be such as to satisfy the truth of 'e2–e4', by executing her action plan.

One may object that making *s* happen and therefore being informed that *p* because of such a making is intertwined with the perception that one is making *s* happen. This is correct. Alice also enjoys the same knowledge that Bob has, insofar as she is also an observer of her own move. This means that Alice may no longer see clearly whether she knows that *p* because she made *s* happen (because of her interaction with the world) or because she perceived herself making *s* happen (because of her perception of the world and her interaction with it). In our example, the solution is to decouple making *s* happen and perceiving oneself making *s* happen. For example, Alice may control Bob's chessboard remotely (correspondence chess). If she knows that Bob's chessboard is in state *s*, then this is so even if she cannot perceive herself making a difference to it.

Let me summarize what conclusions we have reached so far.

First, Alice (the maker) enjoys the same synthetic and contingent information about *s* as Bob and Carol do. The difference among the three agents is not one in terms of different kinds of information (or different kinds of beliefs, or different kinds of propositional contents, to use a more textbook vocabulary). Perhaps this explains epistemology's disinterest in the maker's knowledge tradition. In terms of kinds of information (the *what* is hold not the *how* or the *why*), there is no distinction, so there is no interesting theory to develop about this.

Second, it seems that Alice's knowledge is also *not* a posteriori, at least not in the same sense in which Bob's and Carol's is, because she also enjoys a source's *weak* (a full qualification still pending) a priori account for the information about *s* that she brings about, which both Bob the observer and Carol the receiver of Bob's message lack by definition. Perhaps this explains logic's disinterest in the maker's knowledge tradition:

Since DEL [dynamic epistemic logic] is mostly about information change due to communication, the model transformations usually do not involve factual change. The bare physical facts of the world remain unchanged, but the agents' information about the world changes. In terms of Kripke models that means that the accessibility relations of the agents have to change (and consequently the set of states of the model might change as well). Modal operators in dynamic epistemic languages denote these model transformations.

(van Ditmarsch et al. 2015, pp. 1–2)

The case in which Alice brings about a change in the system is similar to the case in which Alice assigns a particular value to a state of the world. Factual or ontic changes can be modelled by epistemic dynamic logics that include assignment operators in the language for epistemic actions.[14] However, such logics investigate the informational implications of such changes for the agents involved, not what it means for the agent who brings about the change to be able to account for it. In particular, public assignments are such that the whole group of agents is aware of the factual change—compare this to the case in which Alice moves the pawn and both her and Bob then hold the new information that the pawn has been moved—whereas atomic assignments are such that only facts are changed, independently of whether (or which) agents are informed about such changes—compare this to the case in which Alice sweetens the coffee but Bob does not know about it.

The outcome of the previous two points is that a maker's knowledge looks like a hybrid: synthetic and contingent information + a weak a priori account. Is there room for this poietic knowledge in the overall map of distinctions logically available? The answer is yes but, in order to clarify how, I need to add a further conceptual distinction and finally explain what I mean above by 'somehow', 'weak', and 'in a sense'.

4. Maker's Knowledge: *ab anteriori*

Since at least Kant, philosophers have been implicitly using information, and its cognate terms, as the neutral vocabulary to discuss the nature of the three classic couples introduced above. Information has played the role of the least common denominator through which all other epistemic currencies have been related to one another. Or, to use a different metaphor, information has played the role of the perfect butler in an Oxford college: does all the conceptual work impeccably but also invisibly. If we acknowledge information's key role and bring its conceptual contribution to light by formulating it explicitly, in terms of whether a truth is also informative or not, over and above whether it shares any of the other three features, the result is the mapping presented in Figure 30. Bear in mind that the table has a twofold goal: it clarifies the

---

[14] The classic reference is van Ditmarsch et al. (2005); see also van Benthem et al. (2006).

	a	b	c	d	e	f	g	h	i[143]	l	m	n	o	p	q	r
	C					Kr			Ka	A	In				B	C
Analytic	1	1	1	1	1	1	1	1	0	0	0	0	0	0	0	0
A priori	1	1	1	1	0	0	0	0	1	1	1	1	0	0	0	0
Necessary	1	1	0	0	1	1	0	0	1	1	0	0	1	1	0	0
Uninformative	1	0	1	0	1	0	1	0	1	0	1	0	1	0	1	0

	a	b	c	d	e	f	g	h	i	l	m	n	o	p	q	r
Synthetic	0	0	0	0	0	0	0	0	1	1	1	1	1	1	1	1
A posteriori	0	0	0	0	1	1	1	1	0	0	0	0	1	1	1	1
Contingent	0	0	1	1	0	0	1	1	0	0	1	1	0	0	1	1
Informative	0	1	0	1	0	1	0	1	0	1	0	1	0	1	0	1

Figure 30 Mapping the four conceptual distinctions

various positions one can take on the dichotomies, as well as showing what happens if the a priori vs. a posteriori dichotomy is extended to map the couple informative vs. uninformative explicitly.

A few comments are in order. We have sixteen possible combinations.[15] Columns **a** and **r** represent the classic positions. They also represent Carol's predicament. Carol's knowledge of the moves being played in the other room is either analytic, a priori, necessary, but also uninformative, that is, it is entirely and only based on her knowledge of the rules of the game (e.g. she knows that white moves first, and that, after that move, black moves); or it is synthetic, a posteriori, contingent, and informative, yet this is the case only when she receives a message from Bob. Interestingly, the classic, pre-Kantian position and Carol's (the message-receiver's) position are the same, hence the single label C. Centuries before Shannon and any mathematical theory of communication, Francis Bacon's concept of vexation of nature, for example, already fit very well with C, and this was because classic epistemology is largely based on a passive, message-receiving model of information gathering, no matter whether one is in Plato's cave or in front of Descartes' fire. Note also that column **a**, obtained by adding 'uninformativeness' as an explicit feature of a truth, is the source of the scandal of deduction, as Hintikka labelled it: mathematical truths seem to be analytic, a priori, necessary, but also uninformative.[16]

---

[15] An interesting question, to be left unanswered in this chapter, is whether some combinations are provably impossible.

[16] The reader interested in knowing more about the scandal of deduction may wish to read D'Agostino and Floridi (2009).

Column **n** was popular among Platonists and some modern defenders of innate truths, hence the label In. Both C and In were challenged by Kant, to make room for the synthetic a priori (column **l**). Whether this is successful is open to debate ('to say the least', a critic may add). More recently, Kripke's analysis made room for the analytic a posteriori (column **f**). The debates on **l** and **f** are still lively. From Figure 30 it is easy to see how Kant and Kripke hold inverted positions with respect to the synthetic–analytic and a posteriori–a priori nature of the truths in question. Two assumptions shared by Kant and Kripke, and indeed by the debate on the synthetic a priori and the analytic a posteriori, are that:

- the truths in question are informative (they say something about how the world is, e.g. the chess move, or the state of the coffee) and
- a single agent holds such truths.

The latter point is crucial. Whether it is the Cartesian Ego, the transcendental subject, or an ideal, abstract knower, the assumption is that what is predicated of one holder can be predicated of any holder of such truths. Concentrating only on a single, epistemic agent is fine, insofar as the couple necessary vs. contingent and analytic vs. synthetic are concerned. This is so because we saw that these properties qualify the nature of the truths in question first, and then the nature of the knowledge of them. But a monoagent approach is insufficient when it comes to the other two couples, for at least two main reasons.

First, because different epistemic agents may have different ways of accessing a truth, and I mean this in principle, irrespective of individual idiosyncrasies. We saw that our three abstract and idealized epistemic agents Alice, Bob, and Carol have different ways of accessing the same information 'e2–e4': *through* experience (by making *s* to be the case), *by* experience (by observing that *s* is the case), and *by proxy* experience (by being communicated that *s* is the case). The epistemology of trust, witnessing, and testimony, for example, hinges on the distinction between Alice's and Bob's knowledge that 'e2–e4' on the one hand, and Carol's knowledge on the other.

And second, because whether a truth—which is informational about the world, that is, it tells one something about how the world is—is also informative—that is, it tells one something *new* about how the world is—depends on the epistemic status of the epistemic agent, and this may vary from Alice, to Bob, to Carol, again in principle, not in terms of contingent idiosyncrasies. We saw that broadcasting *m* does not upgrade Alice's or Bob's epistemic status. Neither the source nor the sender of the message *m* are informed by *m*; only the receiver can be. Likewise, being the agent that brings about *s* that makes *p* true means having a different access to the truth of *p* from that enjoyed by an agent who merely observes that *p* (more on this presently). Thus, adopting a multiagent perspective and accepting that different agents may have different kinds of access to the same truth enables one to make sense of several other columns in Figure 30. In particular, one can see that Bob's position is represented by **q**. For Bob, who saw the move, the truth 'e2–e4' is synthetic, a posteriori, contingent, but also uninformative, as uninformative as 'bachelors are unmarried men'. His correct reaction, if we were to tell him 'look, Alice moved the King's white pawn from e2 to e4', would be 'I know, I saw it, you are not telling me anything new'. The *synthetic uninformative* characterizes all messages that an epistemic agent receives about states of the world that such an epistemic agent has already witnessed directly. They belong to the logic of communication (redundancy) and confirmation, but not to the logic of informativeness. A crucial clarification is in order here.[17]

An interesting limitation of dynamic epistemic logic is that it is typically presented as a logic of communication, but does not in fact have any explicit way of talking about the 'source' of a message. Strictly speaking, the senders are outside the system, and can only be simulated through the content of the message. In our example, if Bob informs Carol that *p*, this will be modelled as a message that says that Bob knows *p*, yet this message could equally well be sent by an outsider. A corollary of this feature is that observations can be modelled in exactly the same way (a message sent by the system, rather than by an observer of the system). This is very clear in puzzles like that of the wise men or the muddy children (Floridi 2005a). A result of this limitation is that (when seen through the eyes of DEL) the difference between how Bob and Carol came to know that *p* becomes purely temporal: the difference in account/access is merely a difference in who got the information first. On the one hand, this does not pose a problem for the position defended in this chapter; it is just more evidence in favour of the fact that a pure logic of information cannot be used to distinguish between knowledge acquired by observation and knowledge acquired by testimony. On the other hand, the focus on the 'uninformative' makes the (undesirable) temporal reading very plausible. Let me stress that the core difference here is between messages from the system (i.e. observation) and messages from other observers of the system (i.e. communication in the intuitive sense). This is why I wrote 'already witnessed *directly*'. To anticipate: in the commutative diagram in Figure 31, observation matches vertical (model-to-system) arrows, but communication matches horizontal (model-to-model) arrows.

Finally, we can make sense of Alice's (the maker's) knowledge, in terms of column **m** in Figure 30. By drawing a distinction between a priori and a posteriori as if the two were a binary, mutually exclusive couple, we miss the fact that quite a lot happens between the two, neither *before* nor *after* but *through* experience.[18] There is no technical term for the somewhat weak a priori knowledge that *p* enjoyed by an agent responsible for bringing about the truth of *p*. So, I shall use *ab anteriori* to refer to such a third space. We are now ready for a definition:

> The maker's knowledge is *ab anteriori knowledge*. A contingent, synthetic proposition *p* about *s* (the information *p*) is an ab anteriori truth if and only if it can be known by interacting with *s* to make *p* true.

---

[17] I am most grateful to Patrick Allo for this point and its precise formulation because, left implicit, it may mislead more than one reader.
[18] For similar lines of criticism see Jenkins (2008) and Casullo (2013).

In principle, you can figure out an *ab anteriori truth* just by changing the world so that it makes the relevant statement true (it fits it). We saw that among the most obvious examples of ab anteriori truths are performatives, understood in the way Searle (1989) does, not Austin. Anybody who understands the statement 'you are fired' uttered successfully will not need to check any facts to know how the world has changed accordingly, and hence that this statement is true. Note that, given the previous definition, any contingent, synthetic information the truth of which cannot be brought about by interacting with the system it refers to can be a priori, if Kant is correct, or must be a posteriori, if Kant is wrong.

The last step to be taken is to provide a clear representation of Alice's ab anteriori knowledge. To do this I shall borrow and adapt the concept of a commutative diagram from category theory. Consider Figure 31.

On the right side of the diagram, Bob observes the system as it (ontically or factually) changes (m) from S_1 to S_2, and he updates informationally his model M_1, which forward-fits (g) S_1, into his model M_2, which forward-fits (g) S_2. Bob's access commutes: $m \circ g = g \circ l$. His side of the diagram can be translated into a standard Kripke model in dynamic epistemic logic.

Insofar as Alice is also an observer of the same transition, she has the same epistemic access to $m \circ g = g \circ l$ that Bob has. However, on the left side of the diagram, Alice the maker observes the system as it (ontically or factually) implements (h) the virtual system V_2 (e.g. the possible move e2–e4) into the system S_2 (in our example, the actual state of the chessboard after her e2–e4 move) thanks to her interactions, and she updates informationally her blueprint (recall that a blueprint is a model of something that does not yet exist but that we want to design or create, or implement; in our example, her strategy to move e2–e4) B_2, which forward-fits V_2 and backward-fits[19] (k)

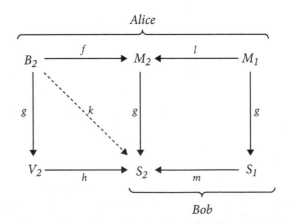

Figure 31 Commutative diagram for the maker's and the witness's knowledge

---

[19] I use 'backward-fits' to indicate that a blueprint is a project that fits a system that does not exist but that will exist if the blueprint is implemented. A model is a project that forward-fits a system that already exists.

S_2, into her model M_2, which forward-fits (g) S_2. Alice's information still commutes: $h \circ g = k = g \circ f$. The difference is that now she has a maker's access to S_2 that Bob cannot have, and can account for the information p in a way that is unavailable to Bob. Finally, the reader may recall the case in which Alice was playing correspondence chess with Bob. This is represented by Alice having access only to the left side of the diagram, not the right side.

Conclusion: Some Consequences of the Analysis of the Maker's Knowledge

By way of conclusion, let me now highlight a few interesting consequences of the previous analysis.

1. It seems clear that references to experience in terms of dependence-independence or before–after, from Kant onwards, are too coarsely grained when it comes to understanding the 'riority' (a priori, a posteriori, ab anteriori) of a truth. For in Carol's case we are talking of experience socially and in terms of communication, as trust in testimony; in Bob's case, we are talking of experience epistemically, in terms of perception; and in Alice's case, we are talking about experience pragmatically, in terms of interaction. These are different senses, which explain why we need more than the equally coarsely grained dichotomy between a priori and a posteriori. For it depends on what kind of experience plays which role, and in which logical order. In more technical terms, we need a better level of abstraction lest the *ab anteriority* of the maker's knowledge escapes our analysis.

2. The definition of what counts as maker's knowledge provides us with a criterion to identify who is the maker in a group of agents, that is, it enables us to identify who plays Alice. For we can exclude first all the agents whose information state can be upgraded by broadcasting the truth in question, and then all the remaining agents whose account for the truth in question can only be based on perceptual experience. If anyone is left, that is the maker. Observations in science may seem to admit no makers, and the passive tradition in epistemology, according to which epistemic agents are mere observers of the world, finds some roots in this, but much of modern and contemporary science is actually interactive— think for example of CERN's main function, which is to provide the particle accelerators and other infrastructure needed for high-energy physics research— and requires a better understanding of the maker's knowledge.

3. We saw that neither Alice nor Bob can be informed by m and this is consistent with an analysis of perception in which the mutual information—in the technical sense of the expression (see Cover and Thomas 2006)—between the state of the system (e.g. pawn moved) and the information about that state (e.g. e2–e4) is 1. I have explored this point in Floridi (2014b).

4. Note that Alice need not be informed about the fact that she is informed about s. The fact that the analysis developed in the previous pages does not require the acceptance of the KK (or in this context II) thesis (aka S4, K3, or the reflective thesis about positive introspection), namely $\Box\varphi \rightarrow \Box\Box\varphi$, is consistent with the modal logic KTB (aka B), which I have argued, in Floridi (2006), may be suitable as a logic for 'S holds the information p'.

5. The consistency of the previous analysis with KTB does not preclude the possibility of $\Box\Box\varphi$. On the contrary, the message m can work as a trigger for both Alice and Bob to make possible, and indeed facilitate, $\Box\Box\varphi$. I have defended this possibility in terms of a double-channel explanation of KK (or II) in Floridi (2006).

6. Bob and Carol are both outside the system producing s and hence making e2–e4 true. Alice is part of the system. As the ontic or factual source of s, Alice holds the information p as part of the system that brings about s. It follows that the maker's knowledge is knowledge of a system from within, not from without, consistent with the Aristotelian view that 'scientia est scire per causas'. This too is in stark contrast with the passive view we inherit from some modern epistemology, and especially from the Cartesian tradition, which is based on a receptive perception of the world, rather than design, intervention, interaction, and control. The problem emerged in nineteenth-century German philosophy of technology, which correctly criticized Kant precisely because of his inability to see that, through technology, agents create, design, and manipulate objects in themselves, not just their phenomenal perceptions. When Alice eats an apple, she eats a noumenal something, whatever else that something may be in itself. Likewise, when she builds an Ikea table, she is building a noumenal something, whatever else that something may be in itself.

7. When only the observer's knowledge is possible, Nature replaces Alice. Imagine the case in which the wind moves the pawn two steps. Teleological interpretations of Nature (or God) the Maker tend to look for the ultimate blueprint of the universe.

8. Most of classic epistemology has focused on a single agent. This is fine, but too restrictive in a world that needs to understand how knowledge and information work within multiagent systems. The previous analysis shows how different even our most fundamental distinctions appear, once we introduce a multiagent perspective.

9. We saw that Alice's ability to give a maker's account of p is based on her ability to remember that she brought about the change in the system modelled by p. This means that it should not be analysed as if it were similar to a Markov chain because it is not 'memoryless': Alice's model of the future state of the system does not depend only on relevant information about the current time, but also on information about its past states. In other words, ab anteriori knowledge is necessarily historical.

10. In ethics (volume two of the tetralogy, Floridi 2013b), I have tried to show that standard approaches are concerned with the source/agent of the action when in fact greater emphasis should be placed on the receiver/patient. In epistemology (volume one of the tetralogy, Floridi 2011c), I have tried to show that standard approaches are concerned with the receiver/observer, when in fact more emphasis should be placed on the source/maker. Relying on the chess example one last time: in ethics, we should be more concerned with the black, while in epistemology we should be more concerned with the white.

We have now come to the very last chapter of this book, where I shall deal with the question: if all the story told so far is plausible, is there a logic of design? And what may be its relation to the logic of information?

10

The Logic of Design as a Conceptual Logic of Information

Summary

Previously, in Chapters 1 and 2, I argued that philosophy could fruitfully be interpreted as conceptual design. In Chapter 3, I offered a constructionist view of such conceptual design in terms of non-naturalism. There I anticipated that more needed to be done on the logic of design. The need for such a logic became pressing in the last chapter, in which I supported a poietic interpretation of our knowledge. The maker's knowledge needs a logic of 'making', that is, a logic of design of the semantic artefacts for which we are epistemically responsible. Thus, in this last chapter, I outline a logic of design of a system as a specific kind of conceptual logic of the design of the model of a system, that is, the blueprint that provides information about the system to be created. In section 1, I use the method of levels of abstraction—introduced in Chapter 2—to clarify that we have inherited from modernity two main conceptual logics of information understood as logics of modelling systems: Kant's *transcendental logic* of *conditions of possibility* of a system, and Hegel's *dialectical logic* of *conditions of in/stability* of a system. Both conceptual logics of information are useful to analyse structural properties of given systems. Therefore, both are implicitly used by many disciplines. Yet I shall argue that, strictly speaking, neither is by nature a conceptual logic of information about (or modelling) the *conditions of feasibility* of a system, that is, neither is a logic of information as a logic of design, even though they have been repurposed to fulfil such a task, partly because they easily lend themselves to this, and partly because they were the only conceptual logics available. A logic of design is a third conceptual logic that is still missing and needs to be developed.[1] Thus, in section 3, I outline this third conceptual logic of information and then interpret the conceptual logic of design as a logic of *requirements*, by introducing the relation of 'sufficientization'. In the conclusion, I shall argue that the logic of requirements is exactly what we need to make sense of, and buttress, a constructionist approach to how we model systems informationally, that is, a shift from a representation-alist (*mimetic*) to a constructionist (*poietic*) understanding of knowledge. Accordingly, this last chapter can also be read as a call to action for, and a first stepping-stone in the

---

[1] As excellent, indeed now classic, examples see Munari (1971), Arup (2012), Norman (2013). For more recent case-based studies see Buurman and Rölli (2016).

direction of, the full articulation of a conceptual logic of design in general, so that we may go beyond practitioners' rules of thumb and recipes for best practices.[2]

1. Introduction: Two Modern Conceptual Logics of Information

When we analyse a system, what kind of structural level of abstraction (LoA) could we adopt? A simple taxonomy may be given in terms of a past-oriented, present-oriented, and, as we shall see, future-oriented approach (let me warn the reader that what follows contains significant simplifications, some probably controversial).

Imagine that one is interested in understanding the genesis of a system, how it came to be, or what brought it about. This is the purpose orienting the choice of LoAs. One then focuses on modelling the *conditions of possibility* of a system under investigation (Figure 32). This is clearly a past-oriented approach, consistent with causal, genetic, or genealogical forms of reasoning that lead to a particular modelling or conceptualization

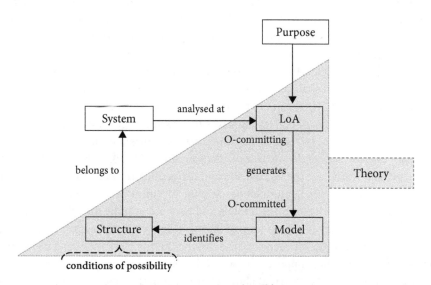

Figure 32 Transcendental logic

[2] This is not a new invitation. In Simon (1996, pp. 121–5), Herbert Simon discusses 'The Logic of Design'. Simon acknowledges that First Order Logic (FOL) does not deliver what is needed. However, his approach moves towards a logic of design as heuristics, i.e. a logic of searching for 'candidates' for a good solution, within a space of possible worlds in which a variety of solutions for a problem is available. As the reader will see, in this chapter I share the same view about FOL, but I take a different direction, in favour of a logic of design in terms of a logic of requirements. The two approaches are not incompatible and probably complementary. To put it simply, in a personal discussion with Simon at Carnegie Mellon, we agreed that his interest was in a logic that would help to identify the right answers, whereas mine was, and still is, in a logic that would help to design the right questions.

of reality, with the identification of necessary and (perhaps) jointly sufficient conditions, with investigations about what must have been the case for something else to be the case. The approach goes hand in hand with an interest in the natural sciences, or any discipline that tries to mimic their logic. One looks at a system and tries to understand what brought it about. As the reader may have already guessed, this conceptual logic finds its roots in Kant's transcendental logic.

It is tempting, and far from impossible, to use Kant's transcendental logic as a logic of construction as design. I mentioned above the compatibility between the natural sciences and Kant's transcendental logic, but the latter has also been employed in jurisprudence, for example, in order to look at normative systems in terms of ideal or hypothetical conditions of construction of a system. This is not an incorrect repurposing of it, but it does stretch its nature. It is true that the reasoning that takes one from a system to its conditions of possibility can also be adopted to move from the conditions of possibility (now to be understood as requirements of feasibility) to the system itself. But while the former move is univocal, the latter is not, unless one of the two following conditions is satisfied, each of which is problematic. Either one already knows what system one is going to obtain anyway, and so it is actually begging the question. Or the system is entirely constrained by its conditions of possibility, which now become both necessary and jointly sufficient to deliver it. In this case, the assumption is that the transcendental conditions constrain the issuing system univocally. This is unlikely to say the least, because it hardly ever happens. Just think of the requirements prompting the design of a house. I shall come back to this limit case of design below, when I shall define it as 'degenerate' (in the mathematical sense of the word already encountered in Chapter 2). For the time being, let me stress that such a degenerate approach seems implicitly adopted by Kant and neo-Kantians of various orientations. The issue may be explained with an analogy. If you have a cake, you can backtrack to the ingredients and the recipe, but if you have the ingredients and the recipe they may lead to a variety of cakes, because there can be quite a lot of room for variations, and the cake you started from is unlikely to be the only one feasible and may not even be the best, or the most interesting, in terms of full exploitation of the ingredients and the recipe itself. In Kant, it is the univocal relation between conditions of possibility of a system and its requirements of feasibility that supports the whole transcendental project. And this is so because Kant is mainly concerned about guaranteeing the objectivity of knowledge even when knowledge is no longer representational. Kant cannot ground the univocal nature of knowledge ('this is what the world looks like') on the univocal nature of the reality it refers to ('this is the way the world is') because this is a strategy open to representationalism but not to constructivism. So, he replaces the latter with the univocal genesis and relationship knowledge enjoys in its encounter with the world. The set of ingredients plus the recipe lead to only one cake and that cake leads back to only one recipe and set of ingredients. Likewise, in Kelsen's (1967) *Pure Theory of Law*, for example, the crucial concept of *basic norm* (*Grundnorm*) seems to play a twofold role.

It is used to refer to the basic order or rule that forms an underlying basis for a legal system understood as a hierarchical relationship of norms, akin to a first principle or axiom. It therefore works as a point of origin or source for all law, which obtains legitimacy from it. Yet it remains inevitably ambiguous whether the *Grundnorm* and the issuing construction is an *as-if* model of how the law that exists may be reconstructed, in closer similarity to a transcendental analysis, or a hypothetical blueprint of how the law that may, but does not yet, exist should be constructed. The tension is unresolvable because the two interpretations look at the same road, from system to model and from model (now blueprint) to system. Thus, from a 'degenerate' analysis, the answer is that the *Grundnorm* is both a blueprint and a model. But this solution is challenged by the fact that, historically, there is a recursive relation between the blueprint for the design of a system that is then analysed by a model that turns into a blueprint for a new system, and so forth. I shall return to the recursive nature of any design process in section 3. For now, what I am suggesting here is that we should take the univocity of the transcendental as problematic, indeed untenable in most cases, and probably in all interesting cases. Certainly the American pragmatists' view of the a priori and hence of the transcendental conditions of possibility of knowledge is already significantly not univocal.[3] In particular, I share C. I. Lewis' neo-Kantian 'conceptualistic pragmatism',[4] according to which empirical knowledge is the outcome of the exercise of the constructive activities of the mind on the data (Lewis' sensuous 'give') offered by the world, but the set of a priori concepts that are used in such a process are not only biologically determined, they are also the historical product of the knower's social and cognitive circumstances; pragmatically and not absolutely, contrary to Kant. In the vocabulary of this chapter, they are historical LoAs, which admit of alternatives and preferential choice, where the choice of the right LoAs (the right set of a priori concepts) depends on purpose-oriented, pragmatic considerations, and it is modifiable and hence improvable, depending on the success achieved. This means that, in Lewis, there is no equation of univocity. Once you socialize and historicize the transcendental—as we should here, given that the *method of abstraction* is driven by a contextually justified choice of purposes—it becomes very difficult to accept the Kantian equation:

$$[\text{conditions of possibility} = \text{requirements of feasibility}] \leftrightarrow [\text{designed system}]$$

in which one set of conditions works both as the set of conditions of possibility and as the set of conditions of feasibility to which only one designed system corresponds, and vice versa. The truth is that, in most design cases, the identity and the double implication

---

[3] See Rosenthal (1987).

[4] See Lewis (1929). As is clear from Chapter 3, I am utterly unconvinced by Lewis' later naturalism as presented in Lewis (1946) because it seems to me to exchange Kant's logical univocity for a biological, impoverished version that is even more controversial. Having freed the transcendental from its univocal relationship with the construct, Lewis seems to put it back inside a smaller cage of univocal relation with successful behaviour and planning. The point is that we should be more, not less Kantian than Kant, so to speak.

are hardly ever justified. Fortunately, instead of resolving the tension, it may be preferable to bypass it by sticking to the natural vocation of transcendental logic as a logic of re-construction. This becomes easier once a proper logic of design as construction becomes available, as I intend to show below. But before this, we need to look at another alternative.

One may wish to understand not the past genesis but the current (present-oriented) state of dynamics of a system. If this is the purpose orienting the choice of the LoA, then one does not look at what brought about the system, but focuses instead on modelling the *conditions of in/stability* of a (transition) system under investigation (Figure 33). This approach is consistent with polarized and procedural ways of reasoning, with the identification of contrasts and their resolutions (or lack thereof), with present-oriented analyses of processes (evolutions, developments), and mutual interactions. The approach goes hand in hand with an interest in the social and human sciences, especially economics, history, law, and political science, although the natural sciences have also been approached from this perspective, if with remarkable lack of persuasiveness (consider Marxist–Leninist analyses of scientific theories such as quantum mechanics). One looks at a system and tries to understand what dynamic equilibria keep it stable or unstable. In this case too, the reader may have already guessed that this conceptual logic finds its roots in Hegel's dialectics. As with transcendental logic, dialectics has been stretched to repurpose it as a logic of design, most famously by Marx. The outcome is unconvincing insofar as the state transitions of the system identified by the logic, for example a specific political organization of a society, are at the same time necessary and yet open to steering or influence. As in Kant, in Hegel too we deal with a logic of necessity: what must have been the case for the system

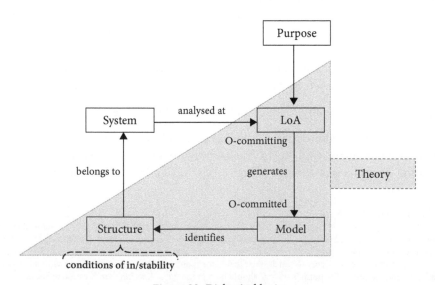

Figure 33 Dialectical logic

to be what it is, or what will have to be the case given that the system is what it is. In fact, design needs a logic of 'sufficiency', as I shall explain presently.

From the previous sketch it follows that modernity has been dominated by two main conceptual logics of information: Kant's and Hegel's. Both can be seen at work, methodologically, in philosophers such as Marx (Hegel) and Husserl (Kant). Yet they are not incompatible and can also easily be found interacting, for example in game theory. Indeed, part of the difficulty in understanding Foucault, for example, is due to the fact that his genealogical approach often switches between a transcendental and a dialectical conceptual logic of information.

Both conceptual logics model systems as something given, whether in the natural universe—as more significantly in Kant—or in human history—as more influentially in Hegel. Thus, both move from the system to the model, broadly understood as a description of (information about) it, looking for generalities and patterns. Both are constructionist in a broad sense of the term: they look at how a system came to be and its dynamics. One is then reminded that German idealism is among the most constructionist-friendly approaches in the history of philosophy. Yet strictly speaking neither is a conceptual logic of *construction as design*, which moves from the model— now understood as a *prescription* or *blueprint*—to its implementation, as a realized system that does not precede the model. That is, neither is in itself primarily a *logic of design*, although both have been stretched and repurposed to fulfil this role. In this case, the goal is to understand the future-oriented possibility of construction of the system. One then focuses on modelling the *conditions of feasibility* of the system under investigation (Figure 34). As I have argued in Chapter 9, one important consequence is that asking whether a logic of design is a priori or a posteriori means not having grasped the shift from *mimesis* to *poiesis*.[5] A designer's knowledge is a very significant case of what is known as the maker's knowledge. This is the sort of knowledge that Alice enjoys when she holds the information (true content) that Bob's coffee is sweetened because she just put two spoons of sugar in it herself, that is, because she designed the system that way. We saw that her knowledge is *contingent, synthetic, weakly* a priori (ab anteriori), and *uninformative*, in the technical sense that she cannot be informed about the sugar in the coffee by hearing a public announcement stating that there is sugar in the coffee. This is why I agree with Ammon (2017) that designing is not an empirical kind of experimenting (contrary to widespread methodological claims) but more an independent epistemic praxis through which one can acquire genuine *ab anteriori* knowledge.

The lack of a logic of design is not just a scholarly gap, or a source of over-interpretations of transcendental logic and dialectical logic in our philosophical reasoning. It is a particularly pressing problem because of a significant shift in how we prioritize forms of knowledge and the sciences in particular.

---

[5] The classic on *mimesis* is of course Auerbach (2003). I have introduced the idea of *homo poieticus* in Floridi (1999) and discussed it further in Floridi and Sanders (2005).

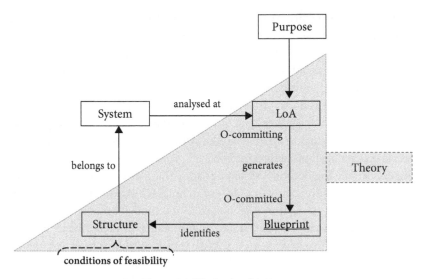

Figure 34 The logic of design

For a long time, and at least since Greek philosophy, our epistemic culture has privileged a *mimetic* view of knowledge and hence science as a description of reality, whether geometrical, physical, biological, chemical, or human, for example. Astronomy provided a kind of regulative ideal. For this reason, even nowadays, our philosophy of science tends to focus more on physics than on any other discipline. However, as our knowledge of reality has progressed and become more refined, as our need to investigate reality has increasingly relied on technology, experiments, and artefacts, and as our ability to create, control, and modify aspects of the world has grown, our epistemic outlook has become increasingly constructionist, that is, *poietic*. Today, it would be perfectly reasonable to say that the most influential sciences and scholarly disciplines that shape our world and our implicit, cultural understanding of it are architecture, computer science, economics, engineering, and law. They all do much more than just describe their objects; they actually contribute to construct them, and, in the case of engineering and computer science, empower other sciences to construct their own, through new artefacts, technologies, simulations, algorithms, and data-based research. *Poietic* as opposed to *mimetic* science relies on a conceptual logic of construction that does not start from the system to analyse it in terms of a model, but actually starts from the model (the blueprint) to realize the system. In this case understanding is constructing. Or, as Vilém Flusser insightfully put it:

the factory of the future will have to be the place where *homo faber* becomes *homo sapiens sapiens* because he has realised that manufacturing means the same thing as learning—i.e. acquiring, producing, and passing on information.   (Flusser 1999, p. 50)[6]

---

[6] Flusser (1999) is a gem, full of remarkable insights.

This information manufacturing, this poietic knowledge, is implicitly based on a logic of design. We find its roots in Kant and Hegel, as I tried to show above, but it is under-theorized. Such a conceptual logic of *semantic information modelling* as *designing* is consistent with creative forms of reasoning, with the identification and exploitation of constraints and affordances, and hence the satisfaction of requirements, with future-oriented analyses of what systems could be built and could work, often recursively, and with engineering sciences broadly understood. It is a logic of sufficient rather than necessary conditions, in a specific sense that I shall explain presently.[7] Before, I need to deal with an issue left implicit since Chapter 2, and now pressing here: the role of contradictions.

2. Design, Contradictions, and Dialetheism

One cannot discuss Hegel's dialectical logic without clarifying what role, if any, contra-dictions may play in a logic of design. The issue can be rather complicated, so let me tackle it by introducing a simple thought experiment.

Suppose we are allowed to play the role of minor gods. We are not just observers of the world, but also makers of it. Using a vocabulary by now standard, let us call the world we are building the *system*, and the output of the observation of such a world its *model*. The system is completely transparent to us, who have engineered it, but rather opaque to its users. The world-system is made of many other sub-systems. One of them is a vending machine: we, the gods, know exactly what goes on inside it, whereas Alice, the user, can only rely on a simpler LoA to understand and operate it. Could there be 'contradictions' inside the system? If we are poor engineers, or rather clumsy gods, the answer is obviously yes. This is not a matter of category mistake: if some parts A of the vending machine click and clang to the effect that state D arises, let us say that the machine dispenses the soft drink, while some other parts B, of the same system, simul-taneously move and change to the effect that the opposite state $\neg D$ also arises, so that the machine does not dispense the soft drink, and this happens at the same time as D, then the physical clash—what conceptually, or in terms of design, is described as a logical inconsistency—between D and $\neg D$ will arise and cause a mess: Alice will not get her drink when she should, or perhaps she will get it randomly, or will get more or sometimes less than what she paid for. Clearly, actual contradictory processes, or events, or patterns, or facts, or features of entities (depending on one's own ontology) may be presupposed to occur in the world. *Metaphysical dialetheism* is perfectly con-ceivable from a God's (sorry, gods')-eye perspective. Alice the observer, however, placed on the other epistemological side (the mortal one) of the LoA, will experience

---

[7] On a poietic epistemology see Floridi (2018). Information manufacturing should not be confused with the contemporary movement known as information architecture, which is really about how to manage available information in ways that make it more accessible; see for the example the entertaining Covert and Fenton (2014) or a standard textbook treatment in Morville and Rosenfeld (2015).

only the *malfunctioning* (Floridi et al. 2015) of the system—for example the delivery of no drinks—not the contradictory double-functioning (both *A* and *B*) that is causing the malfunctioning, that is, she will not experience the machine dispensing and not dispensing the purchased drink at the same time and in the same sense. The example should clarify that wondering whether the world might contain contradictions means wondering whether it is feasible and sensible to adopt an LoA at which some of the states of the world-system are described by the resulting model as the upshot of contradictions intrinsic to the system.

Let us return to our vending machine. Suppose that it is working perfectly well, but that Alice develops an inconsistent model of it and its behaviour. She represents the machine as simultaneously dispensing and not dispensing the right drink for the same correct amount of money, in exactly the plain sense in which you and I understand such contradiction. In other words, her model states that both p and $\neg p$ are true of the targeted system. If asked, she might explain why she gets the right drink every time she inserts the right coins as a case of amazing good luck. In this case, the contradiction is in the model, not in the system. Strictly speaking, there is no reason to assume that the constraints imposed by the world are such that only consistent models are possible. It would be wonderful if the opposite were the case. Unfortunately, *semantic dialetheism* is not only perfectly possible, but probably the norm, given how difficult it is to spot inconsistencies in our ways of handling the world informationally. This point is painfully driven home when we shift our perspective, and instead of talking of contradictory observing models—which requires some conceptual gymnastics, as we have just seen—we concentrate on contradictory *blueprints*, those models that specify the overall design of the systems to be built. Too often contradictory requirements and specifications lead to malfunctioning and even dangerous systems. We expend too much effort and resources debugging and trying to make sure that blueprints are at least internally consistent to have any doubts about the everyday phenomenon of semantic dialetheism.

Contradictory artefacts resulting from contradictory blueprints need not consist of physical bits or digital bytes. They might be social or intellectual constructs as well. Legislation, political institutions, or social practices may easily be contradictory, for example. This not only reinforces the view that metaphysical dialetheism is far from being a mere speculation, it also shows how metaphysical and semantic dialetheism, both viable as independent options, may be combined into a single form of *absolute dialetheism*. Hegel and Marx were keen on explaining contradictory (social, intellectual, political, economic, engineered, and so forth) systems in terms of models capable of handling contradictory descriptions of them.

Does all this mean that, after all, our philosophy of logic should embrace a more contradictory-friendly attitude when it comes to the nature of information? I do not think so. There are pragmatic considerations lying behind the assumption of consistency (and hence the rejection of dialetheism). They should not be dismissed as merely practical, while interpreting the method of levels of abstraction exclusively in epistemological terms (roughly: the models are always descriptions, never blueprints). We saw that we cannot appeal to the consistency of the world as if it were uncontroversial, and we should be aware of the overall cost of maintaining consistency. But the pragmatic dimension of our construction of our models of the world is crucial and cannot be left out or underestimated as merely contextual, because it is there that the previous costs are counterbalanced by overwhelming benefits. We seek and value semantic information not just because we wish to pursue the epistemic goals of *description*, *explanation*, and *prediction*, but also, if not probably mainly, because we want to interact with the world and build it or modify it successfully. It is the pragmatic dimension provided by the goals of *interaction*, *construction*, and *modification* that grants to the virtue of consistency of our models a *normative*, *overriding* value that would otherwise make consistency appear to be on a par with other virtues (thus consistency and elegance, for example, are not on the same plane). It does so in two ways. *Interactively*, being told that one is and is not a vegetarian will not help pragmatically the chef who needs to provide an appropriate meal, exactly in the same way and sense in which being told that one is or is not a vegetarian leaves things unimproved informatively. From a Tarskian perspective, in information transactions, consistency is to be sought because without it there is no useful transaction and not because any transactions will ensue. *Constructively*, a blueprint of a vending machine does not have to have the virtues of being elegant, or simple, or parsimonious, but it must be devoid of contradictory features, or the resulting artefact will malfunction. The same applies to a piece of legislation, a computer program, or the safety system of a nuclear power station. Consistency is a necessary condition for well-functioning. This pragmatic feature cannot be overvalued. That is why in both cases (i.e. interactively and constructively), we should adopt levels of abstraction that generate consistent models. To conclude this brief excursus in the evaluation of dialetheism in the logic of design, there are three informational contexts where consistency plays a crucial role: in (what we take to be) the nature of the world (the system), in how we describe it (the model), and in how we go about engaging with it, including designing it (the blueprint). The difference that information makes is not only epistemic (affecting only the system and its model), it is also, if not primarily, pragmatic (affecting also the praxis and the blueprint), and consistency serves both masters. This is why inconsistent information might make sense descriptively, but has no value normatively. Let us now turn to the logic of design itself.

3. The Logic of Design as a Logic of Requirements

The search for a logic of design is not (and it would be suspicious if it were) entirely new. Carnap, for example, who described philosophy as conceptual engineering, is a great representative of the German tradition, beginning at least with Kant and going all the way at least to Wittgenstein's *Tractatus*, in which philosophical analysis is expected to unearth the deep, conceptual structures of knowledge, language, and semantics. This is design of some sort:

The programme of rational reconstruction set out in 1922–3 had given great prominence to a notion of 'structure' that remained somewhat enigmatic. And though 'structure' itself was purely logical or analytic, its application instance in the 'constructive' project of the Aufbau sought to capture the component of knowledge that Helmholtz and Poincare had said was all we ultimately could know about the world: 'What science can attain to is not the things themselves but only the relations among the things; apart from these relations there is no knowable reality' (Poincare 1904, p. XIII). Carnap, as we saw, had taken this further, and built his project of rational reconstruction on the idea that 'every science is a science only insofar as the study of structures [Strukturlehre] is contained in it' (above, p. 163). Did this make our knowledge of 'structure' itself a form of synthetic knowledge? And finally, even if 'structure' was purely logical, where did the principles of logic come from? All Carnap's great role models in logic had answered this last question by gesturing toward a special source of knowledge, different from the empirical—the principles of logic were synthetic a priori, or traceable to a 'logical source of knowledge' that gives us our ability to grasp 'thoughts' residing in a 'third realm' distinct from the first realm of physical objects and the second realm of subjective consciousness.[8]

However, Carnap, analytic philosophers, and structuralists and deconstructionists of all kinds seem to forget that structures are not only unveiled, investigated, known, discovered, reconstructed, or deconstructed. They are also, and perhaps today above all, built, constructed, engineered, in a word: *designed*. What does this mean?

Keeping in mind the risk just highlighted, it is obvious that architecture, the design discipline par excellence, provides a great heuristics to clarify what a logic of design may be. According to the American Institute of Architects, there are five phases of design.[9] The taxonomy is popular and rather uncontroversial. It provides an excellent starting point. I shall paraphrase and summarize it below, with only minor adaptations and a significant proviso:[10]

> *Phase 1: Originate.*   This is the thinking phase in which one realizes that something new (in our terminology, a new system) needs to be built in order to satisfy a particular purpose. It is the 'needing' moment of the project.
>
> *Phase 2: Focus.*   This is the phase in which one defines the system's *requirements* (these are broadly understood as scope, features, purpose, or functionality, more on this presently) that the system must have in order to satisfy the purpose. It is the 'vision' moment for the project.
>
> *Phase 3: Design.*   This is the phase in which one models the system's requirements. It is the 'shaping' moment of the project.

---

[8] Carus (2007, p. 185).

[9] AIA website: http://howdesignworks.aia.org/fivephases.asp.

[10] I am very grateful to James Williams for having called my attention to the potentially misleading nature of architecture as an apparently non-recursive area of design.

Phase 4: Build. This is the phase in which one constructs the system. It is the 'making' moment of the project.

Phase 5: Use.[11] This is the last phase in which the system is finally available and starts satisfying its purpose. It is the 'testing' moment of the project.

The proviso to be added is that the five phases can easily be *recursive*. If any phase, including *Phase* 5, is unsatisfactory, one may go back all the way to *Phase* 1. Indeed, the phases are often recursive in many design contexts in which fast prototyping has become ordinary. 3D printing has had a profound influence on this more cyclical approach. This holds true in architecture as well. Of course, one does not build whole architectural systems to re-do them if unsatisfied. The difference lies in the longer, diachronic time-scale. For example, the refinement of the Doric, Ionic, and Corinthian orders of architecture took a long time, but it was no less recursive than the trial and error one may experience in designing a web page for a customer. Rome was not built in a day, but this does not mean that it was not built recursively through the centuries. And we saw above that Kant's transcendental logic may be in a recursive relation with the logic of design: what is initially a blueprint is translated into a first system, which is then analysed by a model that can become a new blueprint for a revised system, and so forth. All this highlights the fact that design is not limited to the creation/implementation of systems anew, but also applies to the repurposing or improving of existing systems, relying on repeated iteration with, sometimes, small adjustments, in a variety of time-scales.

As is obvious, the logic of design may cover all five phases. If we ignore *Phase* 1, as the moment when one realizes that a new system to fulfil a specific goal is needed, then during *Phases* 4–5 one *verifies* and *validates* (in the design, not the philosophical sense of the two terms) the system that is being built, that is, one checks its 'fitness for purpose'. During the verification stage, one evaluates whether the system is being developed in the right way, for example by checking for consistency. And during the validation stage, one evaluates whether the right system is being developed, for example by evaluating the correctness of the final system with respect to users' needs. Both stages are methodological. It is the step from *Phase* 2 to *Phase* 3 that is significantly *inferential* and can then be defined correctly as belonging to the conceptual logic of design: the satisfaction of a specific purpose leads to the identification of some requirements which then lead to the design of a specific system that implements them in order to satisfy the purpose, with all the necessary loops in recursive refinements. This should sound familiar: it means that architectural design contains within itself an inferential stage—the passage from *Phase* 2 to *Phase* 3—that is fully captured by system engineering. This is our next step.

---

[11] 'Occupy' in the original text. I modified the terminology slightly to cover all kinds of designs, not just the design of buildings.

In system engineering,[12] one provides the specification for a system (S) to be designed by describing an explicit, non-empty, finite, and complete set of requirements $\{R_1, \ldots, R_n\}$ to be satisfied by S. Such requirements in $\{R_1, \ldots, R_n\}$ can be non-functional or functional, or, to use a more classic terminology, may refer to the *form* or the *function* of the system. Non-functional requirements are also simply known as requirements *tout court*. They define a system's architecture, that is, what the system is *supposed to be*. For example, a refrigerator's main non-functional requirement is that its compartment is thermally insulated and easily accessible in order to store food. Functional requirements are also known as functions. They define a system's behaviour, that is, what the system is *supposed to do*. In our example, a refrigerator's main functional requirement is to maintain a constant temperature a few degrees above the freezing point of water, inside its easily accessible, thermally insulated compartment. The distinction is crucial and it has philosophical implications too, so it is important to keep it clear and firm in mind. For example, Kant's formulations of the categorical imperative have often been seen as formal, motivational features of an agent's behaviour, that is, as functional requirements. However, from a system engineering design perspective, and a more consistent interpretation of Kant's autonomous dictates of reason, they are better understood as non-functional requirements, namely universalizability and non-instrumentalization, that is, what a categorical imperative is supposed to be. Finally, there is a third sense in which one may speak of requirements, and that is when resources needed to build a system are under discussion. This is not going to play a role in the logic of design discussed in this chapter, but it is an obvious constraint, both practically (e.g. funding) and theoretically (e.g. computational power or memory, two resources that translate into time and space, which then translate into complexity issues). Figure 35 summarizes the previous analysis and taxonomy.

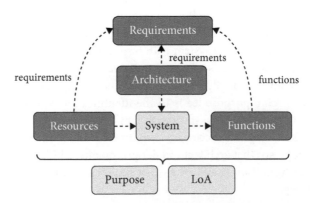

Figure 35 Elements of system design

[12] On the philosophy of design in engineering and architecture see the collection of essays in Vermaas et al. (2007).

It turns out that the inferential step in the logic of design from *Phase* 2 to *Phase* 3 concerns the relation between a set of requirements (in the comprehensive sense of 'requirements' just clarified), on the one hand, and a system that implements them (more or less satisfactorily), on the other. In other words, the (conceptual) logic of design turns out to be the (conceptual) logic of requirements. But then, exactly what kind of designing relation between requirements and system are we discussing? This is not a classic entailment as understood in First Order Logic (FOL).[13] In FOL, we are acquainted with the relation of *satisfaction*: a truth-structure A *satisfies* a set of sentences Γ if and only if A *models* Γ, that is: $A \vDash \Gamma$. By analogy, one may argue that the system S satisfies (models) a set of requirements, that is, we could use the double turnstile to formalize the design relation between a system and the requirements thus:

- $S \vDash \{R_1, \ldots, R_n\}$.

There is, however, a difficulty. Read literally, such a formula would mean that S *necessitates* $\{R_1, \ldots, R_n\}$. This is obviously not true in our case. Recall the difficulty of using transcendental or dialectical logic for design purposes. The set of requirements logically precedes and 'conduces' to S, and S does not have a relation of necessitation with respect to the requirements it implements: a fridge does not necessitate 'preserving food'; it is rather this requirement that makes the fridge a sufficient solution. There is still a relation of satisfaction, but it needs to be re-interpreted. To this end, let me introduce to mean that whatever is on the left 'sufficientizes' ('makes sufficient') whatever is on the right as an implementation. This no longer resembles a deduction.[14] One may object that

The other feasible strategy is the pattern language proposed by Alexander,[15] where a deductive relation, between the design requirements, or as he called it the tendency, and the form [of the system], is constructed.   (Zeng and Cheng 1991, p. 140)

However, it is questionable whether Alexander's work may be so interpreted. For example, in Alexander (1964) he writes:

There is no legitimate sense in which deductive logic can prescribe physical form for us.
(Alexander 1964, p. 8)

And even if there may be some cases in which it may be correct to speak of a deductive relation, this only means that there are some 'degenerate' (once more, in the mathematical, technical sense of the word; see the conclusion of Chapter 2) cases of

---

[13] Opting for a modal logic approach only seems to complicate instead of solve the problem. This is not to say that modal logic cannot be helpful in studying patterns of inference in design reasoning and rationalization; see for example Galle (1997).

[14] Note that this is in contrast with the interpretation provided by Zeng and Cheng (1991), who argue that the logic of design is a recursive kind of deductive logic. Unfortunately, their analysis confuses different levels of abstraction as well as different stages of development of design, and it seems to resemble some kind of Aristotelian practical syllogism.

[15] Alexander et al. (1977), Alexander (1979). Both references are in the original quotation.

design in which the requirements are so completely constraining as to make possible one and only one system that satisfies all of them and no others. We saw above that such cases are neither representative nor interesting. Note, however, that the inferential relation is not an induction or abduction either.[16] One may call it a 'conduction'. We can now write:

- $\{R_1, \ldots, R_n\} \models S$

to formalize the design relation between a set of requirements and what they conduce to in terms of a system that suffices to satisfy them. For example, the set of two requirements that indicate that we should design a system that seats one person 'sufficientizes' several solutions, without necessitating any of them in particular:

- {seat, one-person} $\models$ Chair
- {seat, one-person} $\models$ Stool
- {seat, one-person} $\models$ Pouf

How we identify the requirements is a matter of analysis, sometimes of necessity, but sometimes of choice. Recall the rejection of the 'Kantian equation': the same set of requirements may lead to a variety of systems understood as solutions that satisfy them, and the choice of which solution may be preferable, or whether the set needs to be revised, is pragmatic, but not determined, and can be as much linked to biological and social frameworks as to cultural, personal, or even accidental circumstances. In terms of choice, for example, demaking a video game means remaking it for an older platform, that is, it is a self-imposed challenge to require simpler graphics and sound, and simplified gameplay to see what a video game would be like, if it had been conceived and produced for an older hardware or software generation. The same applies to so-called 'constrained writing'. *Green Eggs and Ham*, the famous children's book, uses only fifty different words because of a $50 bet by Theodor Geisel, also known as Dr. Seuss, with Bennett Cerf.

Once the requirements have been identified (and often this is a process of discovery that needs recursive revisions as the design process progresses) then choosing between the different systems 'sufficientized' by the requirements, and deciding how to implement the preferred choice, become a matter of policy, that is, the application of a deliberate set of principles in order to guide the decision and achieve the wanted outcome. This is why there is no ultimate designed system in the world that does not encapsulate autonomy and choice, even if implicitly and inadvertently.[17]

We can now extend this analysis to make sense of four standard cases, in analogy with the double turnstile in mathematical logic.

---

[16] The temptation of interpreting the logic of design as abduction in Peircean terms is recurrent. March (1984) defends a logic of design as a logic of abduction, but in a problem-solving context; see also Goel (1988), who seeks to extend March's approach. Kroll and Koskela (2015) re-proposes the abductive interpretation but refers only to March (1976) not to March (1984).

[17] I am grateful to Mariarosaria Taddeo for having pointed out the need for this further clarification.

1. If a consistent but boundless set of requirements is provided, that is, if a system can be designed that can satisfy any non-empty set of requirements, then in practice there is no such system, but in theory one may be referring to the set of all systems:

-   $\{R_1, \ldots\} \models \{S_1, \ldots\}$

In FOL, this would be analogous to a boundless set of premises that entails a boundless set of conclusions; more an intellectual curiosity than something useful for any design purpose.

2. If an inconsistent set of requirements is provided, that is, if nothing goes and there is no system that can be designed that can ever satisfy such a set (imagine the requirements for a perpetual motion machine), then there is only the set, not followed by any system (the empty set):

-   $\{R_1, \ldots, R_n, \neg R_1, \ldots, \neg R_n\} \models \{\}$

In FOL, this would be analogous to a contradictory set that entails any conclusion. And in the same way that a contradictory set is false in all possible worlds, likewise a set of requirements that is inconsistent is good for no purpose, which means it is useless for any design. One may use this terminology to speak of impossible systems.

3. If no requirements are provided, that is, if anything goes and there are no constraints (think of the design of a drug that works like a panacea), then the empty set of requirements sufficientizes S:

-   $\{\} \models S$

In FOL, this would be analogous to a tautology. And in the same way as a tautology is true in all possible worlds, likewise a system, the design of which is unconstrained by any requirement, is a system good for any purpose, which means it is magical or, more seriously, useless.

4. Finally, if a consistent and finite set of requirements, for example {seat, one-person, back}, conduces to a unique system, namely a chair, that is, if only one system can satisfy them, then we have a double relation of sufficientization:

-   $\{R_1, \ldots, R_n\} \models\vDash S$.

In FOL, this would be analogous to a relation of double entailment. This is the 'degenerate' case in which a set of requirements sufficientizes only one system which satisfies only one set of requirements.

The previous analysis helps one to see that optimization in design consists in any improvement in the number or nature of the requirements and/or in their implementation according to some pre-established purpose. And efficient design is the implementation of a set of requirements such that it is impossible to satisfy any one of them any more without satisfying at least one of them less (Pareto efficiency).

As in FOL, what interesting systems one may design (what interesting theorems one may prove) is a matter of talent, intuition, hard work, opportunity, good fortune, free thinking, and imagination, and many other variables that are hard to pin down. As Donald Schön correctly put it, the designer (or indeed the logician and the philosopher and anyone who creatively designs solutions) is

like a chess master who develops a feeling for the constraints and the potentials [affordances in the terminology of this chapter] of certain configurations of pieces on the board.[18]

So, the conceptual logic I have suggested here is more in line with an early analysis provided by William Fawcett who was critical of logico-mathematical approaches to the logic of design:

So, what is the distinctive 'logic of design'? The author prefers the point of view that the identity of design lies in empirical considerations, rather than in modes of inference; and in purely empirical terms it has been confirmed that design is a more difficult task than analysis.

(Fawcett 1987, p. 85)

There is no Leibnizian 'calculemus' in the logic of design. There can be very little naturalized expediency as there is a qualitative gap between the design of a nest and the design of NEST (the smart thermostat). Nevertheless, the mechanism lying behind good design and good logic is clear. There are three conceptual logics of information as modelling of a system, and the third one is the logic of design as a logic of requirements.

Conclusion: From *Mimesis* to *Poiesis*

In the previous pages, I have sought to outline a conceptual logic of information under-stood as (i) a transcendental logic of past conditions of possibility of a system (Kant), or as (ii) a dialectical logic of present conditions of in/stability of a system (Hegel), or as (iii) a design logic of future conditions of feasibility of a system. I then characterized (iii) as a conceptual logic of requirements and introduced the relations of 'sufficientiza-tion'. The last comment I wish to make is about why a conceptual logic of information as design is particularly important today. Four reasons seem to be salient.

First, the digital re-ontologizes (Floridi 2014a) our world by transforming the very nature of our concepts and their related phenomena. It does this by decoupling hith-erto coupled elements such as presence and location, law and territoriality, ownership and use, successful agency and intelligence. Such decoupling fluidifies both things and ideas about things, making possible the design and redesign of both. In short, the digi-tal provides more affordances and fewer constraints as new requirements for our creative design efforts. We need a logic of design as a logic of requirements to make the most of such increased opportunities.

Second, the digital poses new challenges, conceptual and ethical. We saw in Chapter 1 that such challenges are open, that is, they are problems that may be solved in more than one way by rational, well-informed, and open-minded (i.e. not stubborn) interlocutors.

---

[18] Schön (1983, p. 104); see also Parsons (2016, p. 49).

This openness calls for a clear understanding of how we design the solutions, how such solutions can better satisfy the requirements that motivate them, and how the requirements may evolve and be improved in order to fulfil the driving purposes. In short, it calls for a logic of design and sufficientization driven by the right policies.

Third, and probably as a consequence of the previous two reasons, a conceptual logic of information as design is particularly important today because our knowledge of the world is increasingly constructionist. I already mentioned the fact that some of the most influential sciences and intellectual endeavours of our time, including Architecture, Computer Science, Economics, and Engineering and Jurisprudence, do not just study their systems, they mainly build and modify them. The more science shifts from a *mimetic* to a *poietic* approach to the world, the more we shall need a logic of design. Kant and Hegel were on the right track.

And finally, because the essence of philosophy is not logic, but design. Logic is only a second best compromise, in the absence of design. It is time for philosophy to equip itself not only with a transcendental and a dialectical logic but also with a logic of requirements to devise new answers to the open questions posed by the information revolution. I argued at the beginning of this book that philosophical questions are ultimate but not absolute questions, which are not answerable empirically or mathematically, but are open to informed and rational disagreement. The best way to address them is by developing philosophy as conceptual design, and this requires its own logic.

Afterword—Rebooting Philosophy

Introduction

We have come to the end of this third volume. Together with the previous two, I hope it provides sufficient clarity and some designing tools for the philosophy of information to enable us to make the next step, which will be to understand and design the human project we may want to pursue in the twenty-first century. As usual, the more one explores, the more one realizes how much more work lies ahead, in terms of better understanding of the challenges we face, and efforts that we must make to devise adequate ways of thinking about our world, our society, and ourselves, in increasingly digitized contexts. By way of conclusion, in this afterword, I shall sketch the direction in which I hope we may make some progress. Many of the problems with which we are dealing and shall be dealing in the infosphere are uncharted territory, but I hope that a few points of reference may help us to get oriented. The actual navigation is left to the next volume, *The Politics of Information*.

Scholasticism as the Philosophical Enemy of Open Questions

When we use a computer, its performance seems to degrade progressively. This is not a mere impression. An old version of Firefox, the free Web browser, was infamous for its 'memory leaks': it would consume increasing amounts of memory to the detriment of other programs. Bugs in the software actually do slow down the system. We all know what the solution is: reboot. We restart the computer, the memory is reset, and the performance is restored, until the bugs slow it down again.

Philosophy is a bit like a computer with a memory leak. It starts well, dealing with significant and serious issues that matter to anyone. Yet, in time, its very success slows it down. Philosophy begins to care more about *philosophers' questions* than *philosophical ones*, consuming increasing amounts of intellectual attention.

The problem with philosophers' questions is not that they are impenetrable to any outsider—although they are, like any internal game—but that whatever the answers turn out to be, assuming there are ones, they do not matter at all, because nobody could care less about the questions in the first place anyway. This is an old problem.

In the sixteenth century, Rabelais satirized in his *Gargantua and Pantagruel* the (really existing) library of St Victor by producing a list of 139 invented titles of books. Centuries later, we seem to be back to the same problem. This is how philosophy speaks today:

(a) 'The Failure of Class: Postcapitalist narrative and textual precapitalist theory'
(b) 'Deconstructing Lyotard: Cultural narrative and premodern dedeconstructivism'
(c) 'As Lewis taught us in a classic series of articles, trope theories Gettierize zombie arguments'.
(d) 'While the contextualist disagrees, we still hold that supposed mind/body "problems" cannot generate an unacceptably Russellian picture of the world'.

Do not try to understand them. I produced (a) and (b) using the 'post-modern gibberish essay generator' (http://www.elsewhere.org/pomo), and (c) and (d) using 'the analytic philosophy generator' (http://www.andrewmbailey.com/Humor/Chart.pdf but try also http://www.gabbay.org.uk/mike-funny/crap-generator.pdf).

The examples above are cases of scholasticism: philosophy talking about itself to itself in its own jargon. Scholasticism is the ultimate freezing of the system, the equivalent of Windows' 'blue screen of death': so many resources are devoted to internal issues that no external input can be processed anymore, and the system stops working. The world may be undergoing a revolution, Rome may be burning, but the philosophical discourse remains detached, meaningless, and utterly oblivious. Philosophy's open questions are closed within some canon of authors to be discussed, and an orthodoxy of theories and issues with which to engage. Scholasticism is intolerant towards intellectual novelties. Time to reboot the system.

The result of a philosophical rebooting today can only be beneficial. Digital technologies are not just tools modifying how we deal with the world, like the wheel or the engine. They are above all formatting systems, which increasingly affect how we understand the world, how we relate to it, how we see ourselves, how we interact with each other, and finally how our hopes for a better future are shaped. We need philosophy to make sense of the radical changes brought about by the information revolution and design the new human project for the twenty-first century. And we need it to be at its best, for the difficulties we are facing are many and truly challenging. Clearly, we need to reboot philosophy now. But then the question is: how? Rebooting is not re-inventing, but rather starting afresh with a system that can perform well if properly used. So, let me sketch three lessons, based on Turing's work, on how we should formulate our new philosophical questions today. I can be very brief about the first lesson we can learn from Turing, because it refers to the use of the *method of abstraction* I outlined in Chapter 2. I shall not repeat here what I wrote there. Without a clear sense of the level of abstraction at which one is working, there is no way of making any sense of the open questions that we are facing. The other two lessons deserve their own sections.

Philosophical Questions Worth Asking

On 23 April 2010, Bill Gates gave a talk at MIT in which he asked: 'are the brightest minds working on the most important problems?' By 'the most important problems' he meant 'improving the lives of the poorest; improving education, health, nutrition'. Unfortunately, the list should probably include improving peaceful interactions, human rights, environmental conditions, living standards, inequalities...and this is only the beginning. Clearly, the brightest *philosophical* minds should not be an exception. They should turn their attention to such pressing challenges. Admittedly, one may stop philosophizing and start doing something about this messy world instead. Someone may be carried away and suggest that we should close down our philosophy departments and never corrupt our brightest youths philosophically, *pace* Socrates, who was accused of doing exactly that. Yet, such a solution smacks of self-defeat. It would be like deciding to burn the wicker basket in which we are travelling, because our hot air balloon is descending too quickly. Philosophy is what you need to keep in a good world, not what you want to get rid of in a bad one. Athens is a better place with Socrates. There must be a different way forward. The fact is that philosophy can be extremely helpful, for it is philosophy, understood as conceptual design, that forges and refines the new ideas, theories, perspectives, and, more generally, the intellectual framework that can then be translated and applied to understand and deal with the ultimate questions that challenge us so pressingly. In the huge team-effort made by the brightest minds, the philosophical ones can contribute insights and visions, analyses and syntheses, heuristics and solutions that can empower us to tackle 'the most important problems'. Every little effort helps in the battle against idiocy, obscurantism, intolerance, fanaticisms, bigotry, prejudice, fundamentalisms of all kinds, populism, and mere ignorance. If this sounds self-serving recall that the longer the jump forward is, the longer the run-up to it should be. Or, with a different metaphor, philosophy takes care of the roots, so that the rest of the plant might grow more healthily.

Suppose we accept all this as a reasonable assumption. Which ideas, theories, perspectives, and, more generally, which intellectual framework should philosophers be designing now and for the foreseeable future, so that their contribution will be timely and helpful? Which philosophical questions should they be addressing? The answer would be inconceivable without Turing's legacy, for it lies in the conceptual threads that run across so many of our 'most important problems'. In globalized information societies, most of the crucial challenges that we are facing are linked to information and communication technologies, in terms of causes, effects, solutions, scientific investigations, actual improvements, conceptual resources needed to understand them, or even just the wealth required to tackle them, as Bill Gates' example clearly shows. Obviously, information resources, technologies, and sciences are not a panacea, but they are a crucial and powerful weapon in our fight against so many evils. The lesson to be learnt from Turing concerns the sort of questions that the brightest philosophical minds should be addressing.

Philosophical 'rebooting' moments are rare. They are usually prompted by unhinging transformations in the surrounding reality. Since the 1990s, I have been arguing that we are witnessing one of those moments. It now seems obvious, even to the most conservative person, that we are experiencing a turning point in our history. The epochal transition from a completely analogue to an also digital world is changing every aspect of our lives, quickly, profoundly, and relentlessly. The list is known but worth recalling: education, work, and entertainment; communication, business, and commerce; love, hate, and anything in between; politics, conflicts, and the peaceful cohabitations; culture, health, and even digital remains of the dead…feel free to add your preferred topics; they are all transformed by technologies that have the recording, transmission, and processing of data as their core functions. In short, we live in an infosphere in which, behind the most important problems evoked by Gates, often lies some digital technology. It is a new world in which we have begun to ask new pressing questions, as I shall argue in the next section.

A Philosophical Anthropology to Approach Philosophical Questions

Oversimplifying, science has two fundamental ways of changing our understanding. One may be called *extrovert*, or about the world, and the other *introvert*, or about ourselves. Three scientific revolutions have had great impact both extrovertly and introvertly. In changing our understanding of the external world and how we can interact with it, they also modified our conception of who we are and may expect to become. After Copernicus, the heliocentric cosmology displaced the Earth and hence humanity from the centre of the universe. Darwin showed that all species of life have evolved over time from common ancestors through natural selection, thus displacing humanity from the centre of the biological kingdom. And following Freud, we acknowledge nowadays that the mind is also unconscious and subject to the defence mechanism of repression, thus displacing it from the centre of pure rationality, a position that had been assumed as uncontroversial, at least since Descartes. The reader who, like Popper and myself, would be reluctant to follow Freud in considering psychoanalysis a strictly scientific enterprise like astronomy or evolutionary theory might yet be willing to concede that contemporary neuroscience is a likely candidate for such a revolutionary role. Either way, the result is that, today, we acknowledge that we are not immobile, at the centre of the universe (Copernican revolution), we are not unnaturally separate and diverse from the rest of the animal kingdom (Darwinian revolution), and we are very far from being Cartesian minds entirely transparent to ourselves (Freudian or Neuroscientific revolution).

One may easily question the value of this classic picture. After all, Freud (1917) himself was the first to interpret these three revolutions as part of a single process of reassessment of human nature (Weinert 2009). His hermeneutic manoeuvre was, admittedly, rather self-serving. But it does strike a reasonable note. In a similar way, when we now perceive that something very significant and profound has happened to human life after the computer revolution, I would argue that our intuition is once again perceptive, because we are experiencing what may be described as a fourth revolution, in the process of dislocation and reassessment of humanity's fundamental nature and role in the universe. This has been going on since the 1950s and Turing is undoubtedly the representative figure of such a revolution. Computer science and the resulting technological applications have exercised both an extrovert and an introvert influence. They have provided unprecedented epistemic and engineering powers over natural and artificial realities; and by doing so, they have also cast new light on who we are, how we are related to the world, and hence how we understand ourselves and who we might become. Today, we are slowly accepting the idea that we are not at the centre of the *infosphere* because we are not the only smart agents able to carry on an increasing number of complex tasks. Our computers have joined us in the infosphere and are often better than us at dealing with it. It follows that, when we define AI as the successful performance, by digital technologies, of tasks that, if left to humans, would require intelligence, we are really telling a new story about ourselves. Add to this the fact that we see ourselves increasingly as informationally embodied organisms (*inforgs*)—think for example of the idea of DNA as software—mutually connected and embedded in an informational environment that we share with both natural and artificial agents similar to us in many respects. And you can see why Turing has changed our philosophical anthropology as much as Copernicus, Darwin, and Freud ever did. This has had a significant impact on what it means to do philosophy after Turing, the last point to which I wish to call the reader's attention.

How to Make Sense of the World and Design It Today

What can enable humanity to make sense of our contemporary world, respect it, and improve it responsibly, and hence help in solving 'the most important problems'? The answer seems quite simple: a new philosophy of information. Among our mundane and technical concepts, information is currently one of the most important, widely used, yet least understood. It is the Cinderella in the history of philosophy. Think of it for a moment. Understanding information is a necessary input for any philosophy of knowledge, no matter whether ordinary (epistemology) or scientific (philosophy of science). There is no ethics without choices, responsibilities, and moral evaluations, yet all these need a lot of relevant and reliable information and quite good management of it. Logic was a matter of dialectics first, and then mathematical proofs, but today it is also if not mainly a question of information extraction, transmission, and dynamics. Ontology without informational patterns—real, virtual, possible, necessary, or even impossible—would be meaningless, and many branches of logic are really branches of information theory. The philosophy of mind needs informational mental states, and the philosophy of language without communication of information is pointless. Any philosophy of the *logos* is a philosophy of information and Christian philosophy of religion is inconceivable without the informational concept of revelation. The list could be extended and refined to aesthetics, hermeneutics, philosophy of biology, philosophy of physics, etc. but the point is clear. To paraphrase Molière, Western philosophy has been speaking informationally without knowing it for twenty-five centuries. To use the initial analogy, we have always relied on Cinderella working hard in the house of philosophy. It is time to acknowledge her great and pervasive services. The brightest *philosophical* minds should turn their attention to it in order to design the philosophy *of* our time properly conceptualized *for* our time. This is a quick and dirty way of introducing the philosophy of information as a much needed development in this history of philosophy. Let me now sketch the longer story that links it to Turing.

Admittedly, it would be too much of a stretch to attribute to Turing the foundation or even the beginning of a new philosophy of information. After all, he never focused on the concept of information itself, or on problems about communication understood as *information flow* or *transmission*, despite the fact that he and Shannon knew each other's work. Thus, the Index of Turing (2004) does not even contain an entry for 'information' and a book like Luenberger (2006) mentions Turing only once, in relation to Bletchley Park. And yet, I would argue that without Turing, his groundbreaking work on *information processing*, the scientific and technological consequences of it, and the lessons outlined above, contemporary interest in the philosophy of information would be very hard to explain. Turing shares with Shannon and Wiener the merit of having called our philosophical attention to the world of information and its dynamics. Without his lessons, there would be no philosophy of information. The fact that nowadays we are more likely to treat computers as communication machines rather than powerful calculators and smartphones as mini computers rather than telephones only indicates how deep the influence of Turing's work has been on our world.

Conclusion: Creative Destruction in Philosophy

The development of new philosophical ideas seems to be akin to economic innovation. For when Schumpeter adapted the idea of 'creative destruction' in order to interpret economic innovation, he might as well have been talking about intellectual development. Philosophy flourishes by constantly re-booting itself. Nowadays, its pulling force of innovation is represented by the world of information, computation, and communication phenomena, their corresponding sciences and technologies, and the new environments, social life, as well as the existential, cultural, economic, and educational issues that they are bringing about. It is a new scenario that owes very much to Turing's work and intellectual legacy. I just outlined the philosophical lessons that we should learn from Turing. I suggested that the philosophy of information, insofar as it brings to fruition Turing's legacy, can present itself as an innovative paradigm that opens up a very rich, helpful, and timely area of conceptual investigations. The philosophy of information seeks to expand the frontier of our philosophical understanding, by providing innovative methodologies to address our most important problems from a contemporary perspective. It relies on Turing's intuition of the crucial importance of the *method of abstraction* to ensure that such problems are addressed in the right way.

The scientific revolution made seventeenth-century philosophers redirect their attention from the nature of the knowable object to the epistemic relation between it and the knowing subject, and hence from metaphysics to epistemology. The subsequent growth of the information society and the appearance of the infosphere, as the environment in which billions of people spend their lives nowadays, have led contemporary philosophy to privilege critical reflection first on the domain represented by the memory and languages of organized knowledge, the instruments whereby the infosphere is managed—thus moving from epistemology to philosophy of language and logic—and then on the nature of its very fabric and essence, information itself and its dynamics, including communication, flows, and processing. As a result, Information has arisen as a concept as fundamental and important as Being, knowledge, life, intelligence, meaning, or good and evil—all pivotal concepts with which it is interdependent—and so equally worthy of autonomous investigation. It is also a more impoverished concept, in terms of which the others can be expressed and interrelated, when not defined. This is why the philosophy of information may explain and guide the purposeful construction of our intellectual environment, and provide the systematic treatment of the conceptual foundations of contemporary society.

The future of the philosophy of information depends on how well we engage with Turing's intellectual legacy, with 'the most important problems' of our time, and with classic philosophical issues. I am optimistic. Thanks also to Turing, the Baconian–Galilean project of grasping and manipulating the alphabet of the universe has begun to find its fulfilment in the computational and informational revolution, which is affecting so profoundly our knowledge of reality and how we conceptualize it and ourselves within it. Informational narratives possess an ontic power, not as magical confabulations, expressions of theological logos, or mystical formulae, but immanently, as building tools that can describe, modify, and implement our environment and ourselves. From this perspective, the philosophy of information can be presented as the study of the informational activities that make possible the construction, conceptualization, and finally the moral stewardship of reality, both natural and artificial, both physical and anthropological. The philosophy of information enables humanity to semanticize (give meaning to and make sense of) the world and construct it responsibly. It promises to be one of the most exciting and beneficial areas of philosophical research of our time.

References

Abelard, Peter. 1976. *Sic et non*. Chicago; London: University of Chicago Press.

Adams, Fred. 2011. "Information and Knowledge à la Floridi." In *Putting Information First: Luciano Floridi and the Philosophy of Information*, edited by Patrick Allo, 84–96. Oxford: Wiley-Blackwell.

Adams, Fred, John A. Barker, and Julia Figurelli. 2012. "Towards Closure on Closure." *Synthese* 188 (2):179–96.

Al-Hakim, Latif. 2007. *Information Quality Management: Theory and Applications*. Hershey, PA; London: Idea Group Pub.

Albert, Hans. 1978. "Science and the Search for Truth." *Boston Studies in the Philosophy of Science* 58:203–20.

Albert, Hans. 1985. *Treatise on Critical Reason*. Princeton, NJ: Princeton University Press.

Alexander, Christopher. 1964. *Notes on the Synthesis of Form*. Boston, MA: Harvard University Press.

Alexander, Christopher. 1979. *The Timeless Way of Building*. New York: Oxford University Press.

Alexander, Christopher, Sara Ishikawa, and Murray Silverstein. 1977. *A Pattern Language: Towns, Buildings, Construction*. New York: Oxford University Press.

Allo, Patrick. 2010. *Putting Information First: Luciano Floridi and the Philosophy of Information*. Oxford: Wiley-Blackwell.

Allo, Patrick. 2011. "The Logic of 'Being Informed' Revisited and Revised." *Philosophical Studies* 153 (3):417–34.

Ammon, Sabine. 2017. "Why Designing Is Not Experimenting: Design Methods, Epistemic Praxis and Strategies of Knowledge Acquisition in Architecture." *Philosophy & Technology* 30 (4):495–520.

Anderson, R. Lanier. 2015. *The Poverty of Conceptual Truth: Kant's Analytic/Synthetic Distinction and the Limits of Metaphysics*. Oxford: Oxford University Press.

Apel, Karl-Otto. 1975. "The Problem of Philosophical Fundamental-Grounding in Light of a Transcendental Pragmatic of Language." *Man and World* 8 (3):239–75.

Aristotle. 1938. *De Sophisticis Elenchis*, trans. E. S. Forster, *On Sophistical Refutations*, The Loeb Classical Library. Cambridge, MA: Harvard University Press.

Arnold, A., and John Plaice. 1994. *Finite Transition Systems: Semantics of Communicating Systems*. Paris; Hemel Hempstead: Masson; Prentice Hall.

Arup, Ove. 2012. *Philosophy of Design: Essays, 1942–1981*. Munich; London: Prestel.

Auerbach, Erich. 2003. *Mimesis: The Representation of Reality in Western Literature*. Translated from the German by Willard R. Trask with a new introduction by Edward W. Said. 50th anniversary ed. Princeton, NJ; Oxford: Princeton University Press.

Austin, J. L. 1962. *How To Do Things with Words: The William James Lectures*. Oxford: Clarendon Press.

Bar-Hillel, Yehoshua. 1951. "A Note on State-Descriptions." *Philosophical Studies* 2 (5):72–5.

Bar-Hillel, Yehoshua. 1964. *Language and Information: Selected Essays on Their Theory and Application*, Addison-Wesley series in logic. Reading, MA; London: Addison-Wesley.

Bar-Hillel, Y., and R. Carnap. 1953. "An Outline of a Theory of Semantic Information." In *Language and Information: Selected Essays on Their Theory and Application*, edited by Y. Bar-Hillel. Reading, MA; London: Addison-Wesley.

Barthes, Roland. 1981. *Camera Lucida: Reflections on Photography*. New York: Hill and Wang.

Barwise, Jon, and Jerry Seligman. 1997. *Information Flow: The Logic of Distributed Systems*. Cambridge: Cambridge University Press.

Batini, Carlo, and Monica Scannapieco. 2006. *Data Quality—Concepts, Methodologies and Techniques, Data-Centric Systems and Applications*. Berlin; New York: Springer.

Baumann, P. 2006. "Information, Closure, and Knowledge: On Jäger's Objection to Dretske." *Erkenntnis* 64 (3):403–8.

Belnap, Nuel D., and Thomas B. Steel. 1976. *The Logic of Questions and Answers*. New Haven; London: Yale University Press.

Bencivenga, E. 2006. "Philosophy: What Is to Be Done?" *Special Issue of Topoi* 25 (1–2).

Blackburn, Simon. 2016. *The Oxford Dictionary of Philosophy*. 3rd edn. Oxford: Oxford University Press.

Blanshard, Brand. 1939. *The Nature of Thought*. 2 vols. London: Allen & Unwin.

Boca, Paul P., J. P. Bowen, and J. I. Siddiqi. 2010. *Formal Methods: State of the Art and New Directions*. London: Springer.

Bogen, James, and James Woodward. 1988. "Saving the Phenomena." *The Philosophical Review* 97 (3):303–52.

Borel, Émile. 1927. "À propos de la recente discussion entre M. R. Wavre et M. P. Levy." *Revue de Métaphysique et de Morale* 34:271–6.

Borges, Jorge Luis. 1964. *Other Inquisitions, 1937–1952*. Austin: University of Texas Press.

Bosanquet, Bernard. 1911. *Logic, or, The Morphology of Knowledge*. 2nd edn. 2 vols. Oxford: Clarendon Press.

Bradley, F. H. 1914. *Essays on Truth and Reality*. Oxford: Clarendon Press.

Bradley, F. H. 1922. *The Principles of Logic*. 2nd edn. 2 vols. London: Oxford University Press.

Bradley, F. H. 1930. *Appearance and Reality: A Metaphysical Essay*. 2nd edn. Oxford: Clarendon Press.

Bregman, M. R., and T. Q. Gentner. 2010. "Syntactically Complex Vocal Systems." In *Encyclopedia of Animal Behavior*, edited by M. D. Breed and J. Moore, vol. 3, 368–74. Oxford: Elsevier.

Bridges, Jason. 2007. "Review of Richard Gaskin, 'Experience and the World's Own Language: A Critique of John McDowell's Empiricism.'" *Notre Dame Philosophical Reviews* 2007 (2).

Burgess, John P. 2009. *Philosophical Logic*. Princeton, NJ; Oxford: Princeton University Press.

Buurman, Gerhard M., and Marc Rölli. 2016. *The Intrinsic Logic of Design*. Zurich: Niggli.

Carnap, Rudolf. 1935. *Philosophy and Logical Syntax*. London: Kegan Paul, Trench, Trubner & Co Ltd.

Carnap, Rudolf. 1951. "The Problem of Relations in Inductive Logic." *Philosophical Studies* 2 (5):75–80.

Carus, André W. 2007. *Carnap and Twentieth-century Thought: Explication as Enlightenment*. Cambridge: Cambridge University Press.

Cassirer, Ernst. 1953. *Substance and Function, and Einstein's Theory of Relativity*. New York; London: Dover; Constable & Co.

Casullo, Albert. 2013. "Four Challenges to the A Priori–A Posteriori Distinction." *Synthese* 192 (9):1–24.

Casullo, Albert. forthcoming. "A Defense of the Significance of the A Priori–A Posteriori Distinction."

Casullo, Albert, and Joshua C. Thurow. 2013. *The A Priori in Philosophy*. Oxford: Oxford University Press.

Census. 2011. "Census Data Quality Assurance Strategy." http://www.ons.gov.uk/ons/guide-method/census/2011/the-2011-census/processing-the-information/data-quality-assurance/2011-census---data-quality-assurance-strategy.pdf.

Chaitin, Gregory J. 2006. *Meta Maths: The Quest for Omega*. London: Atlantic.

Chater, Nick, and M. Oaksford. 2008. *The Probabilistic Mind: Prospects for Bayesian Cognitive Science*. Oxford: Oxford University Press.

Chen, Min, and Luciano Floridi. 2013. "An Analysis of Information Visualisation." *Synthese* 190 (16):3421–38.

Child, A. 1953. "Making and Knowing in Hobbes, Vico, and Dewey." *University of California Publications in Philosophy* 16 (13):271–310.

Chisholm, Roderick M. 1966. *Theory of Knowledge*. Englewood Cliffs, NJ: Prentice-Hall.

Chisholm, Roderick M. 1989. *Theory of Knowledge*. 3rd edn. Englewood Cliffs, NJ: Prentice-Hall.

Cocchiarella, Nino B., and Max A. Freund. 2008. *Modal Logic: An Introduction to Its Syntax and Semantics*. Oxford: Oxford University Press.

Cohen, Felix S. 1929. "What Is a Question?" *The Monist* 39 (3):350–64.

Cover, T. M., and Joy A. Thomas. 2006. *Elements of Information Theory*. 2nd edn. Hoboken, NJ: Wiley-Interscience.

Covert, A., and N. Fenton. 2014. *How to Make Sense of Any Mess*. Createspace Independent Pub.

D'Agostino, Marcello. 2010. "Tractable Depth Bounded Logics and the Problem of Logical Omniscience." In *Probability, Uncertainty and Rationality*, edited by Hykel Hosni and F. Montagna, 245–75. Pisa: Edizioni della Scuola Normale Superiore.

D'Agostino, Marcello. 2013. "Semantic Information and the Trivialization of Logic: Floridi on the Scandal of Deduction." *Information* 4 (1):33–59.

D'Agostino, Marcello, and Luciano Floridi. 2009. "The Enduring Scandal of Deduction: Is Propositional Logic Really Uninformative?" *Synthese* 167 (2):271–315.

Dalal, M. 1988. "Investigations into a Theory of Knowledge Base Revision: Preliminary Report." Proceedings of the Seventh National Conference on Artificial Intelligence (AAAI-88), St. Paul, MN.

De Caro, Mario, and David Macarthur. 2010. *Naturalism and Normativity*. New York: Columbia University Press.

Deacon, Terrence William. 1997. *The Symbolic Species: The Co-evolution of Language and the Brain*. New York: W.W. Norton.

Deleuze, Gilles, and Felix Guattari. 1994. *What Is Philosophy?* London: Verso.

Dennett, Daniel C. 2006. "Higher-Order Truths about Chmess." *Topoi* 25 (1–2):39–41.

Descartes, René. 1984. *The Philosophical Writings of Descartes*. Translated by John Cottingham, Robert Stoothoff, and Dugald Murdoch. 3 vols. Cambridge: Cambridge University Press.

Dessauer, Friedrich. 1958. *Naturwissenschaftliches Erkennen*. Frankfurt am Main: Josef Knecht.

Dewey, John. 1925. *Experience and Nature*. Chicago; London: Open Court.

Dewey, John. 1929. *The Quest for Certainty*. New York: Minton, Balch & company.

Dewey, John. 1938. *Logic, the Theory of Inquiry*. New York: H. Holt and company.

Dewey, Robert E. 1956. "The Future of Philosophy." *Journal of Philosophy* 53 (5):187–96.

Deza, Michel M., and Elena Deza. 2009. *Encyclopedia of Distances.* New York: Springer.

Diamond, Jared M. 2006. *The Third Chimpanzee: The Evolution and Future of the Human Animal.* 2nd edn (original 1991). New York: Harper Perennial.

Dietrich, Eric, and Zach Weber. 2011. "Philosophy's Future: Science or Something Else?" *Special Issue of Essays in Philosophy* 12 (2).

Dretske, Fred. 1981. *Knowledge and the Flow of Information.* Oxford: Blackwell.

Dretske, Fred. 1994. "If You Can't Make One, You Don't Know How It Works." *Midwest Studies in Philosophy* 19 (1):468–82.

Dretske, Fred. 1999. *Knowledge and the Flow of Information.* Stanford, CA: CSLI Publications.

Dretske, Fred. 2006. "Information and Closure." *Erkenntnis* 64 (3):409–13.

Ducasse, Curt John. 1942. "Moore's Refutation of Idealism." In *Philosophy of G. E. Moore*, edited by P. A. Schilpp, 225–51. Chicago, IL: Northwestern University Press.

Dumas, Alexandre. 2008. *The Man in the Iron Mask*, Oxford world's classics. Oxford: Oxford University Press.

Dummett, Michael. 2010. *The Nature and Future of Philosophy.* New York: Columbia University Press.

Dunne, Anthony, and Fiona Raby. 2013. *Speculative Everything: Design, Fiction, and Social Dreaming.* Cambridge, MA: The MIT Press.

Durante, Massimo. 2017. *Ethics, Law and the Politics of Information—A Guide to the Philosophy of Luciano Floridi.* New York: Springer.

Empiricus, Sextus. 2000. *Outlines of Scepticism.* Rev. edn. Cambridge: Cambridge University Press.

English, Larry. 2009. *Information Quality Applied: Best Practices for Improving Business Information, Processes, and Systems.* Indianapolis, IN: Wiley.

Ernvall, Jarmo, Jyrki Katajainen, and Martti Penttonen. 1985. "NP-Completeness of the Hamming Salesman Problem." *BIT Numerical Mathematics* 25 (1):289–92.

Fanelli, Daniele. 2012. "Negative Results Are Disappearing from Most Disciplines and Countries." *Scientometrics* 90 (3):891–904.

Faulks, Sebastian. 2005. *Human Traces.* London: Hutchinson.

Fawcett, William. 1987. "A Note on the Logic of Design." *Design Studies* 8 (2):82–7.

Floridi, Luciano. 1994. "'Objective Knowledge': The Disappearance and Revaluation of 'Knowledges' from John Sergeant to Karl Popper." *Nouvelles de la République des Lettres* 1:97–122.

Floridi, Luciano. 1996. *Scepticism and the Foundation of Epistemology: A Study in the Metalogical Fallacies.* Leiden; New York: Brill.

Floridi, Luciano. 1998a. "The Importance of Being Earnest: Peirce's Interpretation of Scepticism." In *C. S. Peirce Categories to Constantinople*, edited by J. van Brakel and M. van Heerden, 47–60. Leuven: Leuven University Press.

Floridi, Luciano. 1998b. "Mathematical Scepticism: A Sketch with Historian in Foreground." In *The Skeptical Tradition around 1800*, edited by Johan van der Zande and Richard Popkin, 41–60. Dordrecht: Kluwer.

Floridi, Luciano. 1999. *Philosophy and Computing: An Introduction.* London; New York: Routledge.

Floridi, Luciano. 2000. "Mathematical Skepticism: The Cartesian Approach." In *Proceedings of the Twentieth World Congress of Philosophy*, edited by Akihiro Kanamori, 217–65. Bowling Green, KT: Philosophy Doc Ctr.

Floridi, Luciano. 2002a. "On Defining Library and Information Science as Applied Philosophy of Information." *Social Epistemology* 16 (1):37–49.

Floridi, Luciano. 2002b. *Sextus Empiricus, The Recovery and Transmission of Pyrrhonism*. New York: Oxford University Press.

Floridi, Luciano. 2004a. *The Blackwell Guide to the Philosophy of Computing and Information*. Malden, MA; Oxford: Blackwell.

Floridi, Luciano. 2004b. "LIS as Applied Philosophy of Information: A Reappraisal." *Library Trends* 52 (3):658–65.

Floridi, Luciano. 2004c. "Mathematical Skepticism: The Debate between Hobbes and Wallis." In *Skepticism in Renaissance and Post-Renaissance Thought: New Interpretations*, edited by Jose Raimundo Maia Neto and Richard H. Popkin, 143–83. New York: Prometheus.

Floridi, Luciano. 2004d. "On the Logical Unsolvability of the Gettier Problem." *Synthese* 142 (1):61–79.

Floridi, Luciano. 2004e. "Outline of a Theory of Strongly Semantic Information." *Minds and Machines* 14 (2):197–222.

Floridi, Luciano. 2005a. "Consciousness, Agents and the Knowledge Game." *Minds and Machines* 15 (3–4):415–44.

Floridi, Luciano. 2005b. "Is Semantic Information Meaningful Data?" *Philosophy and Phenomenological Research* 70 (2):351–70.

Floridi, Luciano. 2006. "The Logic of Being Informed." *Logique et Analyse* 49 (196):433–60.

Floridi, Luciano. 2007. "In Defence of the Veridical Nature of Semantic Information." *European Journal of Analytic Philosophy* 3 (1):1–10.

Floridi, Luciano. 2008a. "A Defence of Informational Structural Realism." *Synthese* 161 (2): 219–53.

Floridi, Luciano. 2008b. "The Method of Levels of Abstraction." *Minds and Machines* 18 (3): 303–29.

Floridi, Luciano. 2008c. "Understanding Epistemic Relevance." *Erkenntnis* 69 (1):69–92.

Floridi, Luciano. 2009. "Philosophical Conceptions of Information." In *Formal Theories of Information*, edited by Sommaruga Giovanni, 13–53. Dordrecht: Springer-Verlag.

Floridi, Luciano. 2010a. *Information—A Very Short Introduction*. Oxford: Oxford University Press.

Floridi, Luciano. 2010b. "Information, Possible Worlds, and the Cooptation of Scepticism." *Synthese* 175 (supl. 1) (63):63–88.

Floridi, Luciano. 2010c. "Semantic Information and the Correctness Theory of Truth." *Erkenntnis* 74 (2):147–75.

Floridi, Luciano. 2011a. "A Defence of Constructionism: Philosophy as Conceptual Engineering." *Metaphilosophy* 42 (3):282–304.

Floridi, Luciano. 2011b. "The Informational Nature of Personal Identity." *Minds and Machines* 21 (4):549–66.

Floridi, Luciano. 2011c. *The Philosophy of Information*. Oxford: Oxford University Press.

Floridi, Luciano. 2011d. "Semantic Conceptions of Information." In *The Stanford Encyclopedia of Philosophy*, available online, edited by Edward N. Zalta.

Floridi, Luciano. 2012a. "Degenerate Epistemology." *Philosophy & Technology* 25 (1):1–3.

Floridi, Luciano. 2012b. "Semantic Information and the Network Theory of Account." *Synthese* 184 (3):431–54.

Floridi, Luciano. 2012c. "Turing's Three Philosophical Lessons and the Philosophy of Information." *Philosophical Transactions* A (370):3536–42.

Floridi, Luciano. 2013a. "Editor's Cut—The Future of Philosophical Research According to Journal Editors." *Metaphilosophy* 44 (3):191–4.

Floridi, Luciano. 2013b. *The Ethics of Information*. Oxford: Oxford University Press.

Floridi, Luciano. 2014a. *The Fourth Revolution—How the Infosphere Is Reshaping Human Reality*. Oxford: Oxford University Press.

Floridi, Luciano. 2014b. "Perception and Testimony as Data Providers." *Logique et Analyse* 57 (226):151–79.

Floridi, Luciano, ed. 2016. *The Routledge Handbook of Philosophy of Information*. London: Routledge.

Floridi, Luciano. 2018. "What a Maker's Knowledge Could Be." *Synthese* 195 (1):465–81.

Floridi, Luciano, and Jeff W. Sanders. 2005. "Internet Ethics: The Constructionist Values of Homo Poieticus." In *The Impact of the Internet on Our Moral Lives*, edited by Robert J. Cavalier, 195–214. Albany, NY: State University of New York (SUNY) Press.

Floridi, Luciano, Mariarosaria Taddeo, and Matteo Turilli. 2009. "Turing's Imitation Game: Still a Challenge for Any Machine and Some Judges." *Minds and Machines* 19 (1):145–50.

Floridi, Luciano, Nir Fresco, and Giuseppe Primiero. 2015. "On Malfunctioning Software." *Synthese* 192 (4):1199–220.

Flusser, Vilém. 1999. *The Shape of Things: A Philosophy of Design*. London: Reaktion.

Fortnow, L., and S. Homer. 2003. "A Short History of Computational Complexity." *Bulletin of the EATCS* 80:95–133.

French, S., and J. Ladyman. 2003. "The Dissolution of Objects: Between Platonism and Phenomenalism." *Synthese* 136 (1):73–7.

Freud, Sigmund. 1917. "A Difficulty in the Path of Psycho-analysis." *The Standard Edition of the Complete Psychological Works of Sigmund Freud* XVII (1917–1919):135–44.

Fries, Jakob Friedrich. 1807. *Neue Kritik der Vernunft*. 3 vols. Heidelberg,: Bey Mohr und Zimmer.

Gabbay, Dov M., and Karl Schlechta. 2009. *Logical Tools for Handling Change in Agent-based Systems, Cognitive Technologies*. New York: Springer.

Galle, Per. 1997. "Towards a Formal Logic of Design Rationalization." *Design Studies* 18 (2): 195–219.

Gaskin, Richard. 2006. *Experience and the World's Own Language: A Critique of John Mcdowell's Empiricism*. Oxford: Oxford University Press.

Gaukroger, Stephen. 1986. "Vico and the Maker's Knowledge Principle." *History of Philosophy Quarterly* 3 (1):29–44.

Gerbrandy, Jelle, and Willem Groeneveld. 1997. "Reasoning about Information Change." *Journal of Logic, Language and Information* 6 (2):147–69.

Gettier, Edmund L. 1963. "Is Justified True Belief Knowledge?" *Analysis* 23 (6):121–3.

Glaeser, Friedrich. 1969. "The Future of Philosophy." *Philosophy and History* 2 (2):166–9.

Goel, Vinod. 1988. "Complicating the 'Logic of Design'." *Design Studies* 9 (4):229–34.

Greco, Gian Maria, and Luciano Floridi. 2004. "The Tragedy of the Digital Commons." *Ethics and Information Technology* 6 (2):73–82.

Grice, H. P. 1957. "Meaning." *The Philosophical Review* 66 (3):377–88.

Grice, H. P. 1989. *Studies in the Way of Words*. Cambridge, MA: Harvard University Press.

Griggs, R. A., and J. R. Cox. 1982. "The Elusive Thematic-Materials Effect in Wason's Selection Task." *British Journal of Psychology* 73 (3):407–20.

Grim, Patrick. 2003. "Computational Modeling as a Philosophical Methodology." In *The Blackwell Guide to the Philosophy of Computing and Information*, edited by L. Floridi, 337–49. Oxford; New York: Blackwell.

Grundmann, Thomas. 2015. "How Reliabilism Saves the A Priori/A Posteriori Distinction." *Synthese* 192 (9):2747–68.

Hahn, Ulrike, and Mike Oaksford. 2006. "A Bayesian Approach to Informal Argument Fallacies." *Synthese* 152 (2):207–36.

Haller, R. 1974. "Concerning the So-called 'Munchhausen Trilemma.'" *Ratio* 16 (2):125–40.

Haller, R. 1979. "Über die Möglichkeit der Erkenntnistheorie." In *Vernunft, Erkenntnis, Sittlichkeit. Int. Phil. Symp. Göttingen 27–29 Okt. 1974 aus Anlass des 50 Todestages von L. Nelson*, edited by P. Schroeder, 37–54. Hamburg: Meiner.

Hamblin, Charles Leonard. 1970. *Fallacies*. London: Methuen.

Hansen, Hans V., and Robert C. Pinto, eds. 1995. *Fallacies: Classical and Contemporary Readings*. University Park, PA: Pennsylvania State University Press.

Harel, Idit, and Seymour Papert. 1991. *Constructionism*. Norwood, NJ: Ablex Pub. Corp.

Harnad, Stevan. 1990. "The Symbol Grounding Problem." *Physica* D (42):335–46.

Harnad, Stevan. 1993. "Problems, Problems: The Frame Problem as a Symptom of the Symbol Grounding Problem." *Psycoloquy* 4 (34):1–10.

Hawking, S. W., and Leonard Mlodinow. 2010. *The Grand Design*. London: Bantam Press.

Hegel, Georg Wilhelm Friedrich. 1975. *Hegel's Logic: Being Part One of the Encyclopaedia of the Philosophical Sciences (1830)*. 3rd edn. Oxford: Clarendon Press.

Hegel, G. W. F. 1985. "On the Relationship of Scepticism with Philosophy." In *Between Kant and Hegel: Texts in the Development of Post-Kantian Idealism*, edited by George Di Giovanni and H. S. Harris, 311–62. Albany: State University of New York Press.

Heidegger, Martin. 1927. *Sein und Zeit*. Halle a. d. S: M. Niemeyer.

Heidegger, Martin. 1962. *Being and Time*. Oxford: Basil Blackwell.

Heis, Jeremy. 2012. "Attempts to Rethink Logic." In *The Cambridge History of Philosophy in the Nineteenth Century (1790–1870)*, edited by Allen W. Wood and Songsuk Susan Hahn, 95–132. Cambridge: Cambridge University Press.

Helmholtz, Hermann von. 1995. *Science and Culture: Popular and Philosophical Essays*. Chicago: University of Chicago Press.

Herzog, Thomas N., Fritz Scheuren, and William E. Winkler. 2007. *Data Quality and Record Linkage Techniques*. New York; London: Springer.

Hilbert, David. 1971. *Foundations of Geometry*. 2nd edn. La Salle, IL: Open Court.

Hintikka, Jaakko. 1962. *Knowledge and Belief: An Introduction to the Logic of the Two Notions*. Ithaca, NY: Cornell University Press.

Hintikka, Jaakko. 1973. *Logic, Language-games and Information: Kantian Themes in the Philosophy of Logic*. Oxford: Clarendon Press.

Hintikka, Jaako. 1974. "Practical versus Theoretical Reason—An Ambiguous Legacy." In *Practical Reason*, edited by Stephan Körner, 83–102. New Haven: Yale University Press.

Hoare, C. A. R. 1972. "Chapter II: Notes on Data Structuring." In *Structured Programming*, edited by O. J. Dahl, E. W. Dijkstra, and C. A. R. Hoare, 83–174. New York: Academic Press Ltd.

Hobbes, Thomas. 1656. *Elements of Philosophy, the first section, concerning body. Written in Latine... and now translated into English. To which are added Six lessons to the professors of mathematicks of the Institution of Sr Henry Savile, in the University of Oxford. [With plates.]*: 2 pt. London: Printed by R. & W. Leybourn, for Andrew Crooke.

Holm, Ruurik. 2003. "A Constructive Approach to State Description Semantics." *Journal of Applied Logic* 1 (1–2):13–46.

Horrobin, David F. 2001. *The Madness of Adam and Eve: How Schizophrenia Shaped Humanity*. London: Bantam.

Hughes, G. E., and M. J. Cresswell. 1984. *A Companion to Modal Logic*. London: Methuen.

Hume, David. 2000. *An Enquiry Concerning Human Understanding: A Critical Edition*. Oxford: Clarendon Press.

Humphreys, Paul. 2004. *Extending Ourselves: Computational Science, Empiricism, and Scientific Method*. Oxford: Oxford University Press.

Husserl, Edmund. 1950. "Die Idee der Phänomenologie: Fünf Vorlesungen." In *Gesammelte Werke*, edited by Walter Biemel, Band II. Haag: Martinus Nijhoff. These are five lectures delivered by Husserl in Göttingen in 1907, Eng. tr. (1964) *The Idea of Phenomenology*, by W. P. Alston and G. Nakhnikian, The Hague: Martinus Nijhoff.

Illari, Phyllis, ed. 2012. *The Philosophy of Information—A Simple Introduction*. Society for the Philosophy of Information, http://www.socphilinfo.org/teaching/book-pi-intro.

Jacovides, Michael. 2002. "The Epistemology under Locke's Corpuscularianism." *Archiv für Geschichte der Philosophie* 84 (2):161–89.

Jäger, Christoph. 2004. "Skepticism, Information, and Closure: Dretske's Theory of Knowledge." *Erkenntnis* 61 (2–3):187–201.

Jenkins, C. S. I. 2008. *Grounding Concepts: An Empirical Basis for Arithmetic Knowledge*. Oxford: Oxford University Press.

Jenkins, C. S. I., and Masashi Kasaki. 2015. "The Traditional Conception of the A Priori." *Synthese* 192 (9):2725–46.

Joachim, Harold H. 1939. *The Nature of Truth: An Essay*. 2nd edn. London: Oxford University Press.

Josephson, John R. 2000. "Smart Inductive Generalizations are Abductions." In *Abduction and Induction: Essays on Their Relation and Integration*, edited by P. A. Flach and A. C. Kakas. Dordrecht; Boston: Kluwer.

Kant, Immanuel. 1998. *Critique of Pure Reason*. repr. w. corr. edn. Cambridge: Cambridge University Press.

Kant, Immanuel. 2007. *Critique of Pure Reason*. London: Penguin. Translated, edited, and with an introduction by Marcus Weigelt, based on the translation by Max Müller.

Kelsen, Hans. 1967. *Pure Theory of Law*. California Library Reprint Series Edition ed. Berkeley: University of California Press.

Kerr, E. T., and D. Pritchard. 2012. "Skepticism and Information." In *Luciano Floridi's Philosophy of Technology*, edited by Hilmi Demir, 191–200. New York: Springer.

Konstantinidis, Stavros. 2007. "Computing the Edit Distance of a Regular Language." *Information and Computation* 205 (9):1307–16.

Kracht, M., and O. Kutz. 2007. "Logically Possible Worlds and Counterpart Semantics for Modal Logic." In *Philosophy of Logic*, edited by D. Jacquette, 943–96. Amsterdam: Elsevier.

Kroll, Ehud, and Lauri Koskela. 2015. "On Abduction in Design." In *Design Computing and Cognition '14*, edited by John S. Gero and Sean Hanna, 327–44. Cham: Springer International Publishing.

Kuorikoski, Jaakko. 2009. "Simulation and the Sense of Understanding." Conference on "Models and Simulations 3", Charlottesville, Virginia.

Kutach, Douglas. 2006. "Similarity Is a Bad Guide to Counterfactual Truth." APA Pacific Meeting.

Lafage, Celine, and Jérôme Lang. 2001. "Propositional Distances and Preference Representation." *Lecture Notes in Computer Science* 2143:48–59.

Lakatos, Imre. 1978. "Infinite Regress and Foundations of Mathematics." In *Philosophical Papers*, edited by J. Worrall and G. Currie, vol. 1, 3–23. Cambridge: Cambridge University Press.

Larkin, Jill H., and Herbert A. Simon. 1987. "Why a Diagram Is (Sometimes) Worth Ten Thousand Words." *Cognitive Science* 11 (1):65–100.

Le Goc, Marc, and Fabien Vilar. 2017. "Operationalization of the Blending and the Levels of Abstraction Theories with the Timed Observations Theory." *Proceedings of the 9th International Conference on Agents and Artificial Intelligence (ICAART* 2017*)* 2:364–73.

Leaman, Oliver. 1998. *The Future of Philosophy: Towards the Twenty-first Century.* London: Routledge.

Lee, Yang W., Leo L. Pipino, James D. Funk, and Richard Y. Wang. 2006. *Journey to Data Quality.* Cambridge, MA: MIT.

Leibniz, Gottfried Wilhelm. 1951. *Selections.* New York: Charles Scribner's Sons.

Leibniz, Gottfried Wilhelm. 1996. *New Essays on Human Understanding.* Cambridge: Cambridge University Press.

Lewis, Clarence Irving. 1929. *Mind and the World-order; Outline of a Theory of Knowledge.* New York; Chicago: C. Scribner's Sons.

Lewis, Clarence Irving. 1946. *An Analysis of Knowledge and Valuation.* La Salle, IL: Open Court.

Lewis, David K. 1973. *Counterfactuals.* Oxford: Basil Blackwell.

Lewis, David. 1979. "Counterfactual Dependence and Time's Arrow." *Noûs* 13 (4):455–76.

Llewelyn, John E. 1964. "What Is a Question?" *Australasian Journal of Philosophy* 42 (1): 69–85.

Luebke, D. M., and S. Milton. 1994. "Locating the Victim: An Overview of Census-Taking, Tabulation Technology and Persecution in Nazi Germany." *Annals of the History of Computing, IEEE* 16 (3):25–39.

Luenberger, David G. 2006. *Information Science.* Princeton, NJ; Oxford: Princeton University Press.

Luper, Steven. 2006. "Dretske on Knowledge Closure." *Australasian Journal of Philosophy* 84 (3):379–94.

Luper, Steven. 2010. "The Epistemic Closure Principle." In *Stanford Encyclopedia of Philosophy*, edited by Edward N. Zalta.

Maddy, Penelope. 2007. *Second Philosophy: A Naturalistic Method.* Oxford: Oxford University Press.

Mancosu, Paolo. 1998. *From Brouwer to Hilbert: The Debate on the Foundations of Mathematics in the 1920s.* New York; Oxford: Oxford University Press.

Manthey, Bodo, and Rüdiger Reischuk. 2005. "The Intractability of Computing the Hamming Distance." *Theoretical Computer Science* 337 (1–3):331–46.

March, Lionel. 1976. *The Architecture of Form.* Cambridge: Cambridge University Press.

March, Lionel. 1984. "The Logic of Design." Developments in Design Methodology, 265–76. Chichester: John Wiley & Sons.

Marcus, S. L., and L. J. Rips. 1979. "Conditional Reasoning." *Journal of Verbal Learning and Verbal Behavior* 18:199–224.

Marion, Mathieu. 1998. *Wittgenstein, Finitism, and the Foundations of Mathematics.* Oxford: Clarendon.

Maydanchik, Arkady. 2007. *Data Quality Assessment*, Data Quality for Practitioners Series. Bradley Beach, NJ: Technics Publications.

McDowell, John. 1996. *Mind and World: With a New Introduction.* Cambridge, MA; London: Harvard University Press.

McGilvray, Danette. 2008. *Executing Data Quality Projects Ten Steps to Quality Data and Trusted Information.* Amsterdam; Boston: Morgan Kaufmann/Elsevier.

McLuhan, Marshall, and Barrington Nevitt. 1972. *Take Today; the Executive as Dropout.* New York: Harcourt Brace Jovanovich.

Mercier, Desiré. 1923. *Criteriologie Generale: Ou Theorie Generale de la Certitude.* 8th edn. Paris: F. Alcan.

Mitcham, Carl. 1994. *Thinking through Technology: The Path between Engineering and Philosophy.* Chicago; London: University of Chicago Press.

Moor, James. 2003. *The Turing Test: The Elusive Standard of Artificial Intelligence.* Dordrecht; Boston: Kluwer Academic Publishers.

Moore, George Edward. 1925. "A Defence of Common Sense." In *Contemporary British Philosophy, 2nd series,* edited by J. H. Muirhead. London: Allen & Unwin.

Moore, George Edward. 1939. "Proof of an External World." *Proceedings of the British Academy* 25:273–300.

Moore, G. E. 1993a. *Principia Ethica.* Rev. edn. Cambridge: Cambridge University Press.

Moore, G. E. 1993b. *Selected Writings.* London: Routledge.

Morville, Peter, and Louis Rosenfeld. 2015. *Information Architecture for the World Wide Web.* 4th edn. Beijing; Farnham: O'Reilly.

Mulligan, Kevin, Peter Simons, and Barry Smith. 2006. "What's Wrong with Contemporary Philosophy?" *Topoi* 25 (1–2):63–7.

Munari, Bruno. 1971. *Design as Art.* Harmondsworth: Penguin.

Nagel, T. 1974. "What Is It Like to Be a Bat?" *The Philosophical Review* 83 (4):435–50.

Naimpally, S. A., and Brian Warrack. 1970. *Proximity Spaces, Cambridge Tracts in Mathematics and Mathematical Physics.* Cambridge: Cambridge University Press.

Nelson, Leonard. 1908. *Über das sogenannte Erkenntnisproblem, Abhandlungen der Fries'schen Schule Neue Folge.* Göttingen: Vandenhoek & Ruprecht.

Nelson, Leonard. 1965. "The Impossibility of the 'Theory of Knowledge'." In *Socratic Method and Critical Philosophy: Selected Essays,* Eng. tr. by T. K. Brown III, foreword by B. Blanshard, int. by J. Kraft, 185–205. New York: Dover.

Nelson, Leonard. 1970. *Progress and Regress in Philosophy: From Hume and Kant to Hegel and Fries.* 2 vols. Oxford: Blackwell.

Neurath, Otto. 1983. *Philosophical Papers, 1913–1946.* Dordrecht; Lancaster: Reidel.

Newell, A., and H. A. Simon. 1976. "Computer Science as Empirical Enquiry: Symbols and Search." *Communications of the ACM* 19 (3):113–26.

Niiniluoto, Ilkka. 1987. *Truthlikeness.* Dordrecht, Holland; Boston, MA: Reidel.

Nobre, Anna Christina, Angel Correa, and Jennifer T. Coull. 2007. "The Hazards of Time." *Current Opinion in Neurobiology* 17 (4):465–70.

Norman, Donald A. 2013. *The Design of Everyday Things.* Revised and expanded ed. Cambridge, MA: MIT Press.

Norris, Christopher. 2011. "Hawking contra Philosophy." *Philosophy Now* 82:21–4.

Notturno, Mark Amadeus. 1985. *Objectivity, Rationality, and the Third Realm: Justification and the Grounds of Psychologism, a Study of Frege and Popper.* Dordrecht; Lancaster: Nijhoff.

Nozick, Robert. 1981. *Philosophical Explanations.* Oxford: Clarendon Press.

Olson, Jack E. 2003. *Data Quality: The Accuracy Dimension*. San Francisco: Morgan Kaufmann Publishers.

Pagin, Peter. 2008. "Indeterminacy and the Analytic/Synthetic Distinctions: A Survey." *Synthese* 164 (1):1–18.

Papineau, David. 2012. *Philosophical Devices: Proofs, Probabilities, Possibilities, and Sets.* Oxford: Oxford University Press.

Papineau, David. 2015. "Naturalism." In *The Stanford Encyclopedia of Philosophy*, available online, edited by Edward N. Zalta.

Papini, Odile. 2000. "Knowledge-Base Revision." *The Knowledge Engineering Review* 15 (04): 339–70.

Parsons, Glenn. 2016. *The Philosophy of Design*. Cambridge: Polity.

Pascal, Blaise. 1995. *Penseés and Other Writings*. Oxford: Oxford University Press.

Pearl, Judea. 1984. *Heuristics: Intelligent Search Strategies for Computer Problem Solving.* Reading, MA: Addison-Wesley.

Pearson, Karl. 1900. *The Grammar of Science*. 2nd edn. London: A. & C. Black.

Peirce, Charles Sanders. 1877. "The Fixation of Belief." *Popular Science Monthly* 12 (November):1–15.

Pérez-Ramos, Antonio. 1988. *Francis Bacon's Idea of Science and the Maker's Knowledge Tradition*. Oxford: Clarendon.

Philipse, Herman. 2001. "What Is a Natural Conception of the World?" *International Journal of Philosophical Studies* 9 (3):385–99.

Piazza, Tommaso. 2010. "Perceptual Evidence and Information." *Knowledge, Technology & Policy* 23 (1):75–95.

Plato. 1989. *The Collected Dialogues of Plato: Including the letters*, edited by Edith Hamilton and Huntington Cairns, with Introduction and Prefatory Notes. 14th printing edn. Princeton, NJ: Princeton University Press.

Popkin, Richard H. 2003. *The History of Scepticism: From Savonarola to Bayle*. Revised and expanded edn. New York; Oxford: Oxford University Press.

Popper, Karl R. 1968. *The Logic of Scientific Discovery*. 2nd edn. London: Hutchinson.

Popper, Karl R. 1979. *Die beiden Grundprobleme der Erkenntnistheorie: aufgrund von Ms. aus d. Jahren 1930–1933, Einheit der Gesellschaftswissenschaften*. Tübingen: Mohr.

Popper, Karl R. 2002. *The Logic of Scientific Discovery*. London: Routledge Classics.

Popper, Karl R. 2012. *The Two Fundamental Problems of the Theory of Knowledge*, Routledge classics. London: Routledge.

Primiero, Giuseppe. 2009. "An Epistemic Logic for Becoming Informed." *Synthese* 167 (2): 363–89.

Primiero, Giuseppe, and Laszlo Kosolosky. 2016. "The Semantics of Untrustworthiness." *Topoi* 35 (1):253–66.

Quine, W. V. O. 1951. "Two Dogmas of Empiricism." *The Philosophical Review* 60 (1):20–43.

Quine, W. V. 1969. "Epistemology Naturalized." In *Ontological Relativity and Other Essays*, 69–90. New York, NY: Columbia University Press.

Quine, W. V. 1981. *Theories and Things*. Cambridge, MA; London: Belknap Press of Harvard University Press.

Quine, W. V. 1992a. *Pursuit of Truth*. Rev. edn. Cambridge, MA; London: Harvard University Press.

Quine, W. V. 1992b. "Structure and Nature." *The Journal of Philosophy* 89 (1):5–9.

Quine, W. V. 2008. *Confessions of a Confirmed Extensionalist and Other Essays*. Cambridge, MA; London: Harvard University Press.

Raftopoulos, A. 2003. "Cartesian Analysis and Synthesis." *Studies in History and Philosophy of Science* Part A, 34 (2):265–308.

Ramón y Cajal, Santiago. 1999. *Advice for a Young Investigator*. Cambridge, MA; London: MIT Press.

Ramsey, Frank Plumpton. 1990. "Knowledge." In *Philosophical Papers*, edited by D. H. Mellor. Cambridge: Cambridge University Press.

Raper, J. F., David Rhind, and John Feb Shepherd. 1992. *Postcodes: The New Geography*. Basingstoke: Longman.

Redman, Thomas C. 1996. *Data Quality for the Information Age*. Boston: Artech House.

Reichenbach, Hans. 1951. *The Rise of Scientific Philosophy*. Berkeley & Los Angeles: University of California Press.

Reynaert, Peter. 2015. "Does Naturalism Commit a Category Mistake?" *Bulletin d'analyse phénoménologique* 11:3.

Ritchie, Jack. 2008. *Understanding Naturalism*. Stocksfield: Acumen.

Rorty, Richard. 2009. *Philosophy and the Mirror of Nature*. 30th anniversary edn. With a new introduction by Michael Williams and a new afterword by David Bromwich. Princeton, NJ: Princeton University Press.

Rosenthal, Sandra B. 1987. "The Pragmatic A Priori: Lewis and Dewey." *The Southern Journal of Philosophy* 25 (1):109–21.

Russell, Bertrand. 1910. "Knowledge by Acquaintance and Knowledge by Description." *Proceedings of the Aristotelian Society* 11:108–28.

Russell, Bertrand. 1912. *The Problems of Philosophy*. Oxford: Oxford University Press.

Russell, Bertrand. 1914. *Our Knowledge of the External World as a Field for Scientific Method in Philosophy*. Chicago; London: Open Court.

Russell, Bertrand. 1917. *Mysticism and Logic: And Other Essays*. 2nd edn. London: Allen & Unwin.

Russell, Bertrand. 1948. *Human Knowledge: Its Scope and Limits*. London: Allen and Unwin.

Russell, Gillian. 2008. *Truth in Virtue of Meaning: A Defence of the Analytic/Synthetic Distinction*. Oxford: Oxford University Press.

Rysiew, Patrick. 2016. "Naturalism in Epistemology." In *The Stanford Encyclopedia of Philosophy*, available online, edited by Edward N. Zalta.

Sainsbury, R. M. 2001. *Logical Forms: An Introduction to Philosophical Logic*. 2nd edn. Oxford: Blackwell.

Satoh, K. 1988. "Nonmonotonic Reasoning by Minimal Belief Revision." Proceedings of the International Conference on Fifth Generation Computer Systems, Tokyo, Japan.

Schilhab, Theresa, Frederik Stjernfelt, and Terrence William Deacon. 2012. *The Symbolic Species Evolved*. New York: Springer.

Schlette, Heinz Robert, ed. 1968a. *Die Zukunft der Philosophie*. Olten: Freiburg i. Br.

Schlick, Moritz. 1932. "The Future of Philosophy." *College of the Pacific Publications in Philosophy* 1:45–62.

Schlick, Moritz. 1974. *General Theory of Knowledge*. Wien: Springer-Verlag.

Schlick, Moritz. 1979. *Philosophical Papers*. 2 vols. Dordrecht: Reidel.

Schoenbaumsfeld, Genia. submitted-a. "McDowellian Neo-Mooreanism?".

Schoenbaumsfeld, Genia. submitted-b. "Meaning and Conversational Impropriety in Sceptical Contexts."

Schön, Donald A. 1983. *The Reflective Practitioner: How Professionals Think in Action.* New York: Basic Books.

Searle, John R. 1989. "How Performatives Work." *Linguistics and Philosophy* 12 (5):535–58.

Sellars, Wilfrid. 1963a. "Philosophy and the Scientific Image of Man." In *Science, Perception and Reality*, by Wilfrid Sellars, 1–40. London: Routledge & Kegan Paul Ltd (originally published in *Frontiers of Science and Philosophy*, edited by Robert Colodny (Pittsburgh: University of Pittsburgh Press, 1962)), 35–78.

Sellars, Wilfrid. 1963b. *Science, Perception and Reality.* London: Routledge & Kegan Paul.

Shackel, Nicholas. 2006. "Shutting Dretske's Door." *Erkenntnis* 64 (3):393–401.

Shapiro, Stewart. 1997. *Philosophy of Mathematics: Structure and Ontology.* New York; Oxford: Oxford University Press.

Shapiro, Stewart. 2000. *Thinking about Mathematics: The Philosophy of Mathematics.* Oxford: Oxford University Press.

Simon, Herbert A. 1978. "On the Forms of Mental Representation." In *Minnesota Studies in the Philosophy of Science, Vol. IX: Perception and Cognition: Issues in the Foundations of Psychology*, edited by C. W. Savage, 3–18. Minneapolis: University of Minnesota Press.

Simon, Herbert A. 1996. *The Sciences of the Artificial.* 3rd edn. Cambridge, MA: MIT Press.

Sinnott-Armstrong, Walter, and Robert J. Fogelin. 2015. *Understanding Arguments: An Introduction to Informal Logic.* 9th edn, Cengage advantage books. Stamford, CT: Cengage Learning.

Sintonen, Matti. 1990. "How to Put Questions to Nature." *Royal Institute of Philosophy Supplements* 27:267–84.

Sipser, Michael. 2012. *Introduction to the Theory of Computation.* 3rd edn. Boston, MA: Cengage Learning.

Skyrms, Brian. 2010. *Signals Evolution, Learning, and Information.* Oxford: Oxford University Press.

Sorensen, Roy A. 1993. *Pseudo-problems: How Analytic Philosophy Gets Done.* London: Routledge.

Stein, Edward. 1996. *Without Good Reason: The Rationality Debate in Philosophy and Cognitive Science.* Oxford: Clarendon Press.

Stevenson, Charles L. 1944. *Ethics and Language.* New Haven, CT: Yale University Press.

Strandberg, Caj. 2004. "In Defence of the Open Question Argument." *Journal of Ethics* 8 (2): 179–96.

Strawson, P. F. 1985. *Skepticism and Naturalism: Some Varieties, Woodbridge Lectures.* New York: Columbia University Press.

Stroud, Barry. 1981. "The Significance of Naturalized Epistemology." *Midwest Studies in Philosophy* 6 (1):455–72.

Stroud, Barry. 1984. *The Significance of Philosophical Scepticism.* Oxford: Clarendon Press.

Taddeo, Mariarosaria, and Luciano Floridi. 2005. "Solving the Symbol Grounding Problem: A Critical Review of Fifteen Years of Research." *Journal of Experimental & Theoretical Artificial Intelligence* 17 (4):419–45.

Taddeo, Mariarosaria, and Luciano Floridi. 2007. "A Praxical Solution of the Symbol Grounding Problem." *Minds and Machines* 7 (4):369–89.

Tasić, Vladimir. 2001. *Mathematics and the Roots of Postmodern Thought.* Oxford: Oxford University Press.

Theys, Philippe P. 2011. *Quest for Quality Data.* Paris: Editions TECHNIP.

Thorpe, Vanessa. 2005. "How a Novelist's Twist Sparked Academic Feud." *The Observer* (Sunday 21 August).

Toffler, Alvin. 1980. *The Third Wave*. London: Collins.

Tozer, Guy V. 1994. *Information Quality Management*. Oxford: Blackwell.

Tully, James. 1980. *A Discourse on Property: John Locke and His Adversaries*. Cambridge: Cambridge University Press.

Turing, Alan M. 1950. "Computing Machinery and Intelligence." *Mind* 59 (236):433–60.

Turing, Alan Mathison. 2004. *The Essential Turing: Seminal Writings in Computing, Logic, Philosophy, Artificial Intelligence and Artificial Life, plus the Secrets of Enigma*. Oxford: Clarendon Press.

United States Congress. House Committee on Government Reform. Subcommittee on Regulatory Affairs. 2006. *Improving information quality in the federal government: hearing before the Subcommittee on Regulatory Affairs of the Committee on Government Reform, House of Representatives, One Hundred Ninth Congress, first session, July 20, 2005*. Washington: US GPO.

United States Federal Trade Commission. 2010. *Social Security Numbers and ID Theft, Privacy and Identity Protection Series*. New York: Nova Science Publishers.

Uygur, Nermi. 1964. "What Is a Philosophical Question?" *Mind* 73 (289):64–83.

van Benthem, Johan, Jan van Eijck, and Barteld Kooi. 2006. "Logics of Communication and Change." *Information and Computation* 204 (11):1620–62.

van Ditmarsch, H., W. van der Hoek, and B. Kooi. 2007. *Dynamic Epistemic Logic*. New York: Springer.

van Ditmarsch, Hans P., Wiebe van der Hoek, and Barteld P. Kooi. 2005. "Dynamic Epistemic Logic with Assignment." *ACM—Proceedings of the fourth international joint conference on Autonomous agents and multiagent systems*, 141–8.

van Ditmarsch, H., W. van der Hoek, and B. Kooi. 2015. *Dynamic Epistemic Logic*. The Internet Encyclopedia of Philosophy, available online.

Vermaas, P. E., P. Kroes, A. Light, and S. Moore. 2007. *Philosophy and Design: From Engineering to Architecture*. Dordrecht: Springer.

Verschueren, N., W. Schroyens, W. Schaeken, and G. d'Ydewalle. 2001. "Why Do Participants Draw Non-Valid Inferences in Conditional Reasoning?" *Current Psychology Letters: Behaviour, Brain, & Cognition* 6:57–70.

Walton, Douglas, and Alan Brinton. 2016. *Historical Foundations of Informal Logic*. London: Routledge.

Wang, Richard Y. 1998. "A Product Perspective on Total Data Quality Management." *Communications of the ACM* 41 (2):58–65.

Wang, Richard Y., and Henry B. Kon. 1992. *Toward Quality Data: An Attributes-based Approach to Data Quality*. Cambridge, MA: MIT.

Wang, Richard Y., Elizabeth M. Pierce, Stuart E. Madnik, Vladimir Zwass, and Craig W. Fisher, eds. 2005. *Information Quality, Advances in Management Information Systems*; volume 1. Armonk, NY; London: M. E. Sharpe.

Wason, P. C. 1966. "Reasoning." In *New Horizons in Psychology*, edited by B. M. Foss, 135–51. Harmondsworth: Penguin.

Weinert, Friedel. 2009. *Copernicus, Darwin, and Freud: Revolutions in the History and Philosophy of Science*. Oxford: Blackwell.

Wheeler, Gregory. 2015. "Is There a Logic of Information?" *Journal of Experimental and Theoretical AI* 27—special issue on "Inforgs and the Infosphere: Themes from Luciano Floridi's Philosophy of Artificial Intelligence" (1):95–8.

White, James L. 1991. "Knowledge and Deductive Closure." *Synthese* 86 (3):409–23.

Whitehead A. N., 1978. *Process and Reality: An Essay in Cosmology*. Corr. ed. New York: Free Press.

Williamson, Timothy. 1987. "Invertible Definitions." *Notre Dame Journal of Formal Logic* 28 (2):244–58.

Winograd, Terry, and Fernando Flores. 1986. *Understanding Computers and Cognition: A New Foundation for Design*. Norwood, NJ: Ablex.

Wiśniewski, Andrzej. 1994. "Erotetic Implications." *Journal of Philosophical Logic* 23 (2): 173–95.

Wittgenstein, Ludwig. 1975. *On Certainty*. Repr with corrections edn. Oxford: Blackwell.

Wittgenstein, Ludwig. 2001. *Philosophical Investigations: The German Text with a Revised English Translation*. 3rd edn. Oxford: Blackwell.

Wood, Allen. 2006. "Philosophy, What Is to Be Done?" *Topoi* 25 (1–2):133–6.

Woods, John, and Douglas N. Walton. 1982. *Argument: The Logic of the Fallacies*. Toronto: McGraw-Hill Ryerson.

Yue, Anbu, Weiru Liu, and Anthony Hunter. 2008. "Measuring the Ignorance and Degree of Satisfaction for Answering Queries in Imprecise Probabilistic Logic Programs." *Lecture Notes in Computer Science* 5291:386–400.

Zagorin, Perez. 1984. "Vico's Theory of Knowledge: A Critique." *The Philosophical Quarterly* 34 (134):15–30.

Zeigler, Bernard P. 1976. *Theory of Modelling and Simulation*. New York; London: Wiley-Interscience.

Zeng, Y., and G. D. Cheng. 1991. "On the Logic of Design." *Design Studies* 12 (3):137–41.

Index